YOUNG PEOPLE READING

The value of small-scale qualitative research projects into young people's reading is often underestimated. Yet these finely tuned studies, with a precise focus and highly specialised approach, can provide us with profound insights into the richness and variety of young people's reading practices.

Bringing together contributors from six continents, this fascinating volume explores researchers' experiences of investigating the reading habits, preferences and practices of young people aged 12–21. Detailing a variety of empirical methodologies and research methods, its chapters also consider reading in an array of contexts, in various languages and using diverse media.

Key issues addressed in the book include:

- the complexity of sociocultural similarities and differences in young people's reading in international contexts
- multilingual, bilingual and monolingual readers' experiences of reading
- how young readers use a range of different print and digital media
- how our understanding of the range of texts available to young readers and the different contexts of and purposes for reading can be enhanced through small-scale qualitative research.

Providing in-depth discussion of contributors' research and findings, and touching on many different contexts, text types and media, this volume will support and inspire current and future researchers, lecturers and teachers interested in young people's reading.

Evelyn Arizpe is Senior Lecturer at the School of Education, University of Glasgow, UK.

Gabrielle Cliff Hodges is former Senior Lecturer in Education at the University of Cambridge, UK.

YOUNG PEOPLE READING

Empirical Research Across International Contexts

Edited by Evelyn Arizpe and Gabrielle Cliff Hodges

Routledge
Taylor & Francis Group
LONDON AND NEW YORK

First published 2018
by Routledge
2 Park Square, Milton Park, Abingdon, Oxon OX14 4RN

and by Routledge
711 Third Avenue, New York, NY 10017

Routledge is an imprint of the Taylor & Francis Group, an informa business

British Library Cataloguing in Publication Data
A catalogue record for this book is available from the British Library

Library of Congress Cataloging in Publication Data
Title: Young people reading.
Description: Abingdon, Oxon ; New York, NY : Routledge is an imprint of the Taylor & Francis Group, an Informa Business, [2018] | Includes bibliographical references and index.
Identifiers: LCCN 2017054401 | ISBN 9781138291577 (hbk) | ISBN 9781138291584 (pbk) | ISBN 9781315265216 (ebk)
Subjects: LCSH: Reading–Research. | Young adults–Books and reading.
Classification: LCC LB1050.6 .Y68 2018 | DDC 428.4072–dc23
LC record available at https://lccn.loc.gov/2017054401

ISBN: 978-1-138-29157-7 (hbk)
ISBN: 978-1-138-29158-4 (pbk)
ISBN: 978-1-315-26521-6 (ebk)

Typeset in Bembo
by Out of House Publishing

CONTENTS

FIGURES AND TABLES

Figures

Tables

CONTRIBUTORS

Nayla Aramouni was born and grew up in Lebanon. She completed her undergraduate degree in Education at the American University of Beirut while working in what was the Middle East's first and only children's bookstore at the time. Following university, she spent the early days of her career working to encourage reading, first as a primary school teacher then as a children's educational bookstore manager. She also headed up the teacher training department at a Beirut-based educational company, which served the Middle East. In 2008, she travelled to the United Kingdom to complete an MPhil in Children's Literature at the University of Cambridge and then stayed on to complete a PhD in Education. She currently manages the development of new curricula in a wide range of subjects and countries at Cambridge Assessment International Education, a part of the University of Cambridge. She continues to devote time to young people and their reading and works with a social enterprise to strengthen empathy through reading in primary schools.

Evelyn Arizpe is originally from Mexico but has lived in the UK for more than 20 years. She is a Senior Lecturer at the School of Education, University of Glasgow, where she coordinates the MEd Programme in Children's Literature and Literacies and supervises doctoral students working in these fields. Her teaching and research attempt to bridge the gap between children's literature and literacy, and she has taught and published widely in both these areas. She has worked on a number of studies related to reading and response, involving both children and adolescents in various international contexts. She co-authored *Visual Journeys through Wordless Narratives* (Bloomsbury, 2014) with Teresa Colomer, Carmen Martínez-Roldán and other colleagues, and also a new edition of *Children Reading Picturebooks* (Routledge, 2016) with Morag Styles. Her most recent book is *Children as Readers in Children's Literature*, co-edited with Vivienne Smith (Routledge, 2016).

Lucia Cedeira Serantes was born and grew up in A Coruña, Spain. Her academic life took her to Pittsburgh, Pennsylvania in the United States and London, Ontario in Canada. Now she works as an Assistant Professor at the Graduate School of Library and Information Studies, at Queens College, City University of New York where she also coordinates the Certificate for Children and Young Adult Services in Public Libraries. Her primary research lies at the intersection of young adults, reading and public libraries, with an emphasis on the reading experience from the reader's perspective. She has received several awards, among them the John A. Lent Scholarship in Comics Studies at the International Comics Arts Forum. She has presented her research in both library-focused and interdisciplinary conferences and has provided contributions to *Transforming Young Adult Services: A Reader for Our Age* (Neal-Schuman, 2013) and *Plotting the Reading Experience: Theory/Practice/Politics* (Wilfrid Laurier University Press, 2016). She is involved with the Young Adult Library Services Association, where currently she is part of the editorial committee of *The Journal of Research on Libraries and Young Adults*. As a professional librarian, she was honoured to have worked as a young adult librarian and researcher for the (now sadly closed) International Centre for Children's and Young Adults' Books (Salamanca, Spain).

Su Li Chong was born and raised in Malaysia and read for her MPhil and PhD in Education at the University of Cambridge in England. While in Cambridge, she received the St Edmund's College Dean's Award for supererogation work. Currently, she is a Senior Lecturer at the Universiti Teknologi PETRONAS, Malaysia, where she teaches and supervises postgraduate students on the use of qualitative research methodology in social sciences research. Having thrived in both the Malaysian and UK systems of higher education, Su Li brings to bear a perspective that is broad and inclusive. She has spent the past two decades teaching, researching and publishing on issues related to language and literacy education. She believes that the experience of reading in many languages deserves particular attention. She is a member of the United Kingdom Literacy Association and the Qualitative Research Association Malaysia.

Gabrielle Cliff Hodges was born and grew up in England. She is a former Senior Lecturer in Education at the University of Cambridge, where she coordinated and taught on the secondary English Postgraduate Certificate in Education (PGCE) course as well as supervising Masters and PhD students. Previously, she had taught in three 11–18 comprehensive schools in Cambridgeshire, in the last as Head of the English department, before moving into teacher education in 1993. She has written many articles and chapters about secondary English teaching. She is an active member of the National Association for the Teaching of English and the United Kingdom Literacy Association. She is also a Fellow of the English Association. Her main area of research is reading, especially young people's development as readers within and beyond the classroom. In addition, she is very interested in histories of reading and how reading has been taught in the past, whether in the home, at school or within teacher education. Her most recent book is *Researching and Teaching Reading: Developing Pedagogy through Critical Enquiry* (Routledge, 2016).

Osman Coban was born on the Mediterranean coast of Turkey. Before moving to the UK, he completed an MEd in Turkish Language and Literature Teaching and taught this subject in supplementary schools and secondary schools (11–18) in East and Central Anatolia for six years. In 2013 he obtained an MEd in Children's Literature and Literacies from the University of Glasgow with a dissertation focusing on the representation of refugees in children's literature. He has recently submitted his PhD thesis, focusing on the reading choices of adolescent readers in Turkey and the effects of reading fiction. He has presented papers at international conferences held by organisations such as the International Research Society for Children's Literature (IRSCL), the United Kingdom Literacy Association and the International Board on Books for Young People (IBBY). He is a member of IRSCL and IBBY UK. His research interests include young people's reading practices in and out of school, reading-writing stories on online sites, reader response theory, immigration literature and children's literature. In particular, he is interested in developing inclusion and tolerance in multicultural communities through children's and young people's books.

Laura Guerrero Guadarrama was born and grew up in Mexico City. She has a PhD in Modern Languages and is a full-time professor at the Department of Literature of the Universidad Iberoamericana there. She is the director of the electronic journal, *LIJ Ibero, Review of Contemporary Children's and Youth Literature* [*Revista de Literatura Infantil y Juvenil Contemporánea* (Universidad Iberoamericana/Textofilia, 2016)]. She also coordinates a University Diploma on Children's and Youth Literature. She has been a member of the National System of Researchers (level 1) since 2006. She has received the Basic Scientific Research Grant awarded by the Ministry of Public Education and the National Council of Science and Technology twice. She is a member of the International Thematic Network on Children's and Youth Literature in the Iberian and Iberoamerican countries. She has taught in several universities in Mexico, Argentina and Spain, and has authored numerous articles, books and book chapters. Her most recent book is *Neo-Subversion in Contemporary Children's and Youth Literature: An Approach to Mexico and Spain* [*Neosubversión en la LIJ Contemporánea: Una Aproximación a México y España* (Universidad Iberoamericana, 2016)]. She is also interested in women's literature, specifically in the work of Rosario Castellanos, and in the relationship between mass media and literature.

Jia Wei Lim is currently a Senior Lecturer in the Faculty of Education at the University of Malaya, Malaysia. She was born in Malaysia and completed most of her education in Kuala Lumpur. After graduating with a degree in education in teaching English as a second language, she pursued an MA in English literature while she taught A-level English literature for four years in Methodist College Kuala Lumpur. She then continued her studies at the University of Cambridge, where she completed her doctoral thesis on the development of post-16 English Literature in Malaysia. On returning to her country, she continued working with Methodist College Kuala Lumpur to develop a Diploma in English Literature programme. She now lectures on undergraduate and graduate courses, supervises graduate students and serves on the editorial board of her faculty's journal. Her main research interests and publications are focused on literature pedagogy, literature assessment and post-compulsory education. Her latest project is to explore the effectiveness of introducing reflective critical thinking tools for developing readers' responses to literature texts.

Mireia Manresa was born in Catalonia, Spain. She holds a PhD in Language and Literature Education from the Universitat Autònoma de Barcelona (UAB). She has been an Associate Lecturer in the Language and Literature Didactics Department at UAB since 2005 and is a member of the Research Group on Books for Children and Youngsters and Literacy Learning (GRETEL). She has also taught in secondary education since 1997 and now she is working on distance and e-learning education at secondary level for adults. She has collaborated with several institutions and public administrations in different countries as a teacher trainer, consultant and designer of both educational devices and Massive Open Online Courses. Her latest publications, *The Teenager's Reading Universe: From Reading Habits to Literature Teaching* [*L'Univers Lector Adolescent: Dels Habits de Lectura a la Intervenció Educativa*] (Rosa Sensat, 2013) and the recent *Digital Literature for Children: Texts, Readers and Educational Practices* (Peter Lang, 2015), which she has co-edited, stand out among her research output. She is keen on the study of how reading habits are constructed in and out of school and on literary education.

Rebecca Nambi was born and educated mainly in Uganda, East Africa. She is currently a full time Lecturer at Makerere University Kampala in the School of Education where she coordinates the English and Literature Unit and the PhD programme. She teaches on the Masters, the Postgraduate Diploma in Education and the undergraduate programmes in addition to supervising PhD and Masters students. Rebecca has extensive experience as a secondary school teacher having taught English, Literature in English and the General Paper for more than ten years in schools around Kampala. She heads up the committee that organises annual conferences for secondary teachers of English and Literature in Uganda which helps her make connections between theory and practice as she engages on a regular basis with teachers in the field, including the ones she has trained. Rebecca is interested in enhancing reading among adolescents in Uganda and she has undertaken an initiative to introduce a community library at her home with the hope of attracting young people who are either in or out of school, encouraging them to read both local and global texts at no cost to themselves.

Erin Spring was born and raised in Huntsville, Ontario in Canada. Her studies and work as a teacher have taken her to many different places across Canada and beyond. She is is currently an Assistant Professor in the Werklund School of Education at the University of Calgary, Canada. As a settler scholar in this place, Erin is a guest on Treaty 7 territory, home of the Blackfoot, Tsuut'ina and the Stoney Nakoda First Nations. Erin's interdisciplinary research focuses on young people's texts and cultures. She has written extensively on the intersections of place and identity construction in the lives of adolescent readers. She teaches courses for undergraduate and graduate students in Literacy and Culture as well as Indigenous Education. She completed her doctoral work in the Faculty of Education at the University of Cambridge. As part of her study, she worked with young adults, including recent migrants, living in diverse Canadian geographies. Her doctoral thesis was awarded the United Kingdom Literacy Association student research prize in 2014. She is an active member of the Association for Research in the Cultures of Young People, and the International Research Society for the Study of Children's Literature.

WORLD MAP

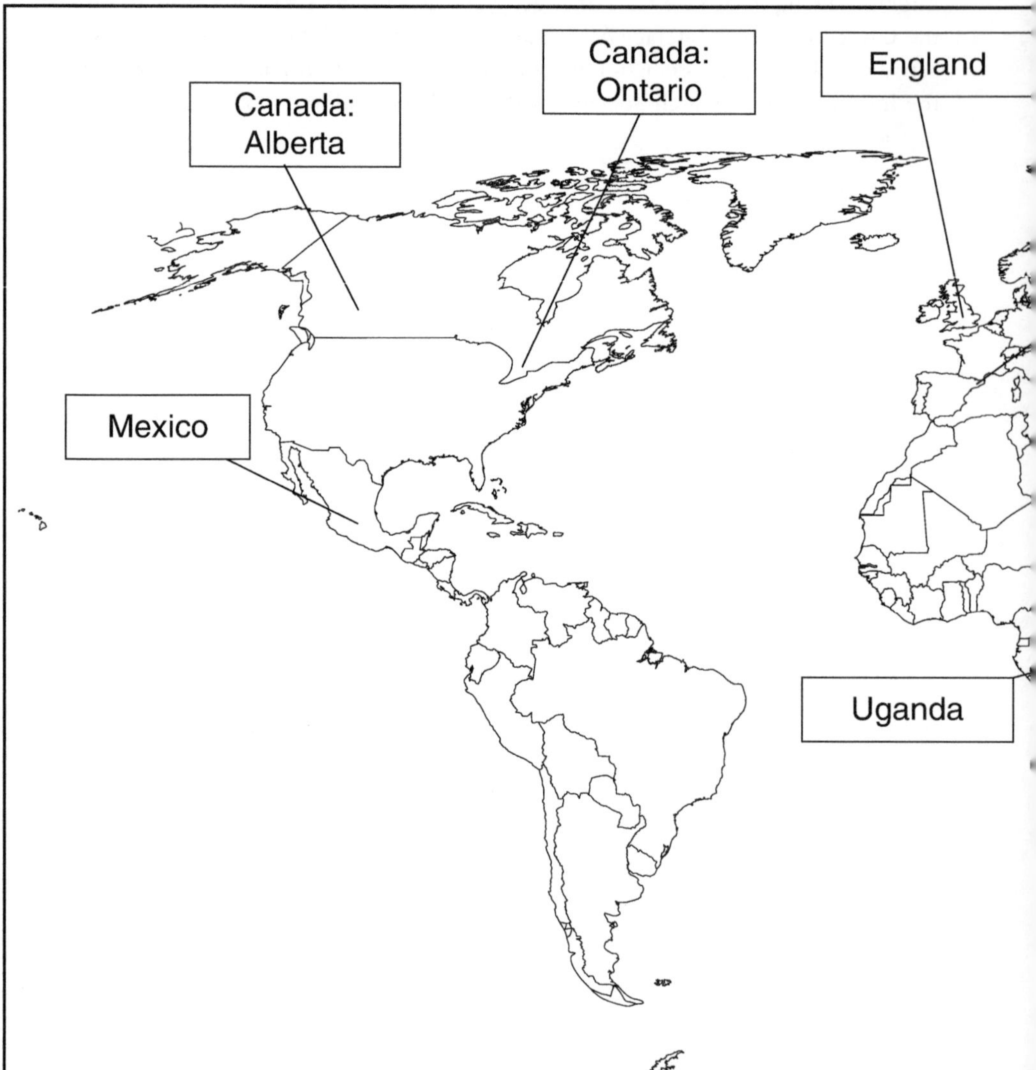

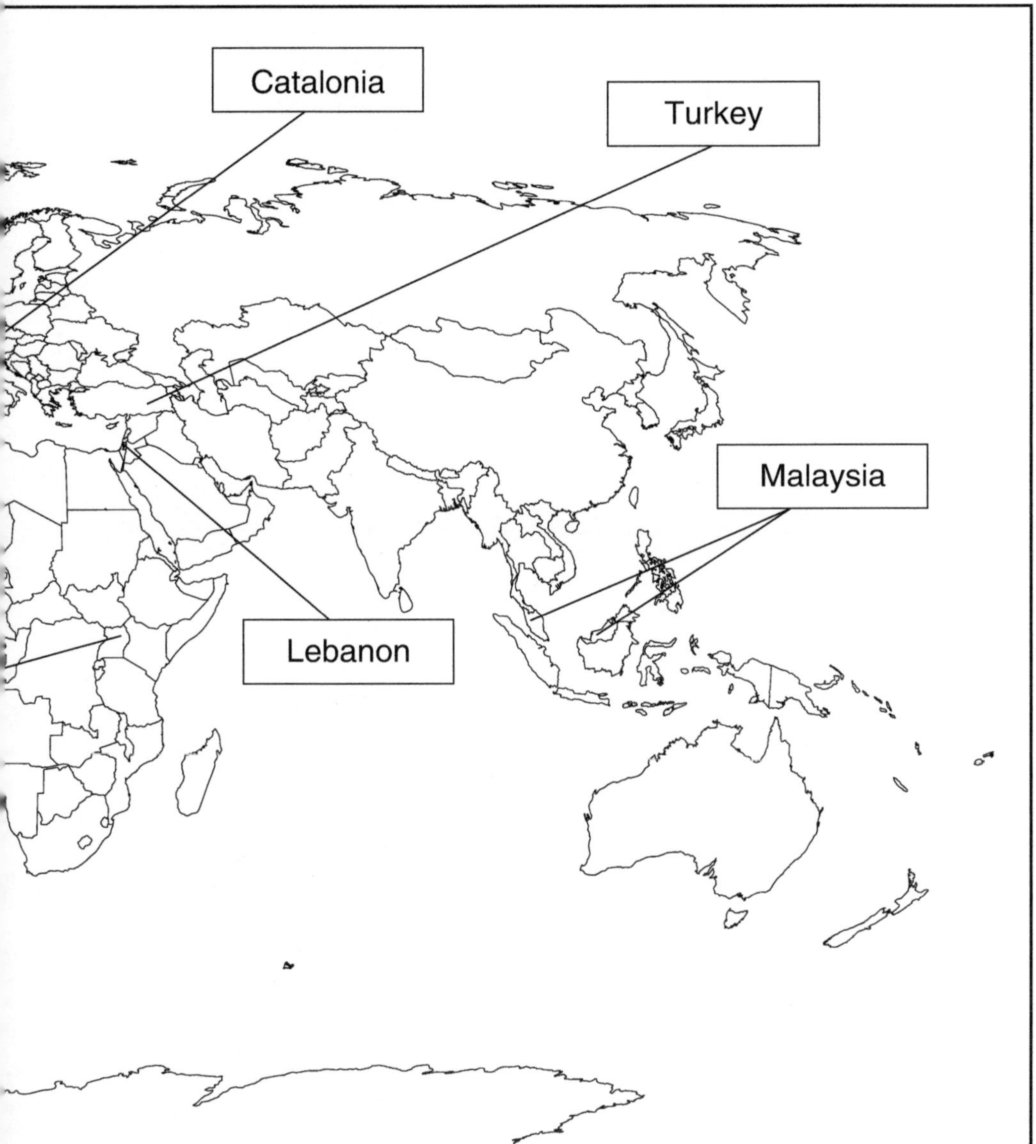

Catalonia
Turkey
Malaysia
Lebanon

INTRODUCTION

Evelyn Arizpe and Gabrielle Cliff Hodges

A rationale for the book

In the summer of 2014, Evelyn Arizpe and Gabrielle Cliff Hodges were examiners for a PhD thesis on the subject of young adult reading. Some years beforehand, their own doctoral studies had focused on young adult readers, which was a life-long interest for both of them. In discussion, they realised that they had also, between them, supervised a number of higher degree students who were themselves researching young adult readers and reading in a variety of different countries around the globe. Evelyn and Gabrielle therefore decided it would be both valuable and interesting to draw some of these diverse studies together into a single edited compilation as a way to ensure that the research was not only shared widely but that it would also enable readers of the book to explore possible correspondences between different doctoral studies. They hoped that such a book would potentially strengthen the rather precarious reputation that such research all too often acquires.

One reason for this precarious reputation is that both quantitative and qualitative research methods have limitations for the capture and analysis of reliable data on reading and other literacy practices, the former because they cannot provide the nuances of personal choice and response and the latter because they cannot offer generalisable results for large populations. However, another reason may have to do with the particular group of readers this book focuses on, a group that ranges from those who have recently left childhood behind to those who are moving into adulthood. How this transition from childhood to adulthood is understood differs between cultures and over time. At the turn of the twenty-first century, definitions of adolescence have become even more fluid, as established models of family and community change and the physical effects of puberty and the cognitive and emotional signs of maturity extend beyond both the earlier and later traditional age boundaries. The frontiers between childhood and adulthood in some contexts have also been blurred, on the one hand as a result of digital technology, which allows access to knowledge and information previously barred to those on the younger end of the spectrum, and on the other hand it promotes to those on the older end of the spectrum forms of play and entertainment traditionally left behind with childhood. The lack of distinct boundaries and the shifting roles that young people must assume result in tensions and contradictions that are reflected and played out in their literacy practices, such as Yolanda, in Arizpe and Guerrero Guadarrama's chapter who was simultaneously reading Disney fairy tales, de Saint-Exupéry's *The Little Prince* (1945) and E. L. James' *Fifty Shades of Grey* (2011). The expectations of society, and particularly parents and educators, have played an important role in these contradictions because their insistence on certain approved reading and other literacy practices often leads to outright rejection of what adolescents enjoy, or to more subtle subversion on the part of adolescent readers. Even from the middle of the twentieth century, young people were developing their own sense of themselves as readers in opposition to the authorities and gatekeepers; as 16-year-old Holden Caulfield explains in J. D. Salinger's classic novel from 1951, *The Catcher in the Rye* (originally written for adults but since appropriated by adolescent readers), 'I'm quite illiterate, but I read a lot' (Salinger, 1951: 18). With these challenges and complexities in mind, we need to approach the subject of young adult readers through research that is rigorous and valid but also flexible and creative, as are the studies collected in this volume.

The chapters that follow this Introduction are a direct outcome of Evelyn and Gabrielle's discussion mentioned in the first paragraph. They include two chapters written by Evelyn and Gabrielle in which they go back to their own doctoral research. Evelyn returns to Mexico where, with Laura Guerrero Guadarrama, she reruns her original doctoral study 25 years on. Gabrielle revisits one of her doctoral research methods, the 'rivers of reading' collages, to see what further reflection since the year 2011 – when she completed her doctoral study – might reveal about its apparent popularity. All but one of the remaining chapters are written by Evelyn's and Gabrielle's doctoral students, each exploring in fascinating detail what selected young adult participants have to say about reading in whichever part of the world the research was conducted. An eighth contributor likewise writes about research arising out of her doctoral work. She was supervised by colleagues in Canada, but was known to Evelyn and Gabrielle through meetings at conferences and via online blogging. Together, the chapters form an unusual collection of contemporary thinking about young adult reading, greatly enriched by being brought into such close proximity and hence making any similarities and distinctions really stand out.

An outline of the Introduction

In this Introduction, we provide a brief summary of some of the many ways in which research into young adult readers and reading is often characterised. We then go on to explain why we think this compilation offers a rather different approach. We consider the chief methodologies that the researchers in this book have chosen to adopt and the wealth of different research methods used to generate rich data about multiple ways of reading diverse texts, whether print, digital, paper-based or online. We conclude the Introduction with a brief outline of each chapter, showing how it is simultaneously distinctive and yet connected to the others. Together, we argue, the chapters form a cumulative whole, which we hope will serve to stimulate further thinking about young adult readers and thereby change the way teachers, parents, librarians and – crucially – young people themselves perceive readers and reading. We also explore some of the reasons why arguments put forward by the twentieth-century reading theorist Louise Rosenblatt have been so important to all our work. Finally, we write a few words about the ethical approaches adopted by the researchers in this volume so that we avoid repetition in each chapter about common procedures such as gaining participants' consent or assuring their anonymity. In summary, the Introduction stresses the urgent need for both teachers and researchers to read about and conduct qualitative, empirical research of the kind represented here because of the vital insights it affords, whether through individual projects or through reading about them in conjunction with one another. The authors intend the book to reach reading researchers and teachers in all parts of the globe, especially those embarking on their own empirical projects, who may find reassurance, inspiration and companionship from the researchers whose work is shared here.

The importance of bringing small-scale qualitative studies together

In this compilation, we argue very strongly that bringing small-scale qualitative studies together is one way of doing what Jason Jensen and Robert Rodgers describe as cumulating 'intellectual gold' (2001: 235). Writing specifically about case studies and the charge that they have often in the past been dismissed as poor-quality research on the grounds that they are both small in size and do not afford generalisability, Jensen and Rodgers state the following: 'when the findings of case studies are analyzed cumulatively, the foundation for both criticisms vanishes because the generalizability of each study is addressed while the richness of detail is preserved' (237). Other researchers before them have argued similar points. Here, for example, is the educator Lawrence Stenhouse distinguishing between the value of linear interpretations and comparative historical interpretations. In both, the reader has an active part to play. With linear interpretations, readers' capacity for interpretation is tacit, and requires them to bring their own prior experience to bear on the research. Comparing different interpretations, however, says Stenhouse, is a more explicit process, whether to the readers themselves or to others. As far back as 1978, Stenhouse was therefore arguing for bringing different small-scale research projects together, just as we are here in this volume, because as Jensen and Rodgers contend, explicit comparisons afford them cumulative value and readers cannot avoid beginning to evaluate – even generalise – from them collectively:

> Linear interpretation is the characteristic of narrative, and it supports the kind of history which is a story of events. Underlying linear interpretation is implicit generalisation about the nature of human action and human purposes. The historian appeals, not only to his sources, but also to his reader's experience. Comparative history is explicitly concerned with generalisation. It depends upon distinguishing classes of institution or activity which are taken to have some identity, and attempting to generalise about them.
>
> (Stenhouse, 1978: 25)

Helen Simons, a former colleague of Stenhouse, develops this argument further, suggesting that it is imperative to change the way we research as well as the way research is perceived, such that it affects not only researchers but participants and readers as well:

> there is a real urgency for educational researchers to rethink and restructure the way we represent what we see, for others too – the policy makers, practitioners and programme developers we seek to serve – have to construct their own meanings from the evidence we offer. That being the case, we would be wise to maximize the possibilities of different ways of seeing how we represent research evidence.
>
> (Simons, 1996: 232)

David Bridges (2017) draws on both Stenhouse and Simons among others in his discussion of the value of single case study research. He suggests three ways in which individual case studies may be valuable. All of them require the reader to be actively engaged with the case studies about which they are reading. He argues that case studies may be 'a source of refutation and conjecture' (244), or encourage readers to relate 'the particular to the particular' (245), or offer 'vicarious experience' (246). Whichever of these three stances readers take up, they deepen understanding and develop learning. Connecting research projects in similar ways is, in part, what we hope to achieve within this book. We also hope that readers' own understanding is deepened and that future research may be developed as a result of learning about the studies presented in these chapters, individually and cumulatively. It would also mean, of course, that more young readers' voices would be heard through their participation in the research, and their experiences made more visible.

Although some recent research into reading has adopted a slightly more inclusive stance towards young adult readers (e.g., Rothbauer et al., 2016; Goodwyn et al., 2018), such a stance is relatively unusual. Moreover, research in some parts of the world remains extremely scarce, for example in places affected by poverty or political upheaval. From an Anglo-centric position, there may be reasons for this situation. As John McMullen (2017) argues, research in war-affected or low-income countries is often difficult, if not non-existent, because 'the places in need of evidence-based support are often the places with the poorest resources and the fewest trained professionals' (8) and for researchers attempting to work there and carry out interventions, there are often 'personal challenges of finance, transport, language, health, time pressure and security' (ibid.). In this present compilation, however, what characterises the research is that it is – almost entirely – conducted by researchers working in their home countries where they are familiar with the languages, have places to stay and hence know how to navigate practicalities such as transport, finance and so on. In addition, they tend to be more familiar with the cultures, communities, languages and practices they are researching than incomers from elsewhere might be. That, coupled with research methodologies designed to learn more about individuals rather than implement interventions, is what makes the work in this volume unusual.

Some prior approaches to reading research

Current approaches to reading research within education have often been determined by contemporary practices in the teaching and learning of reading in schools. In many parts of the world, however, teaching and learning have recently been increasingly dominated by ideas about young people's performance as readers. In a desperate bid for measurable successes, governments have often put almost intolerable pressure on schools to produce results from tests and examinations which, they say, will demonstrate the extent of reader development. To that end, research methodologies such as surveys and questionnaires have been favoured approaches: not only are they relatively easy to administer but they can also generate quantitative data that can readily be translated into student (and hence teacher or school) performance. In parts of the developed world where a wide range of books may be available along with space and time to read them, young adults ironically often appear to be put off reading, precisely because the kind of attention they are required by teachers (and sometimes parents) to pay to the very texts they are encouraged to read is off-putting to them. Meanwhile, in many other parts of the world, very different factors may also be off-putting, for example a serious lack of reading material, very large classes where creative approaches can be extremely difficult to implement, as well as recognisable pressure to perform well in tests and examinations. Whatever the reasons for pressure on readers and a corresponding squeezing of research approaches, current writing about reading research all too often ends with a plea for closer attention to be paid to readers and their reading and for young adult readers' voices and experiences to be much more distinctive.

A great deal of reading research with young adults in different social and cultural contexts in various parts of the world therefore ends up at the same point, namely an impassioned call for more in-depth studies that will help us understand better what part reading really plays in the lives of young adults. Here, for example, are two seasoned Australian researchers, Don Carter and Jacqueline Manuel, writing in the *Australian Journal of Language and Literacy* in 2015. While the statistics they cite (e.g., book sales) appear to show young adult reading in a healthy state in Australia, Carter and Manuel are quick to acknowledge that '[f]rom these statistics, however, it cannot be assumed that purchase patterns in any category of books are directly indicative of young people's actual reading lives, within and beyond the parameters of formal school-based education' (115). Despite criticisms of various prior surveys into young people's reading, Carter and Manuel nevertheless use in their own study what they describe as 'an online survey instrument … [which] required participants to respond to a series of multiple choice questions, each with an open field, along with short-answer items, seeking responses to questions' (118). Their analysis of the data generated by the survey is not uninteresting, but it is perhaps not surprising that they conclude as follows: 'The findings of this research highlight the pressing need to re-focus on the actual and potential significance of reading in the lives of the young people we teach' (126).

Some such research does exist, of course. We are thinking, for example, of work such as Michael Smith and Jeffrey Wilhelm's intriguing study of young American men in which they make use of interesting research methods such as think-aloud protocols and reading logs to tease out the distinctiveness of the boys they are working with. As they say quite emphatically:

> the boys were very different. They had different values, interests, and goals. Consequently we're wary of lumping them together in a category called 'boys', and we're suspicious of research which homogenizes them … Instead of identifying their achievements and needs through statistical averages in which their differences are lost, we need to recognize and work with individual difference, variety, and plurality and make that diversity a strength of our classroom … We want the research we have undertaken on boys and literacy to matter.
>
> (Smith and Wilhelm, 2002: 183–184)

Other research that attempts to understand young adult reading as it is experienced by young readers in different social and cultural contexts includes John Yandell's study of reading literature in urban classrooms over several years, exploring how diverse young adults engage with literature teaching. In his study, *The Social Construction of Meaning: Reading Literature in Urban English Classrooms* (2014), the voices of students and their teachers (and, indeed, the researcher) are clearly heard. However, Yandell's broad intention is to explore reading as it occurs in school rather than in young adults' lives beyond. By contrast, Lynne Wiltse's (2015) research in Canada and Elizabeth Moje et al.'s (2008) study in the United States both attempt to explore young readers' lived experiences of reading, in Wiltse's case within a broadly educational context and in Moje et al.'s case on the city streets beyond. In these kinds of studies, young people who might otherwise be marginalised for reasons of ethnicity, gender or socioeconomic status are at the centre of the researchers' and authors' attention. What our own edited compilation – this very book – also does, however, is bring a much wider variety of both students and researchers into conjunction with one another so that young adult readers and their researchers in Uganda or Malaysia, for example, jostle with others from Turkey, Mexico and Lebanon, allowing for a collection that is global in its scope and mix.

Diverse research

The research projects described here – by contrast with much young adult reading research to date – not only span a diverse range of young readers in different parts of the world; they also employ a variety of methodologies and research methods. The two most popular methodologies are case study and hermeneutic phenomenology. That is perhaps not surprising, given that the authors' chief aims are to research young adult readers' reading as it is actually experienced. As Jensen and Rodgers (2001) explain, case studies are valuable if what is required is 'in-depth understanding of cause and effect relationships that other methodologies find difficult to achieve' (235). Moreover, since the researchers may well end up finding, like Smith and Wilhelm (2002), that their participants are all very different, then they may find solace in Simons' contention that case studies are useful because they form a paradox and that is, precisely, where their value rests. Simons writes: 'case study celebrates the particular and the unique and frequently yields outcomes that are inconclusive. The paradox is that therein lies its strength for policy making' (1996: 227). Hermeneutic phenomenology offers similarly productive opportunities to explore complex phenomena in depth, acknowledging in particular the inevitability that the researcher needs to adopt an interpretative stance. As Catherine Adams and Max van Manen (2008) suggest, 'Phenomenology becomes hermeneutical when its method is taken to be interpretive' (615) rather than merely descriptive. Once, therefore, we do attempt to describe a phenomenon or lived experience in words, we also need hermeneutics to interpret the very language being used to describe it. Hence the researcher has to be not only closely attentive to whatever phenomenon is being explored, but also – in due course – adopt a hermeneutical approach to try and make sense of it. In the case of a deeply complex activity such as reading, the researcher, therefore, faces great difficulties. It is interesting to read how several researchers within this volume have adopted just such a methodology, as well why they did so.

Creative research methods

In addition, both these methodologies require creative research methods, as the contributors to this edited compilation demonstrate, because how young adults experience reading is such a diverse and complex matter. Within the pages of this book, therefore, readers will find a wide variety of methods being used to generate a rich array of data. Readers can gain insights from the detailed consideration to which the research methods and the data they generate are subjected within the chapters of this book. Some research methods are particularly popular, such as semi-structured individual or small-group interviewing, classroom observation, and small-group discussion; others are rather less common – for example, rivers of reading collages, visual depictions of reading memories, and reading journals. The intention is, however, that there should be enough description of each method for it to be replicable by other students or researchers. In terms of data analysis, many of the contributors here not only use common approaches such as thematic coding, but elements of discourse analysis as well.

The range of texts, languages, reading spaces and participants

Another feature of this book is its coverage of an enormously wide range of text types including comics, graphic novels, novels, play texts, films, digital texts, and so on. Some of those mentioned were read by the participants in their own first languages, either because that was the only language in which they were available or because they had been translated into it from English. The texts that were read form a very important element of the research, so readers may well wish to follow some of them up. We have, therefore – wherever possible – referenced versions available in English. Where such versions do not exist, we have left the reference in the original language.

In addition, the researchers consider spaces for reading ranging from school libraries and classrooms to out-of-school bookshops, cafés and bedrooms. Because the projects span such a wide range of countries across the world, there is considerable diversity in young people's access to resources, whether for cultural reasons such as those experienced by young Aboriginal readers on a reserve in northern Canada, or for reasons of national instability or poverty in Lebanon or Mexico. Some of the research also touches on thought-provoking and relatively underexplored issues such as the concept of time as it relates to reading and how memories of reading in the past might inform young people's identities in the present. The question of the extent to which institutional power can support or hinder young people's development as readers emerges frequently. Whatever the focus, because the book spans research with readers aged from 12 to 21 in different parts of the world, it has three particularly unusual affordances, namely the capacity for readers to:

- compare and contrast different sociocultural and geopolitical reading experiences in diverse parts of the world;
- compare and contrast reading patterns across and beyond the teenage years, an age group that has hitherto tended to be neglected;
- focus on young adults in the upper part of the 12–21 age range, a group that – at least in Latin America – is emerging as the most frequent readers of books and digital texts but one that is relatively under-researched.

The influence of Louise Rosenblatt

Although the contributors to this volume draw on a wide variety of theorists in the realms of both reading and research methodology, one theorist in particular has informed more of our research than most: Louise Rosenblatt (1904–2005). For that reason, we discuss in the Introduction the importance of one of her key theoretical ideas – the transactional theory of reading. It underpins almost all the research discussed in this book and we feel it is therefore valuable to outline it in some depth here so that each chapter author is not obliged to keep repeating it. Rosenblatt's two most influential works are *Literature as Exploration* (1938/1995) and *The Reader, the Text, the Poem: The Transactional Theory of the Literary Work* (1978/1994). Both works offer a fascinating exploration of the literary theories she developed. There were several important impulses informing them at the time – political, historical and theoretical – which it is helpful to remember. For example, especially in the earlier part of the twentieth century, she was substantially influenced by the philosophical theories of pragmatists such as John Dewey, Charles Peirce and William James. She was also unusually familiar with the work of various anthropologists, including the very well-known Margaret Mead. However, as a lecturer of literature students, she was very conscious of contemporary political movements in the US that advocated strict conformism and popular approaches to literary study at the time, such as New Criticism, which, she argued, likewise positioned her students as compliant rather than enquiring or even divergent. As she demonstrates beautifully in the second chapter of *The Reader, the Text, the Poem*, no two readers read the same text in exactly the same way and although there might be more or less likely readings, there could never simply be one correct interpretation. It was certainly wrong to try and guess the intention of the author. Instead, she developed an extremely compelling theory of reading as a transaction. She spelled out very clearly that it was a transaction she meant, not an interaction, drawing a distinction between interaction as a mechanical process between objects that remain unchanged as a result of the interaction, and transaction as an organic process between objects that change and are, in turn, changed by the connections they make. In a reading transaction, what takes place is that reader and text work together to create – afresh each time – a poem (or what we might call now a 'reading'). The readings that are created are part of the transaction; they change the reader and the text so that a second reading of the same text by the same reader is always different. Rosenblatt describes the process as ecological (a term she openly adopts from John Dewey), which is to say that it is a living, growing, changing process, not one that is fixed and static (never mind right or wrong). Her theory of transactional reading has been very popular and, as such, has been somewhat abused in the usage, particularly as people have interchanged the words 'interaction' and 'transaction' in ways of which Rosenblatt disapproved. In an article entitled 'Viewpoints: Transaction versus interaction – a terminological rescue operation' (1985), she firmly sets the record straight.

Rereading Rosenblatt's original works is a clear reminder as to why her theories of reading have been so valuable within the research outlined in this volume. Her work gives status and credence to readers themselves (where, before, reading had been dominated by the hegemony of the text and the notion of the writer's intention). Since one key aim of the research outlined here is to try to deepen our understanding of how young adult readers experience reading in all sorts of diverse ways, it is perhaps unsurprising that Rosenblatt's theories chime so well. As already suggested above, the chapters that follow are particularly interesting for the array of qualitative research methods that are employed, often very creatively, to help us see more clearly what these readers can be like and what they do with the vast panoply of texts they read in many different media. Added to that, the researchers who have authored these chapters also demonstrate a strong interest in their participants' geographical and spatial contexts and the ways in which these might affect their reading. The studies show that readers are all different, as is the case with organisms that comprise any ecosystem, so perhaps we should not be surprised. Rosenblatt probably would not have been; but she would, we think, have been pleased!

Another key tenet of Rosenblatt's theorising is the now well-known idea of aesthetic and efferent reading. When complex theories are widely referred to and pared down, as is often the case, they can lose a lot in the process. Sometimes the aesthetic and the efferent are used as simple binaries, which is not at all what Rosenblatt intended. Although she did argue for the idea of a continuum between the two, she also acknowledged that the same text could afford both kinds of reading, not necessarily at the same time but consecutively, rather than the text itself being either at one end or the other of the continuum. Again, within this volume, we see these different ways of reading being minutely explored by the chapter authors in conjunction with their participants, perhaps no more so than with Su Li Chong's Malaysian participant, a law undergraduate studying in an English university, who reads the Malaysian Federal Constitution both for pleasure and solace as well as for information.

Ethics

Rather than each chapter author stating the ethical procedures they adopted, readers should note that in every chapter, all participants' names and the names of any schools referred to have been changed to ensure anonymity (despite, in some cases, being all too well aware of the compromises involved in relation to the young adults' distinctive voices). The pseudonyms selected were either chosen by the students themselves to convey something of their characters (as is the case in Chapter 2) and/or were appropriate to the original names (e.g., the rural school in Chapter 4 had a Nahuatl pseudonym). Because all the studies were conducted in close conjunction with an educational institution, they adhered to the ethics protocols of the respective institutions. These included obtaining consent for participants' involvement and ensuring they understood that they could, if they wished, withdraw at any point without having to give a reason. Where relevant, consent was also sought from school principals as well as from the students' parents/carers. In some of the countries involved, government departments were consulted where the research sites required that level of permission; in Mexico, a risk assessment of the field, in consultation with the school authorities, was carried out before the study: the situation raised issues in terms of the ethics and positionality of the researchers as well as in terms of the group discussions and the interpretation of the readers' responses to the texts. In all cases within this book, the chapter authors were also the researchers in the projects. Their contributions are signalled by their initials, for example, in transcripts of small-group discussions. Where the students' own writing is quoted, the spelling, grammar and punctuation have been left as they were originally. What comes across clearly in all the chapters is the respect that the authors accorded to their participants, whether observing in schools, libraries and classrooms or reporting discussions with them. The fact that such creative and collaborative research methods were also used to generate data is an additional measure of the extent to which these authors wanted their activities to engage young adult readers as fully as possible, not merely use them as objects of enquiry.

The book's three sections

The book is divided into three broad sections: Section 1: 'Making adolescent reading choices visible', Section 2: 'Adolescent reading in times of crisis' and Section 3: 'Young adult readers' experiences within and beyond school and university'.

Section 1: Making adolescent reading choices visible

In Chapter 1, 'The possibilities of comics reading: Uncovering a complex and situated reading experience in Canada', Lucia Cedeira Serantes outlines a research project that sought to explore and understand the role of comics in the lives of young people, emphasising the experience of the readers themselves. In her project, Cedeira Serantes investigated how these comics readers constructed and understood their experience of comics as reading material and what this said about their reader identities and the social contexts of reading comics. The study was initially conceived as shifting the perspective away from previous research that had primarily focused on comics fans and comics as cultural products. Instead, one of the main concerns of this project was to engage teenagers and young adults who self-identified as comics readers and who read beyond superhero narratives. Cedeira Serantes interviewed different readers in a range of sites such as public libraries, comics stores and a university. The term 'comics' was used as an umbrella term to cover the wide variety of formats comics assume (comic books, webcomics, manga, *bande dessinée* and graphic novels, among others). The chapter not only reinforces the complexity of studying comics reading experiences, but also exposes the possibilities that the comics form, often described as light reading or recommended to reluctant readers, can offer in the exploration of young adult reading practices.

In Chapter 2, 'The residue of fiction in the memory of adolescence: The potential effect of reading fiction in Turkey', Osman Coban presents findings from an empirical research project that investigated reading choices of young adult readers, including books from the social media site Wattpad. The research involved a survey and follow-up reading sessions with successful and keen readers. For the reading sessions, students elected to read a book of their own choice. Findings from the data analysis suggested both short- and long-term effects of reading fiction including changing views of a particular issue, developing an understanding of self and diverse others and taking social action.

In Chapter 3, 'Rivers of reading: A research method to explore young adults' personal reading histories', Gabrielle Cliff Hodges revisits one research method employed in her doctoral study of young adult readers: creating critical incidents collages of readers' personal reading histories. The collages not only proved valuable as one research method within a larger case study, but they went on to do the same for many other teachers and researchers. Their popularity may have been because they were a way of conceptualising students' reading that emphasised multiplicity and future transformation rather than more familiar essentialist categories. They were also helpful as a means to bridge the gap between home and school reading, enabling teachers and researchers to find out what young people were reading outside school. Here, Cliff Hodges reconsiders the value of this kind of approach, likening it to aerial photography as a research method that enables a long-distance rather than solely a close-up view of a phenomenon.

Section 2: Adolescent reading in times of crisis

Chapter 4 is entitled 'Reading fears and opportunities: Researching changes over 25 years in the literacy practices of Mexican adolescents'. In it, Evelyn Arizpe and Laura Guerrero Guadarrama consider the findings of a research project that looked at how literacy practices had been changing among young people in Mexico within the past 25 years. While they found evidence that global factors were prompting and shaping some of these changes (the increase in publications for young adults and the presence of digital technology and social media), they also found evidence that, because of deeply rooted traditional perspectives, these changes were still being ignored within certain national contexts (in particular, the official school curriculum). They found that the circumstances of precariousness and insecurity in which adolescents were living were having significant impact on the ways in which they interacted with and responded to texts. As the students responded to the texts they read and reflected on the role of reading in their lives, references to the circumstances of insecurity in Mexico began to emerge and they mentioned not only their own personal fears and anxieties but also the challenges of growing up with considerable risks due to economic instability, political corruption, criminality and violence. These issues are taken up in this chapter, along with the conclusion that the participatory and creative research methods provided a space not only for investigating and reflecting on the changes in literacy practices together with the young people but also expressing hope for the future.

In Chapter 5, 'Young adults' attitudes towards reading in Lebanon', Nayla Aramouni reflects on her doctoral case study, which explored young adults' attitudes towards reading in Lebanon. It took place at two privately run, secular, mixed-sex schools with libraries on site, where English was the language of instruction. Aramouni examines the experiences and opinions of 12 young adults with a range of reading attitudes selected on the basis of their responses to a large-scale survey questionnaire. The relatively small number of books read by keen readers in Lebanon was found to be partly due to the difficulty and expense of obtaining suitable reading material but partly also to the country's unstable environment. The participants' direct experience of war and its effects led to an aversion to books that dealt with what are described as gruesome or depressing issues.

In Chapter 6, '"I think I was born with a suitcase": Blackfoot adolescent readers' responses to Sherman Alexie's *The Absolutely True Diary of a Part-Time Indian*' (Alexie, 2012), Erin Spring focuses on an empirical research study with Blackfoot youth who live on a reserve in Alberta. Her participants read and discussed several Indigenous texts, one of which was set on their reserve. Drawing on what she learned from her doctoral research, she explored ways in which Blackfoot adolescent readers' identities were tied to their understanding of social, cultural and physical places, plus whether and how the experience of reading culturally relevant, local fiction incited these readers to deliberate on the role of places within their lives. She was particularly interested in the role of place — as a geographical, social and cultural construct — in the reading experience. Her research, therefore, explored how her adolescent reader participants reflected on their place-identities while discussing culturally relevant fiction, and to what extent these texts encouraged Blackfoot readers to contemplate, share and celebrate the values and identities that were stripped from their Elders and communities through cultural assimilation.

Section 3: Young adult readers' experiences within and beyond school and university

'Adolescent reading habits: The effect of school activities on reading practices' is the title for Chapter 7, Mireia Manresa's study of young adult readers in Catalonia. The chapter reports the results of a longitudinal socioeducational research project that was designed to explore the influence of school reading planning on the structure of personal reading habits in young people. The characteristics and evolution over a three-year period of the extra-curricular reading of 80 adolescents in a Catalan high school were described and the effects of an independent reading programme on these habits were observed. Three particular aspects of reading were analysed in an attempt to offer a global perspective on reading habits: the quantity of reading, the typology of books read and the forms of evaluating the readings. The research also highlighted the importance of mediation in encouraging young people to read, for example schools' planning for independent reading, and the impact it could have on adolescents' ongoing evolution as readers.

Chapter 8, 'Young people reading in Uganda: Making connections between literature and reality' draws on one aspect of Rebecca Nambi's doctoral research, namely the reading practices and interests of 13–18-year-old adolescents in one secondary school in Uganda. In particular, she was interested in learners' literacy practices and, hence, whether and how learner-centred pedagogy impacted on their learning. Her analysis of the data revealed that although her research participants' reading was mainly guided by the requirements of the Ugandan National Curriculum Development Centre (NCDC), many of the learners were also motivated to read a wide range of texts that related to other contexts beyond the curriculum. However, to a large extent, the school itself as an institution appeared to influence the learners' reading choices and experiences since it was a major source of their reading material. Despite the pessimistic picture painted by some reports regarding the reading attainment of secondary school learners in developing contexts such as Uganda, the findings of Nambi's project revealed that some learners also had a heartening ability to make connections between literature and reality.

In Chapter 9, 'Exploring post-16 literature in English in a Malaysian classroom: A hermeneutic phenomenological perspective', Jia Wei Lim explores reading as a social activity within the public sphere of a classroom, one that is also inescapably determined by curriculum design, in this case the syllabus constructed by the examination board. In her research, she adopted a hermeneutic phenomenological perspective, grounded in teacher and student classroom experiences, to explore the issue of curriculum implementation and understand how post-16 literature was experienced by teachers and students in Malaysia in a subject entitled 'Literature in English', locally known as *Sijil Tinggi Pelajaran Malaysia* (STPM). She demonstrated how teacher and student classroom experiences could be perceived as a cycle of interpretation, conceptualisation and actualisation.

Finally, in Chapter 10, 'Pressure, pleasure and function: Malaysian undergraduates reading across boundaries in a university in England', Su Li Chong discusses research prompted by the concept of aliteracy of undergraduates who appeared to be only marginally interested in academic reading and completely uninterested in wider reading, a phenomenon that was often attributed to low levels of reading motivation. Hitherto, discussions about literacy, illiteracy or aliteracy, fuelled by binaries of function or pleasure, had tended to be based on an assumption that these concepts were situated on a linear continuum. However, research into the lived experiences of young people reading within their own particular contexts on a daily basis generated data that painted a very different picture. Prompted by this anxiety, Chong questioned whether the act of reading might be better explained by exploring not only reading of both academic texts and non-academic texts but also reading for functional purposes as well as for pleasure. A sample of multilingual Malaysian undergraduates in an English university shared their thoughts about their literate lives through a series of in-depth interviews and weekly diary entries. Narratives of the undergraduates' past and current experiences of reading across the boundaries of academic and non-academic materials were collected. Their reading included a fascinating mix of academic and non-academic texts, both print-based and digital, in English, Chinese and Malay. What emerged were complex patterns, one of which is presented here as an example.

References

Adams, C. and van Manen, M. (2008). Phenomenology. In L. M. Given (Ed.), *The Sage Encyclopaedia of Qualitative Research Methods*. London: Sage, pp. 614–619.

Alexie, S. (2012). *The Absolutely True Diary of a Part-Time Indian*. New York: Hachette Book Group.

Bridges, D. (2017). *Philosophy in Educational Research: Epistemology, Ethics, Politics and Quality*. Cham, Switzerland: Springer International Publishing.

Carter, D. and Manuel, J. (2015). Current and historical perspectives on Australian teenagers' reading practices and preferences. *Australian Journal of Language and Literacy*, 38 (2), 115–128.

de Saint-Exupéry, A. (1945). *The Little Prince*. London: Heinemann.

Goodwyn, A., Durrant, C., Reid, L. and Scherff, L. (Eds.), (2018). *International Perspectives on the Teaching of Literature in Schools: Global Principles and Practices*. Abingdon, Oxfordshire: Routledge/NATE.

James, E. L. (2011). *Fifty Shades of Grey*. London: Vintage.

Jensen, J. and Rodgers, R. (2001). Cumulating the intellectual gold of case study research. *Public Administration Review*, 61 (2), 235–246.

McMullen, J. (2017). Delivering and evaluating interventions in war-affected, low-income countries. *Research Intelligence*, 133, 8–10.

Moje, E., Overby, M., Tysvaer, N. and Morris, K. (2008). The complex world of adolescent literacy: Myths, motivations and mysteries. *Harvard Educational Review*, 78 (1), 107–154.

Rosenblatt, L. M. (1938/1995). *Literature as Exploration* (5th ed.). New York: Modern Language Association of America.

Rosenblatt, L. M. (1978/1994). *The Reader, the Text, the Poem: The Transactional Theory of the Literary Work*. Carbondale & Edwardsville: Southern Illinois University Press.

Rosenblatt, L. (1985). Viewpoints: Transaction versus interaction – a terminological rescue operation. *Research in the Teaching of English*, 19 (1), 96–107.

Rothbauer, P., Skjerdingstad, K. I., McKechnie, L. E. F. and Oterholm, K. (Eds.), (2016). *Plotting the Reading Experience: Theory /Practice/Politics*. Waterloo, Ontario: Wilfrid Laurier University Press.

Salinger, J. D. (1951). *The Catcher in the Rye*. London: Little Brown.

Simons, H. (1996). The paradox of case study. *Cambridge Journal of Education*, 26 (2), 225–240.

Smith, M. W. and Wilhelm, J. D. (2002). *'Reading Don't Fix No Chevys': Literacy in the Lives of Young Men*. Portsmouth, New Hampshire: Heinemann.

Stenhouse, L. (1978). Case study and case records: Towards a contemporary history of education. *British Educational Research Journal*, 4 (2), 21–39.

Wiltse, L. (2015). Not just 'sunny days': Aboriginal students connect out-of-school literacy resources with school literacy practices. *Literacy*, 49 (1), 60–68.

Yandell, J. (2014). *The Social Construction of Meaning: Reading Literature in Urban English Classrooms*. London: Routledge.

[illegible]
[illegible] (20[illegible]) [illegible]
[illegible] (20[illegible]) [illegible] [illegible]
[illegible]
[illegible] (20[illegible]) [illegible] [illegible]
[illegible]
[illegible] (20[illegible]) [illegible] [illegible]
[illegible]
[illegible] (20[illegible]) [illegible]
[illegible]
[illegible] (20[illegible]) [illegible]
[illegible]
[illegible] (20[illegible]) [illegible]
[illegible]
[illegible] (20[illegible]) [illegible]
[illegible] (20[illegible]) [illegible]
[illegible] (20[illegible]) [illegible]
[illegible]
[illegible] (20[illegible]) [illegible]
[illegible]
[illegible] (20[illegible]) [illegible]
[illegible]
[illegible] (20[illegible]) [illegible]
[illegible]

SECTION 1

Making adolescent reading choices visible

1

THE POSSIBILITIES OF COMICS READING

Uncovering a complex and situated reading experience in Canada

Lucia Cedeira Serantes

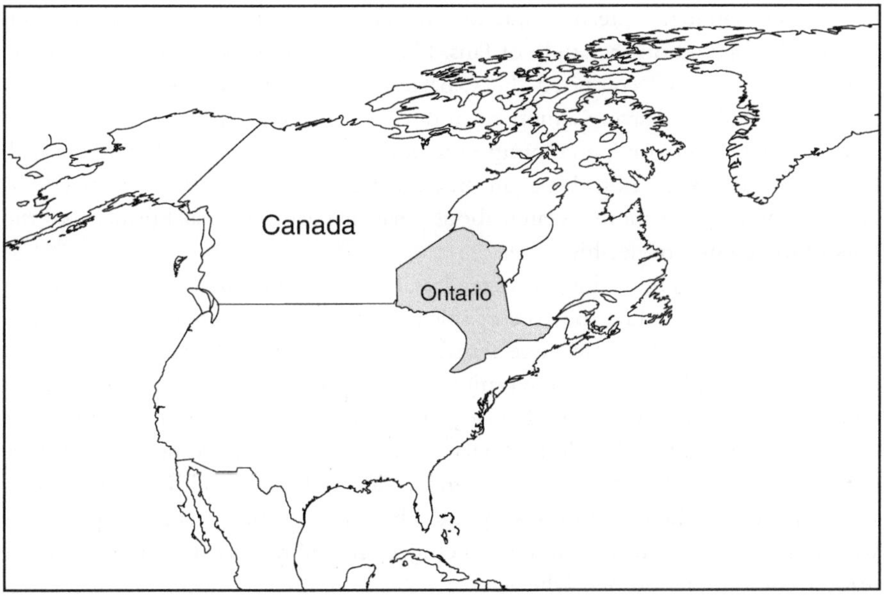

MAP 1

Changing perspectives on comics and their readers

Close your eyes and imagine someone reading comics. I will give you ten seconds and then ask that you come back to this page. Without being presumptuous, my guess is that you imagined a child or a teenager, probably male, reading superhero comics. Inspired by the typical answer to this exercise and personal conversation, I detected a lack of information about why teens and young adult readers are attracted to and read comics. The research work discussed here (Cedeira Serantes, 2014) responds to gaps in the research about comics reading, exploring and bringing to light the diversity and richness of the experience, using readers themselves as the core voices. For example, comics are increasingly characterised as rich, complex, challenging, diverse and multilayered reading materials. Despite this, it is commonplace to present teen readers of comics as readers who lack reading skills or discriminatory taste: reluctant readers, English as a Second Language (ESL) readers, at-risk readers or visual readers. Historically, comics have been popular reading materials for youth, and their content and communities an important part of youth culture (Wright, 2001). By contrast, educational and cultural institutions and the mainstream media have consistently diminished or attacked their value (e.g., Groensteen, 2000; Lopes, 2009).

These divergent attitudes towards comics have attracted the attention of researchers, educators and librarians, who try to explain the appeal of the format or to find an appropriate use of comics in their institutional settings. However, most research has focused primarily on the texts themselves, either from the perspective of the form, the narratives or their production. In comparison, the topic of reception (audiences, readers and/or fans) has been less prominent and is often specifically focused on the study of fans. The association between the fan experience and comics has colonised the experience of reading comics, especially in mainstream culture, leaving almost no room for the possibility of other recognisable experiences: if you are committed to reading comics, inevitably you are, will become, or are expected to be, a fan. In contrast, Gabilliet (2010) or Pustz (1999) point to the need for more research about what they label as 'casual readers', or the bulk of the comics readership.

Because of my genuine interest in readers, I made their thoughts and experiences relative to comics reading the core of this project and due to their centrality, they are introduced straight away: nine females and eight males, between the ages of 17 and 25 years old. They were recruited at three different sites: a public library, a comics store and a university with a large undergraduate population. All of them at the time were living in London, Ontario in Canada although some of them were not originally from that city or even from Canada itself. Some of their pseudonyms were selected by them and others by me. These participants' reading experiences with comics also varied, with some being beginner readers and others comics readers since childhood (see Table 1.1)[1].

Finding comics readers among scholarly disciplines

This study uses 'comics' as an umbrella term that refers to different expressions and formats the medium takes, for example webcomics, comic strips, manga, graphic novels, trade paperbacks, albums. When a participant refers to a specific format, the particular term will be used.

Comics studies is not a single discipline; it is multidisciplinary by nature, with slippery boundaries that extend from art history and literature to media studies

TABLE 1.1 Participants' comics reading experiences

Pseudonym	*Age*	*Last comics read (title + main creator)*	*Recruitment site/Occupation*	*Reader status*
Alison	23	*Black Hole* by Charles Burns, *Scott Pilgrim* series by Bryan Lee O'Malley, and *Lucky* by Gabrielle Bell	University/Graduate student	Intermediate/Avid
Baa	17	Reread *Watchmen* by Alan Moore; *Daytripper* by Fábio Moon and Gabriel Bá; and the 2nd volume of *Phonogram* by Kieron Gillen and Jamie McKelvie	Public library/High school student	Intermediate/Avid
Daniel	23	*Mome* anthology (Fantagraphics); an omnibus *Captain American* by Ed Brubaker; *Shortcomings* by Adrian Tomine; and *Torpedo* by Enrique Sánchez Abulí et al.	Comic book store/Undergraduate student, comic book store staff	Avid
Devi	18	*Squee* and *I Feel Sick* by Jhonen Vasquez, and *Hellsing* by Kouta Hirano	University/Undergraduate student	Intermediate/Avid
HunterS	19	First three trade paperbacks in *The Sandman* series by Neil Gaiman; fifth instalment of *Transmetropolitan* by Warren Ellis and a collection of *Dr Who* stories	University/Undergraduate student	Beginner
Jacob	17	*The Wonderful Wizard of Oz* by Eric Shanower and Skottie Young, an adaptation of *Frankenstein* by Jason Cobley, and a comic in French about the history of rock and roll	Snowball sampling/High school student, library volunteer	Intermediate
Kalo	24	*Filth* by Grant Morrison; *Ex-Machina* by Brian K. Vaughan; *Skim* by Mariko Tamaki and Jillian Tamaki	University/Graduate student	Avid
Lorraine	19	Fifth volume of the *Wet Moon* series by Sophie Campbell; the first volume of *Akira* by Katsuhiro Otomo; and the first trade paperback of the new *Tank Girl* by Jamie Hewlett	Snowball sampling/Undergraduate student	Avid
Marian	24	*Unwritten* by Mike Carey and Peter Gross and *Beast* by Marian Churchland	Public library/Intern.	Avid

(*continued*)

TABLE 1.1 (*Cont.*)

Pseudonym	*Age*	*Last comics read (title + main creator)*	*Recruitment site/Occupation*	*Reader status*
Oracle	23	*Power Girl* with Amanda Conner as the artist; *Batgirl* by Gail Simone, and *Muppet King Arthur* by Roger Langridge	University/Graduate student	Avid
Preacher	18	*Maus* by Art Spiegelman, *Preacher* by Garth Ennis, and *Y: The Last Man* by Brian K. Vaughan	University/Undergraduate student	Intermediate
Promethea	21	Second volume of *Promethea* by Alan Moore and J. H. Williams III and *The Swamp Thing* by Alan Moore	Public market/Undergraduate student	Beginner
Selina	24	*Ex-Machina* by Brian K. Vaughan; *Street Angel* by Jim Rugg and Brian Maruca; and volume one of *Strangers in Paradise* by Terry Moore	University/Graduate student, bookstore staff	Intermediate/Avid
Shade	24	*The Changing Man* by Peter Milligan, but especially because of the artist Brendon McCarthy; a single issue of *Sweet Tooth* by Jeff Lemire, and the first issue of *Flash* by Geoff Johns	Snowball sampling/IT professional	Avid
Shalmanaser	20	Richard Wagner's T*he Ring of the Nibelung* adapted by Roy Thomas, *Maus* by Art Spiegelman, and a collection of short stories based on H. P. Lovecraft works	Public library/IT professional	Intermediate
Templesmith	20	Omnibus for *Silent Hill* by Scott Ciencin; a manga based on the television series *Battlestar Galactica*, and *Maus* by Art Spiegelman	Snowball sampling/Undergraduate student	Avid
Walker	23	*V for Vendetta* by Alan Moore; the graphic novel adaptation of the animation movie *Waltz with Bashir* by Ari Folman and David Polonsky, and a Frank Miller comic he could not remember the title of	Snowball sampling/Undergraduate student	Sporadic

and gender and ethnic studies (Jenkins, 2012). Similarly, reading is also approached from different perspectives. For example, Littau in her *Theories of Reading* (2006) touches on reading in the context of literary theory, feminism, cultural studies and book history, a broad coverage despite missing the rich production from education and literacy-focused projects (e.g., Alvermann and Hinchman, 2012; Cliff Hodges, 2016). One major difficulty (and, in the end, reward) of my own study was to locate and engage with relevant scholarly literature on the rather narrow but intricate duo of comics and readers, making it mandatory to examine three fields of study: media studies, library and information studies (LIS) and education. My approach to reading in this study emerges from a tradition of scholars from LIS and closely related disciplines that have examined the experience of pleasure reading from the reader's perspective (e.g., Fuller and Rehberg Sedo, 2013; Mackey, 2007; Ross et al., 2006, 2018; Sweeney, 2010). These researchers situate adult, teen and child readers at the centre of their studies and, with different objectives in mind, explore the many elements that are intertwined in the experience of reading and being a reader.

Historically, the fields of cultural and media studies are the main sources for studies about readers and fans of comics, with the first tracking back to the wave of popularity for comics during the 1930s and 1940s (e.g., Wolf and Fiske, 1949). These disciplines focus much of their research on the response, influence or interaction between readers/fans as audience, and comics as cultural artefacts. As mentioned earlier, researchers such as Pustz (1999) and Brown (2001), joined later by Gabilliet (2010) and Woo (2011), started problematising the focus on fans and made visible the analytical possibilities opened up by interviewing actual readers to explore issues such as composition and diversity in the comics audience.

Education and LIS share a historical and contemporary interest in developing an understanding of and, more significantly, an applicability of the medium of comics. In their historical overviews, Nyberg (2002) and Tilley (2007, 2012) thoroughly review these fields. In relation to comics, both are in the process of evolving from generally negative attitudes that question their worthiness to positive ones focused on legitimisation and appropriate uses. However, one characteristic that connected both positive and negative views is the lack of readers' research and evidence (Ellis and Highsmith, 2000; Tilley, 2007), a gap this chapter begins to bridge.

The LIS professional literature tends to have a utilitarian goal, offering librarians the necessary information and tools to select, acquire and organise comics as well as ideas to develop programmes and activities that use those comics, leaving little room to explore the reasons for readers' attraction to comics (Cedeira Serantes, 2013). Snowball is one of few researchers (others are Ziolkowska and Howard, 2010; Zabriskie, 2010) who examine the triangle formed by libraries, graphic novels and their readers. Although Snowball's thesis project perpetuates, to a degree, the link between reluctant readers and graphic novels, it also points to previously unexplored topics such as the role of the family in the development of an interest in graphic novels and challenges other unquestioned assumptions such as the idea that all teens enjoy reading graphic novels (Snowball, 2007, 2008, 2011). In education,

Sabeti notes that comics are 'usually synonymous with low literacy levels, reluctant readers and a predominantly male audience' (2011: 137); comics are often presented as tools to achieve other objectives; for example, engagement in the classroom or with a topic, new language learning or even self-esteem. To surpass this narrow understanding, literacy researcher Botzakis invites researchers to see 'what people do with texts' (2009: 58) before attributing meanings, uses and functions to texts to be used in the classroom.

Although this utilitarian focus is understandable, a more expansive understanding is developing due to a combination of several factors: the slow inclusion of comics in teachers' and librarians' education (e.g., Williams and Peterson, 2009), the recognition of comics in awards or the development of comics-focused lists, comics' presence in new curricular requirements, such as the Common Core in the United States (e.g., Clemmons and Olvey, 2015; Monnin, 2013) and the diversification of the comics publishing field, for example, with the increasing availability of informational comics.

Why and how do we speak with comics readers?

In the conclusion of her work on romance reading, Radway claims a focal point in research for 'real people with previously existing needs, desires, intentions, and interpretative strategies' because 'the essentially human practice of making meaning goes on even in a world increasingly dominated by things and by consumption' (1991: 221). I embrace this call, understanding comics readers as living in a complex world where the experience of reading comics brings a particular significance or meaning to their lives and consequently affords comics readers the role of experts.

Epistemologically, I see meaning as created by my participants' interactions with the world; they interpret this complex world and their interactions with it using the language and classification schemas in their mind. To support this constructivist/interpretative approach (Creswell, 2007), a qualitative methodology, and hermeneutic phenomenology specifically, enabled me to study 'how people interpret their lives and make meaning of what they experience' (Cohen, Kahn and Steeves, 2000: 5). Prominent LIS scholar Budd notes, citing Scheler, that 'phenomenology is not a methodology … it is an attitude, a way of preparing oneself for inquiry, for seeing' (2005: 45). Following Budd, I concluded that I also needed to be clear and transparent about my attitudes, about the way I was inquiring and seeing. Achieving clarity and transparency in my methodological work became paramount, with reflexivity as the perfect tool. Using reflexivity I recognised that I was a key instrument in the research process and the importance of making this role visible, in this case through a process of self-reflection that articulated how knowledge was constructed and how biases and assumptions were part of the interpretative process. Finlay points at reflexivity 'as one way to begin to unravel the richness, contradictions, and complexities of intersubjective dynamics', adding that a reflexive analysis 'can only ever be a partial, tentative, provisional account'

(2002: 542–543). I experienced reflexivity as a process that strengthened the trustworthiness of my data and analysis as well as my contribution to other scholars who might be considering a similar methodological path.

As part of this reflexive work, disclosing my own history as a comics reader was integral to revealing myself as a researcher. My deep interest in readers was mostly ignited by the previously noted scarcity of readers' voices in comics reading-related research. However, this was not my only motivation. I have been reading comics since childhood, more or less intensely at different stages of my life, and have had the opportunity to explore different comics traditions (mainly European, American and Japanese). In addition, the rise of the graphic novel intrigued me, especially because of its influence on the contemporary awareness of graphic storytelling in mainstream media and society. The interaction between these three matters (the scholarly gap, my personal history and the rise of the graphic novel) made me wonder about the status, stereotypes and experiences related to comics reading in contemporary society and prompted the following research questions:

- What does it mean to be a comics reader in contemporary society?
- How do comics readers construct and understand their experience of comics as reading material?
- What might be learned about comics readers' identities and the social contexts of reading comics?

Focusing on methods and how I operationalised these questions, I conducted semi-structured interviews. Kvale and Brinkmann (2009) posit that the semi-structured lifeworld interview is based on the idea that knowledge is neither in the interviewee nor in the researcher but in the process they share of being co-constructors of knowledge. To create my interview schedule, I followed their suggestions about how to conceptualise it: it included using thematic questions that helped to produce knowledge and dynamic questions that helped to build rapport and a relationship between interviewer and interviewee (Kvale and Brinkmann, 2009). Moreover, the information and issues raised by participants enriched and expanded the interview process and the schedule itself. During the interview process, my main intention was to bring a sense of acceptance, respect and value towards the experience of reading comics and especially in relation to the participants' individual experiences. Interviews themselves lasted between 50 minutes and two hours and were audio-recorded and transcribed. To complement this interview data, I designed a think-aloud activity where readers explained how they chose the texts they enjoyed reading in the same places where they usually accessed them: libraries, comics stores or any other site they suggested. Interestingly enough, this activity was not as informative as the interviews, but it nevertheless proved to be an important way of building rapport and sharing specific examples of titles they liked. That was valuable since my main methodological concern for this project was to be able to keep the readers' voices at the centre of my analysis.

Four dimensions of the comics reading experience: Developing as a comics reader; the materiality of comics; time constraints; the role of educational institutions

From the analysis of the semi-structured interviews emerged four dimensions of the reading experience on which I will now elaborate: 1) the development of comic readers; 2) the significant role of the materiality of comics; 3) the unique temporal aspects of comics reading in contemporary society; 4) the unfulfilled role of educational institutions. These four dimensions helped me to tease apart different aspects of the participants' reading experiences and to convey their situatedness and complexity. While I examined the dimensions separately throughout the analysis, they also worked together, intertwined in different ways to converge at the moment of reading a text.

'There's always people out there who read more than you' (Alison): Developing as a comics reader

Historically, reading comics was described as something that readers eventually grow out of, thus constructing this kind of reading experience as transient and trivial, with hopes of no permanent damage being done as readers moved up the reading ladder. Parents, teachers and librarians expected comics reading to be a phase and if readers became committed to the form, their experience was linked to the fan identity and the practices that come with it. Comics readers were therefore intended either to learn what they needed and leave comics behind or to become dedicated comics fans. Although Alison's words in the sub-heading for this section could be read as an obvious statement, they end a longer quotation that deserves our full attention in connection with this process of being and becoming a comics reader:

> Actually, I wasn't sure if I should sign up for this study because I wasn't sure that I read enough … I've read [comics] fairly intermittently throughout my life like, there's been times when I've read a lot of them and times where I haven't … like in middle school I don't think I touched a single graphic novel … I don't like getting anything from Heroes [the comics store] and I'm not familiar or superfamiliar with the Marvel and DC universes … there's always people out there who read more than you.

Alison's words are a reminder of the constant comparison between comics readers' practices and experiences and those of the fan. Comics readers negotiate this process overtly, both with and against the comics community, as well as internally, as a process of identity construction. Fiske defined the boundaries of fandom in terms of an insider/outsider relationship, with 'strongly marked and patrolled' boundaries between fans and non-fans (1992: 34–35). The diversity of experiences present in my study's participants exemplifies, however, that these boundaries are active not just in that dichotomy, but also in an in-between territory. For example, Kalo says 'I'm not casual, but I'm not super, super intense', and another participant, Baa, states, 'I am an enthusiast in some aspects but there is a lot that I don't know in superheroes'. Thus, what is the experience of a reader who does not want to become a normative insider – the fan – but who is also not just an outsider? Woo invites researchers interested in comics to

> replace the ideal reader (usually just the fan) … with a more realistic – which is to say, theoretically and empirically adequate – account of individuals as socially embedded agents, some of whom may not identify as part of the audience for comics and graphic novels.
>
> (2011: 133)

My participants' thoughts and experiences clearly align with Woo's call and, in exploring this in-between territory, I highlight three intersecting topics that define the experience of developing as a comics reader.

First, although scholarly interest in social reading practices has increased (e.g., Long, 2003; Fuller and Rehberg Sedo, 2013), reading has often been conceptualised and studied as a solitary activity. In contrast, the central role of fans in comics culture has helped to conceptualise comics reading as a social activity deeply connected to the comics store and/or comics events. The participants in my study offered a wide array of scenarios and experiences that challenge the idea of comics reading as either solely social or solely solitary. Individual and social reading practices coincided in time, evolving and adapting to readers' lives. For participants Daniel and Marian, social reading was more strongly connected to their adolescence and their discovery process of the medium. Alison started reading comics as a solitary activity but at the time of the interview she happily shared the development of a small supportive social group. For Lorraine, comics reading had always been social, from starting reading with her family to becoming the host of a radio show about women in comics while in university. For Selina, comics reading was primarily solitary, except when she shared it with her sister. Finally, Preacher enjoyed both aspects, the solitary because of its 'therapeutic' effects and the social because it tends to become instructive. These rich perspectives clearly complicate a homogeneous discourse on comics reading, for example comics reading as a practice that allows an individual to be part of a fan community. Comics reading is often a solitary act, as most reading is, that becomes social because of the need for sharing, for discussion or for companionship.

Second, the acquisition and possession of knowledge plays an identifiable function in the reader/fan tension and in the cohabitation of individual and social reading practices: knowing about creators, publishers, plotlines and the industry influences participants' current reader status and their desired relationship with comics reading. For example, for Baa, learning about comics was connected to achieving a constant awareness of quality comics to read. Likewise, Preacher tried to select readings that are 'relevant to pop culture … culturally relevant things'. Alison connected knowledge to any reading experience; she saw herself as, and aspired to become, an informed reader. The process of acquiring knowledge about comics became a personal project, part of the discovery and construction of being a reader.

Third, and equally important, is how knowledge strongly intersects with issues of gender. Female participants were more sensitive to or aware of the value of knowledge as a signifier of status in their constant struggle to be admitted as part of the comics community. Selina was one of the most conflicted readers and she noted several 'epiphany' moments during our conversation. This is one of them:

> I'm sitting here criticising what I think is maybe the access point to a medium as being extraordinary inaccessible ... But then I'm going on about how I really have to be precise ... which is all I think evidence of the fact I have this unbelievable impulse to fit into that thing [the community].

Selina thought that the comics community – especially the superheroes community – was rather inaccessible for beginners but at the same time she wished to be part of it. The need for knowledge and to fit in was not unique to the comics community and she referred to other fan communities, like Trekkies. Oracle, Devi and Selina mentioned the lack of female staff in comics stores, something that is slowly changing. Despite this lack of public female presence, Daniel, HunterS, Selina, Devi and Promethea reported that they started reading comics because their mothers or sisters supported them, invited them or encouraged them. Oracle, Devi and Alison spoke about female creators and characters, as well as the treatment of gender-related narratives. The combination of these public and private behaviours could be behind the increasing visibility and success of those comics (Macdonald, 2017). In the end, these readers seemed to be, again, in a middle ground: they might become part of comics culture but, doing so, seek to change the culture and carve out their own space in it.

Readers like HunterS, Shade, Selina, or Walker frequently mentioned their other reading interests during the conversation and Jacob stated that: 'I just like comic books, like most people like books.' The three topics that I have briefly examined above speak of both the invisibility and complexity of being a comics reader and invite researchers and practitioners to think of this practice not as one that readers should grow out of, but as one that must be examined and understood as a diverse and cumulative experience that can be cultivated and connected with other media and life experiences.

'[T]he paper, the book, the whole package of it in one physical thing, I guess I prefer that' (Shade): The materiality of comics

Readers and texts both produce and encounter each other in the midst of cultural, social and historical contexts. Chartier goes as far as to say that

> there is no text apart from the physical support that offers it for reading (or hearing), hence there is no comprehension of any written piece that does not at least in part depend upon the forms in which it reaches its reader.
>
> (1994: 9)

From a historical perspective, texts have certain material circumstances and those circumstances affect the modes of reading, the habits and practices of reading over time. My participants connected the print format to a certain reading experience, where pleasure was related not only to the fact that they were mainly speaking of leisure reading, but also to the use of sensory and affective terms to describe their preference for print comics. It would be easy to link this preference for print to luddite or technophobe behaviours, but many of the participants were video gamers who used different technologies in their educational and working environments, and owned hardware that could be used for reading. Baa and Shade discussed the potential benefits of reading comics in a digital format, mostly related to issues of convenience, connectivity and multitasking, ease of storage and transportation, and access for readers who do not live close to a comics store. In comparison with these affordances, they highlighted print as a choice because its intrinsic limitations can become considerable advantages; for example, when the choice of print becomes the choice of disconnecting, of isolating ourselves. Technology is increasingly difficult to leave behind, so the efforts to distance oneself from it are also harder; taking a day off from technological devices is more and more challenging. In this context, the print book becomes an easy object with which to sustain a practice such as reading without the burden or the pressure to multitask or to be connected.

Kalo speaks of the uniqueness of 'picking up a book'; Templesmith talks about enjoying 'holding a book, and smelling it'; while Preacher says that 'nothing compares to actually holding the story in your hand'. They are not the first to say these kinds of things; researchers (e.g., Ytre-Arne, 2011; Mangen, 2016) have reported similar experiences when examining haptics and the print versus digital reading dichotomy. Such comments highlight the importance of embodiment in the reading experience and the vital function that currently print comics perform in such embodiment. As described in the following paragraphs, this is expressed and appreciated in different ways by different participants.

For example, Marian makes the need for a physical object evident when she says that

> sometimes I'll buy a book and it's just, it's almost as much for the story as it is for 'I want that object'. I just think it's really neat, it's like having a piece of art in your wall in a way.

The comic does not become just any object, but an art object for her. This understanding of the comic, for instance, also explains why she has acquired some webcomics in print. She is not the only one; both Kalo and Daniel mention Montreal comics publisher Drawn & Quarterly and Seattle's Fantagraphics as their favourites, not just because of the content, but also because they care about the quality of the container, about the material quality of their comics production.

Meanwhile, Morineau et al. explore the affordances of the e-book versus the paper book as an 'external memory trigger' (2005: 329) and conclude that 'it does not provide the external indicators to memory that the classical book does, in that it does not serve as an unambiguous index to indicate a field of knowledge on the basis of its particular physical form' (346). I believe that this idea of the book as a contextual index can be expanded to serve as an index for one's reading history. Kalo describes her comics as saying 'they are in my condition': she writes on them, marks them, and rereads them. In this process she creates traces of herself that can be preserved and revisited. Philosopher Mark Johnson explores the idea that '[a]n identifiable, meaningful experience is neither merely emotional, nor merely practical, nor merely intellectual. Rather, it is all of these at once and together' (2007: 74). This effort to bring emotion, practice and intellect into the full experience of reading highlights the importance of the recurrent use of the verb *feel* to explain the experience of looking at the art of print comics or simply reading in print. For these readers, reading a print comic *feels* like a whole experience 'pervaded by unifying qualities that demarcate them within the flux of our lives' (Johnson, 2007: 75). Therefore, connecting Johnson's conceptualisations with Shade's quotation in the sub-heading above, we can say that print comics are memorable because there is one reader, one context, one narrative and one book that can help make one experience whole and identifiable.

However, the question has not been and should not be whether reading in print is better or worse, or more effective or less effective, than reading in digital form. These readers opened up the exploration to a more encompassing question: how the change of media can potentially change our relationship to reading, our relationship to the reading material, and perhaps even to our self-identification as readers.

'If I don't have very much time I might stop reading as much in the future' (Shalmanaser): Time constraints

The reading experience is bounded by spatial and temporal dimensions and consequently time (especially the lack thereof) was repeatedly raised by my participants. I accorded special importance to the temporal requirements and experiences because they highlight human agency and an active and reflective re-engagement with time and temporality (Keightley, 2013). Undermining the study of temporal experiences and time availability obscures one of many factors that could influence these participants' future status as readers. Shalmanaser carefully explains it when he says that:

> if I don't have time to read I tend to read less and less and mainly even when I do have time again I might not think of reading because I just got out of practice, but if I do have time to read typically I will, I will use all of it, I have a limit to how long I can read for one stretch of time but otherwise I try to use [it] to its fullest extent. If I don't have very much time I might stop reading as much in the future.

If lack of time affects the practices of readers and can potentially affect their identities as such, time (and its availability or scarcity) should be a variable included more often in discussions about the reading experience. Daniel 'steal[s] time for myself whenever I can' and Marian describes the opportunity to go to the public library as a 'luxury'. I should clarify that I am not the first researcher to speak about the connection of time, reading, and comics but most scholars examine the possibilities that the medium of comics offer to represent or play with time, for example, with the breakdown of the story, the size of the panels, page layout or the gutter within the medium itself. Sabeti, however, starts grappling with how the medium influences the perception of time, shifting the focus to her participants' reading experiences (2012). I followed a similar path but I saw that comics reading could be examined even more broadly, in connection with lived time and contemporary experiences of time. Sociologist Rosa (2010) was key to informing my own understandings of contemporary time and acceleration and these understandings helped me to contextualise and explain how comics reading relates to issues of time scarcity.[2]

If reading is conceptualised as a focal practice (Sumara, 1996) that rearranges readers' lives, one might wonder how current temporal structures can potentially affect participants' identities as readers. Rosa points to the relevance of this question when he says that 'changes in the temporal structures of modern societies transform the very essence of our culture, social structure, and personal identity' (2003: 17–18). Therefore, when Daniel 'steal[s] time for [him]self' or Kalo describes her lack of time for pleasure reading as 'heart-breaking', it indicates the reality of time scarcity and points to issues of shortage as well as the need for control. For Selina, reading is a powerful force in her life. Without time for reading, she sometimes thinks she would 'go off the deep end'. In a period of her life when it is rather difficult to develop structured and solid routines, Selina establishes a simple but effective strategy: always travelling and moving with reading material; it does not matter how small the time period, she always uses it for reading. Therefore, Selina needs reading material that can both fulfil her need for reading and adapt to her pace of life. Lately, that reading material has been comics.

Reading has often been linked to processes of slowing down, creating time or taking time for oneself. For example, Radway (1991) determined that romance readers used reading as a way to carve out their own space and time in the midst of demanding roles in domestic life. My participants constructed comics as complex narratives that smoothly adapted to the temporal requirements connected to a current social state of time scarcity. Readers considered comics to thrive on the time requirements prevalent in the digital era, inserting themselves between work routines and successfully adjusting to the high volume of activities that young people try to fit into their lives. They also seem to provide a high level of satisfaction without requiring a substantial time investment. Baa powerfully reinforces these conclusions with one sentence: '[Comics] can tell you so much and you can finish them in a day.' It is tempting to equate quick with easy, but this fast experience is also demanding because it requires textual and visual literacy skills as well as knowledge about the medium itself (Ziolkowska and Howard, 2010). In the current age, where time seems to be defined by acceleration and instantaneity, readers appreciated the quality of comics to allow for moments of contemplation. Preacher connects comics reading to relaxing and explains his reading routine as a reaction to chaotic university hall of residence life. He likes to read when 'everyone is asleep or everyone is chilled out a little bit or while they're studying', looking for 'privacy, away from everybody'. The combination of all these reasons situates his reading at night, in bed or on a couch, physically and emotionally comfortable. Reading helps him to find or create a moment for himself. However, as I have said, this is a characteristic that is not unique to reading comics, but supported by many reading experiences. So, what is actually unique about time and comics?

Daniel talks about not reading 'too quickly' to be able to take everything in. Devi describes a similar deceleration process when she characterises comics as treats because she 'can take time' with them, especially in contrast with her academic reading. She connects complexity with pleasure in her comics reading; at the same time, she looks for intricate plots and actively engages in a poised and deliberate reading experience: 'I spend a lot of time on a page. I'll go through the writing while I'm looking at the images but then look at the images on their own and then look at the writing on its own.' An obvious characteristic that makes this act of contemplation possible is the dual nature of comics: text and image. As a quite experienced reader of comics, Devi knows that text and images need to be read together, but she likes to appreciate the images on their own and also needs sometimes to revisit the text. She quickly says that the visual part is what helps her to feel like she 'can take time with it'. The uniqueness of comics, then, is that they create the possibility for a double speed during the same reading experience. This duality gives readers the agency to choose. Kalo explains it as follows:

> I just think that comics as a medium is so cool, it fascinates me how much you can do with what you have, with the panels, with what you can do between the panels, how you can control the flow of time and also leave it up to the reader to go through at their pace.

Although the experience of reading comics is often linked to simple, high-speed reading, it should not be essentialised but rather opened up to multiplicity and, in some cases, even as resistance to contemporary experiences of time. The experience of reading comics gives readers a clear possibility not just to challenge time but almost to make it malleable, potentially contributing to the development of lines of resistance (Leccardi, 2003) to a single fast-paced time experience.

'[S]chool really limits the time, the time for comic books unfortunately, but I try to read' (Lorraine): The unfulfilled role of educational institutions

In 'Beyond market models and resistance', Pawley examines the role institutions play in the history of reading; she states that '[u]sing organizations as a middle layer of analysis can bridge the gap between structure and agency and between macro and micro views' (2009: 74). Many reading researchers know that this function is not limited to the past; institutions such as libraries, schools, the family and media companies are still highly influential in what reading is, what counts as reading or what we read. For example, during the think-aloud protocol, Marian shared her surprise and happiness when she discovered that Brussels devotes a museum to *bande dessinée* (French/Belgian comics) and Tintin. For her, the existence of such an institution symbolises the different status that *bande dessinée* enjoys in comparison to North American comics culture. Readers in my study were aware of the powerful influence of institutions and discussed it at length, pointing to the power of media industries and the past, present and potential roles of libraries and educational institutions in relation to their comics reading.

I am choosing to narrow the discussion to educational institutions because required reading and schoolwork dominate much of my participants' past and present free time. Although educational institutions are mentioned in both positive and negative terms, many of the negative comments strongly link reading to the work done for school or university and, in many cases, it is not perceived as a pleasurable activity. For example, Walker refers to reading as 'the last thing I want to do' and Lorraine explains that 'school really limits the time, the time for comic books unfortunately, but I try to read'. As introduced before, one result of this time scarcity is that participants make careful and informed choices to engage with comics, taking advantage of the little time at their disposal. On the positive side, educational institutions and the professionals who work in them emerge as places and people with the potential to play an important role in the status and development of comics as a well-regarded form of reading material, both for pleasure and for schoolwork. Participants' comments reveal that the use of comics by educators could support a general process of acceptance and increased cultural respectability for comics. Promethea recalls several enriching encounters with *Maus* (Spiegelman, 1986) in classes about twentieth-century history and politics. Templesmith comments on the fact that many people think of comics just as the superheroes genre and for little kids. She used to agree with those opinions until she was exposed to a graphic adaptation of William Shakespeare's *Hamlet* in high school that made visible the possibilities and diversity of the medium. Alison remembers how *Persepolis* (Satrapi, 2003) was selected in her first year at university as the reading choice for a common reading experience. Alison praised the events and lectures organised around this one title; this selection gave her the opportunity to meet other students interested in comics but it is also important to note that choosing a work such as *Persepolis* can potentially help expose students to the diversity of the medium, beyond the ubiquitous American superheroes. These different examples support the idea that when students can use comics in their schoolwork, an opportunity is created for them to show their interest for the form. They share an intrinsic eagerness to explore comics, not just as meaningful reading material but also as an educational tool and cultural reference point (e.g., Fox, 2007; Versaci, 2001).

As mentioned previously, this study was situated in London, Ontario, a predominantly Anglophone city in Canada; however, some of the participants referred to childhood experiences in other cities with stronger bilingual traditions. Kalo was one of a group of readers who recalled *bande dessinée* titles such as Hergé's *Les Adventures de Tintin* (1930–1986), Goscinny and Uderzo's *Astérix* (1961 onwards), and Velter's *Spirou et Fantasio* (1948–1968) as among her first encounters with the form:

> No, they didn't use them in class. They were in the library, we had a library class so we would go and sit around and read … those were often the books that were taken off, they were good. But I really didn't have a big conception of what comics were then.

Other participants mentioned French albums as part of their exposure to French language and culture, something not surprising because of the important cultural impact that *bande dessinée* has in France and Belgium. However, this exposure did not happen in the classroom, but at the library. Although the educational possibilities of comics are being slowly embraced (e.g., Miller, 2015; Brozo et al., 2014), it is not yet a medium completely embedded in teaching activities and environments. This slow process also reveals intriguing tensions that might be worth future research. For example, Kalo again mentioned taking a university course on comics; although her comments about it were extremely positive, she also pointed to some resistance from certain students who 'didn't want it to be "academicised" … I'm trying to think of a word, like, taking into the world of academia'. Differences in exposure, knowledge and relationship to the comics medium might get magnified in classes. At the same time, a beginner reader such as HunterS comments on the need to learn comics literacy:

> we have to spend so much time in class, in tutorial explaining people how to read comics and because they come across 'oh, I've never read a comic before' … they wouldn't touch a graphic novel, they wouldn't touch anything, so they don't get the whole concept of like, left to right, then down but then occasionally … When it comes to people who reads a lot of comics it's just sort of intuitive knowledge of how the story supposed to [work], how text … progressing through it, it confuses the hell out of a lot of people that haven't read it before and then it gets harder to have a discussion with them.

HunterS points to the fact that there is a set of skills that are not intuitive and in need of teaching support; being born in a society that heavily relies on visual messages does not always correlate with being an expert on deciphering them. Conversely, HunterS also challenges the stereotype that presents all young people as naturally interested in or inclined to comics reading (Snowball, 2011). In the interaction of comics readers and educational institutions, many possibilities and tensions open up; listening to readers talk about the absence and presence of comics in educational institutions shows researchers and practitioners paths where comics reading is integrated and supported, trying to leave behind a past where comics were not just absent but denigrated.

Comics readers' contribution to reading research

The end goal of this chapter is to be a stepping stone in the process of diversifying the identities and voices that construct the research discourse about comics reading and about teens and young adults as readers among increasingly visible communities, such as the comics community. These groups of readers' thoughts and experiences have revealed an intricate set of complex and diverse variables to consider when addressing the overall question of what it means to be a comics reader in contemporary society. Beyond comics, participants' thoughts help us deepen our understanding of the conversation about how the change of media can potentially change our relationship to reading and to the reading material. Other issues such as the need for isolation, the relationship between solitary and social reading, and embodiment may connect comics reading to other reading experiences and, potentially, media experiences in general. Therefore, it complicates the boundaries of the research about comics reading and readers, offering points of contact between some of the mentioned disciplines. Although these findings are not intended to be generalisable, they open the door to the possibility of a different kind of comics reader, someone who experiences her relationship with comics in a less normative way, differently from the ones that have been traditionally studied, i.e., fans and collectors. This study increases the awareness of the role of these reading materials in the development of a reading history and identity and, finally, it supports the recognition of the reading and cultural practices of a group of readers who have been historically neglected.

Notes

1 These titles were taken from interviews – either semi-structured and/or think-aloud – which explains why I have not provided a reference list for any of the texts referred to.
2 For an extended examination of this topic, I invite the reader to consult my chapter in *Plotting the Reading Experience* (Cedeira Serantes, 2016). This section is a brief reflection on this topic, but primary to highlight the richness and complexity of the comics reading experience.

References

Alvermann, D. E. and Hinchman, K. A. (2012). *Reconceptualizing the Literacies in Adolescents' Lives: Bridging the Everyday/Academic Divide* (3rd ed.). New York: Routledge.

Botzakis, S. (2009). Adult fans of comic books: What they get out of reading. *Journal of Adolescent & Adult Literacy*, 53 (1), 50–59.

Brown, J. A. (2001). *Black Superheroes, Milestone Comics, and Their Fans*. Jackson: University Press of Mississippi.

Brozo, W. G., Moorman, G. B. and Meyer, C. K. (2014). *Wham! Teaching with Graphic Novels across the Curriculum*. New York: Teachers College Press.

Budd, J. M. (2005). Phenomenology and information studies. *Journal of Documentation*, 61 (1), 44–59.

Cedeira Serantes, L. (2013). Misfits, loners, immature students, reluctant readers: Librarianship participates in the construction of teen comics readers. In A. Bernier (Ed.), *Transforming Young Adult Services: A Reader for Our Age*. New York: Neal-Schuman, pp. 115–135.

Cedeira Serantes, L. (2014). *Young Adults Reflect on the Experience of Reading Comics in Contemporary Society: Overcoming the Commonplace and Recognizing Complexity*. PhD dissertation, University of Western Ontario, Canada.

Cedeira Serantes, L. (2016). When comics set the pace: The experience of time and the reading of comics. In L. McKechnie, P. Rothbauer, K. Oterholm, and K. I. Skjerdingstad (Eds.), *Plotting the Reading Experience: Theory/Practice/Politics*. Waterloo, Ontario: Wilfrid Laurier University Press, pp. 217–232.

Chartier, R. (1994). *The Order of Books: Readers, Authors, and Libraries in Europe between the Fourteenth and Eighteenth Centuries*. Stanford, CA: Stanford University Press.

Clemmons, K. R. and Olvey, H. A. (2015). Graphic texts as a catalyst for content knowledge and Common Core Content Literacy standards in science, technology, engineering, and mathematics classes. In J. A. Hayn, J. S. Kaplan and A.L. Nolen (Eds.), *Young Adult Nonfiction: Gateway to the Common Core*. Lanham, MD: Rowman and Littlefield, pp. 101–118.

Cliff Hodges, G. (2016). *Researching and Teaching Reading: Developing Pedagogy through Critical Enquiry*. London: Routledge.

Cohen, M. Z., Kahn, D.L. and Steeves, R.H. (2000). *Hermeneutic Phenomenological Research: A Practical Guide for Nurse Researchers*. Thousand Oaks, CA: Sage.

Creswell, J. W. (2007). *Qualitative Inquiry & Research Design: Choosing among Five Approaches*. Thousand Oaks, CA: Sage.

Ellis, A. W. and Highsmith, D. (2000). About face: Comic books in library literature. *Serials Review*, 26 (2), 21–43.

Finlay, L. (2002). Negotiating the swamp: The opportunity and challenge of reflexivity in research practice. *Qualitative Research*, 2 (2), 209–230.

Fiske, J. (1992). The cultural economy of fandom. In L. A. Lewis (Ed.), *The Adoring Audience: Fan Culture and Popular Media*. London: Routledge, pp. 30–49.

Fox, C. (2007). History, war and politics: Taking 'comix' seriously. In V. Ellis, C. Fox and B. Street (Eds.), *Rethinking English in Schools: A New and Constructive Stage*. London: Continuum, pp. 89–101.

Fuller, D. and Rehberg Sedo, D. (2013). *Reading Beyond the Book: The Social Practices of Contemporary Literary Culture*. New York: Routledge.

Gabilliet, J. (2010). *Of Comics and Men: A Cultural History of American Comic Books*. Jackson: University Press of Mississippi.

Goscinny, R., ill., and Uderzo, A. (1961 onwards). *Astérix*. France: Dargaud.

Groensteen, T. (2000). Why are comics still in search of cultural legitimization? In A. Magnussen and H. Christiansen (Eds.), *Comics and culture: Analytical and Theoretical Approaches to Comics*. Copenhagen: Museum Tusculanum Press, University of Copenhagen, pp. 29–41.

Hergé. (1930–1986). *Les Adventures de Tintin*. Belgium: Casterman (and others).

Jenkins, H. (2012). Should we discipline the reading of comics? In M. J. Smith and R. Duncan (Eds.), *Critical Approaches to Comics: Theories and Methods*. New York: Routledge, pp. 1–14.

Johnson, M. (2007). *The Meaning of the Body*. Chicago: University of Chicago Press.

Keightley, E. (2013). From immediacy to intermediacy: The mediation of lived time. *Time & Society*, 22 (1), 55–75.

Kvale, S. and Brinkmann, S. (2009). *InterViews: Learning the Craft of Qualitative Research Interviewing*. Thousand Oaks, CA: Sage.

Leccardi, C. (2003). Resisting 'Acceleration Society'. *Constellations*, 10 (1), 34–41.
Littau, K. (2006). *Theories of Reading: Books, Bodies, and Bibliomania*. Cambridge: Polity Press.
Long, E. (2003). *Book Clubs: Women and the Uses of Reading in Everyday Life*. Chicago: University of Chicago Press.
Lopes, P. D. (2009). *Demanding Respect: The Evolution of the American Comic Book*. Philadelphia: Temple University Press.
Macdonald, H. (June 2017). This week's Bookscan chart is a wake-up call for the comics industry. *The Beat: The Newsblog of Comics Culture*. Retrieved 21 June 2017 from: www.comicsbeat.com/this-weeks-bookscan-chart-is-a-wake-up-call-for-the-comics-industry/
Mackey, M. (2007). *Literacies across Media: Playing the Text* (2nd ed.). New York: Routledge.
Mangen, A. (2016). What hands may tell us about reading and writing. *Educational Theory*, 66 (4), 457–77.
Miller, M. (2015). *Class, Please Open Your Comics: Essays on Teaching with Graphic Narratives*. Jefferson: McFarland & Company.
Monnin, K. (2013). Aligning graphic novels to the common core standards. *Knowledge Quest*, 41 (3), 50–56.
Morineau, T., Blanche, C., Tobin, L. and Guéguen, N. (2005). The emergence of the contextual role of the e-book in cognitive processes through an ecological and functional analysis. *International Journal of Human-Computer Studies*, 62 (3), 329–348.
Nyberg, A.K. (2002). Poisoning children's culture: Comics and their critics. In L. Cushman Schurman and D. Johnson (Eds.), *Scorned Literature: Essays on the History and Criticism of Popular Mass-Produced Fiction in America*. Westport, CT: Greenwood Press, pp. 167–186.
Pawley, C. (2009). Beyond market models and resistance: Organizations as a middle layer in the history of reading. *The Library Quarterly*, 79 (1), 73–93.
Pustz, M. (1999). *Comic Book Culture: Fanboys and True Believers*. Jackson: University Press of Mississippi.
Radway, J. A. (1991). *Reading the Romance: Women, Patriarchy, and Popular Literature*. Chapel Hill: University of North Carolina Press.
Rosa, H. (2003). Social acceleration: Ethical and political consequences of a desynchronized high-speed society. *Constellations*, 10 (1), 3–33.
Rosa, H. (2010). *Alienation and Acceleration: Towards a Critical Theory of Late-Modern Temporality*. Malmö: Nordic Summer University Press.
Ross, C. S., McKechnie, L. and Rothbauer, P. M. (2006). *Reading Matters: What the Research Reveals about Reading, Libraries, and Community*. Westport, CT: Libraries Unlimited.
Ross, C. S., McKechnie, L. and Rothbauer, P. M. (2018). *Reading Still Matters: What the Research Reveals about Reading, Libraries, and Community*. Santa Barbara, CA: ABC-CLIO.
Sabeti, S. (2011). The irony of 'cool club': The place of comic book reading in schools. *Journal of Graphic Novels and Comics*, 2 (2), 137–149.
Sabeti, S. (2012). 'Arts of time and space': The perspectives of a teenage audience on reading novels and graphic novels. *Participations*, 9 (2), 159–79.
Satrapi, M. (2003). *Persepolis: The Story of an Iranian Childhood*. London: Jonathan Cape.
Snowball, C. (2007). Researching graphic novels and their teenage readers. *LIBRES*, 17 (1), 1–20. Retrieved 8 February 2018 from: www.libres-ejournal.info/603/
Snowball, C. (2008). Teenagers talking about reading and libraries. *Australian Academic and Research Libraries*, 39 (2), 106–118.
Snowball, C. (2011). *Graphic Novels: Enticing Teenagers into the Library*. PhD dissertation, Curtin University.
Spiegelman, A. (1986). *Maus*. London: Pantheon.
Sumara, D. J. (1996). *Private Readings in Public: Schooling the Literary Imagination*. New York: Peter Lang.

Sweeney, M. (2010). *Reading Is My Window: Books and the Art of Reading in Women's Prisons*. Chapel Hill: University of North Carolina Press.

Tilley, C. L. (2007). *Of Nightingales and Supermen: How Youth Services Librarians Responded to Comics between the Years 1938 and 1955*. PhD dissertation, Indiana University.

Tilley, C. L. (2012). Seducing the innocent: Fredric Wertham and the falsifications that helped condemn comics. *Information & Culture*, 47 (4), 383–413.

Velter, R. (1948–1968). *Spirou et Fantasio*. France-Belgium: Spirou Magazine.

Versaci, R. (2001). How comic books can change the way our students see literature: One teacher's perspective. *The English Journal*, 91 (2), 61–67.

Williams, V. K. and Peterson, D. V. (2009). Graphic novels in libraries supporting teacher education and librarianship programs. *Library Resources & Technical Services*, 53 (3), 166–174.

Wolf, K. and Fiske, M. (1949). The children talk about comics. In P. Lazarsfeld and F. Stanton (Eds.), *Communications Research, 1948–1949*. New York: Harper and Bros, pp. 3–50.

Woo, B. (2011). The Android's Dungeon: Comic-bookstores, cultural spaces, and the social practices of audiences. *Journal of Graphic Novels and Comics*, 2 (2), 125–136.

Wright, B. W. (2001). *Comic Book Nation: The Transformation of Youth Culture in America*. Baltimore: Johns Hopkins University Press.

Ytre-Arne, B. (2011). 'I want to hold it in my hands': Readers' experiences of the phenomenological differences between women's magazines online and in print. *Media, Culture & Society*, 33 (3), 467–477.

Zabriskie, C. (2010). Graphics let teens OWN the library. In R. G. Weiner (Ed.), *Graphic Novels and Comics in Libraries and Archives: Essays on Readers, Research, History and Cataloging*. Jefferson, North Carolina: McFarland & Co, pp. 167–176.

Ziolkowska, S. and Howard, V. (2010). 'Forty-one-year-old female academics aren't supposed to like comics!' The value of comic books to adult readers. In R. G. Weiner (Ed.), *Graphic Novels and Comics in Libraries and Archives: Essays on Readers, Research, History and Cataloging*. Jefferson, North Carolina: McFarland & Co, pp. 154–166.

2

THE RESIDUE OF FICTION IN THE MEMORY OF ADOLESCENCE

The potential effect of reading fiction in Turkey

Osman Coban

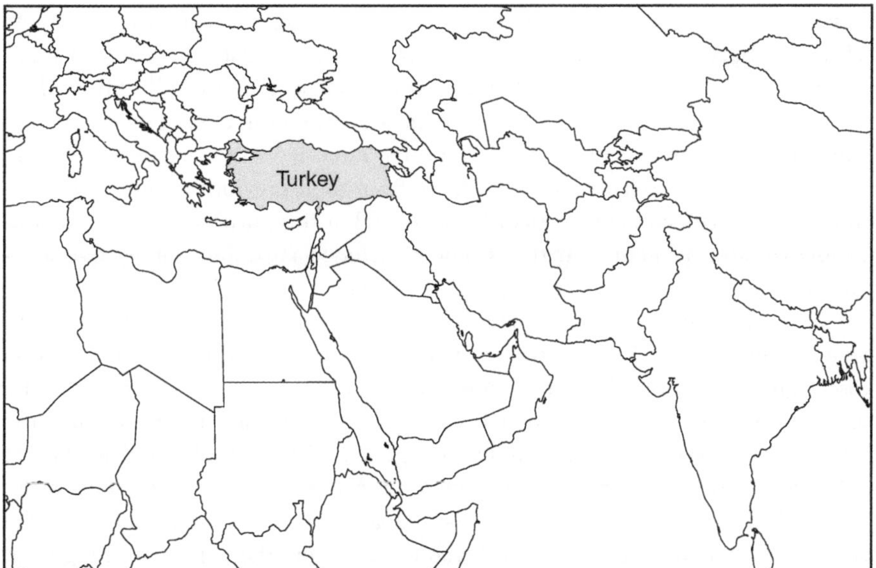

MAP 2

The Japanese psychologist and semanticist, Samuel Ichiyé Hayakawa, noted that: 'It is not true that we have only one life to lead; if we can read, we can live as many more lives and as many kinds of lives as we wish' (1990: 84). Presumably, while reading a literary text, readers enter new worlds and the lives of others. While 'living' the 'life' presented by the text, readers tend to develop similar attitudes to those of the characters presented in the stories. In particular, when a reader 'identifies with a protagonist', this may lead to developing a liking for the protagonist and cause the reader to adopt some of the protagonist's attitudes (Mar and Oatley, 2008: 182). Therefore, the act of 'living as many kinds of lives as we wish' may bring many new kinds of characteristics and perspectives to the reader's own self and this may cause a transformation in the reader. The fictional text can make the readers examine or change their own moral values (Currie, 1995), influence their psychology and behaviour, and perhaps even shape their personality (Djikic et al., 2009; Kaufman and Libby, 2012). This effect occurs even if the reader is aware that the text and the events are depicted in the story are not factual and true (Marsh and Fazio, 2006). According to Markus Appel and Tobias Richter's research (2007), the information presented in fictional texts can turn into real-world beliefs in readers' minds.

In order to understand what happens in the reader's mind in the transaction between reader and text, I wanted to investigate the long-term effects (the residue) of reading fiction on adolescent readers. One of my main research questions was whether reading fiction affects adolescent readers and, if so, what kind of effects does it have? To begin with, I had to consider the reading choices that adolescent readers make or that are imposed on them. As a Turkish researcher conducting a doctoral study, I decided to undertake the fieldwork among young people in my country. As well as investigating selection and choice, I proposed to look at adolescents' 'reading memories', in other words, the particular memories that readers recollect from their previous readings such as a quote, an incident, a picture from a book or a particular feeling they had while reading a book. Through interviews and reading discussions, I wanted to find out what they might recall from their previous readings and how it might have changed their views or behaviours. For this purpose, I employed both quantitative and qualitative methods. These included an online survey questionnaire, semi-structured interviews and focus groups.

The overall aim was to investigate individuals through their active participation in the reading process. To place the research within a theoretical framework, Louise Rosenblatt's transactional/reader response theory (1978/1994) was selected. Because the focus was on the effects of reading on young readers and their reading choices, the philosophical approaches of interpretivism, together with the tools and principles of reader response theory, seemed appropriate to carry out this investigation successfully.

This chapter will focus on what the participants retained in their memories, the residue of fiction, from their previous readings and how they made meaning from these readings. After briefly describing the methodology, sampling and location, I will draw on some of the results of the questionnaire that are illuminating for this chapter. I will concentrate on the analysis of reading activities and interviews to show how reading fiction enabled young readers to explore their memories.

Curriculum and reading campaigns in Turkey

In Turkey, there are both public and private schools, but they both follow the National Curriculum. At the time this study was undertaken, the Board of National Education in Turkey (BNET) (2011a, 2011b), suggested – in the sections on

'Turkish literature' and 'language and expression' within the secondary education curriculum – that the main purposes of language and literature teaching were skills and understanding. The curriculum did not, however, address certain crucial points such as lifelong reading attitudes, online reading practices or reading for pleasure. Moreover, within the assessment objectives, none of the learning outcomes were related to these important aspects. In the Turkish classroom, reading activities were left to teachers without suggesting any strategies that might make reading more attractive (Dilidüzgün, 2006).

At that time, too, despite the fact that there was a lack of encouragement for reading fiction in the National Curriculum, there were many local and national reading promotion campaigns across the country between 2005 and 2012 led by the government. For example, in 2005, the National Ministry of Education prepared a list of 100 Basic Works for primary and secondary students (Çotuksöken, 2007). As a result, discussions and studies about reading, the number of published books (Balcı, 2009), as well as the number of people who read 'as an intellectual and aesthetic activity' (Nikolajeva, 2014: 1), were found to have increased (Turkish Statistical Institute, 2013; Ünal, 2013). Various other reading events such as 'Turkey is Reading' and 'The Speaking Book Festival', took place at national level in different parts of Turkey between 2008 and 2014 (Türkiye Okuyor Kampanyası, 2008; Konuşan Kitap, 2008; Coban, 2015). Non-governmental organisations, such as the Turkish branch of the International Board on Books for Young People (IBBY) helped to promote these campaigns. Because of restrictions on the freedom of expression in the current situation, it has since become harder to organise these kinds of activities.

A snapshot of the study location and the schools

The study took place in Adana, which is the fifth largest city in Turkey with a population of just over 2,000,000 (Adana Governorship, 2015a). Most adults worked in farming, industry and the civil service (Çevre ve Şehircilik Bakanlığı, 2011). In 2015, approximately 10% of the total population were university graduates, and nearly 0.7% of them had a postgraduate degree (Adana Governorship, 2015b).

There were seven libraries in the city, which, at the time of the study, had 214,457 books in their collection and a total membership of 5,215 in 2013 (Neyi ile Meşhur, 2013; Adana Governorship, 2015c). According to the Turkey Reading Culture Map research (Ministry of Culture and Tourism, 2011), approximately 2.5% of the total population in Adana were library members and about 6% of people used public libraries. This means that Adana was among the cities with the lowest library usage in the country. School libraries had limited funding, and the variety of books in libraries was dependent on the creativity and enthusiasm of the teachers responsible for libraries. (Because there were no school librarians in Turkey, school libraries were managed by one of the teachers with the support of students in schools.) Parallel to library usage, the average number of books read per person in one year in Adana was between six and seven, which is lower than the average for Turkey, 7.2 (Türkiye'nin Okuma, 2011).

There were different types of private and public schools in the area including Anatolia schools, science schools, *imam hatip* schools (which aim to provide Islamic education) and vocational schools (which aim to prepare students for a particular vocation such as being a nurse, carpenter or hairdresser). The schools chosen for the focus groups were different types and in different council areas in Adana, namely Seyhan and Çukurova, and had different student profiles. Both the schools chosen were among the most successful ones in the city. One of them had boarders who came from different cities and counties.

Methodology and sampling

Case studies are often used in research that involves small groups or individuals and is qualitative in nature (Lodico et al., 2010). Because I wanted to explore deeply personal issues with young people as they discussed books and real-life situations in detail, case study methodology seemed the best approach (Cohen et al., 2013). However, the data collection also entailed mixed methods: questionnaires were used to provide a platform for the qualitative methods (Jick, 1979). The online questionnaire investigated aspects such as the amount of reading, attitudes towards reading, reading choices and reading memories. The aims were, first, to have a general picture of adolescent reading choices, and second, to choose a purposive sample for the reading sessions and interviews. Although it was an online questionnaire, I spoke to all of the participants who did it in order to explain the study and invite them to participate. The decision to speak to the participants face-to-face was to reduce the disadvantages of the questionnaire being an online tool (Gordon, 1975, cited in Barriball and While 1994). Such disadvantages include issues related to validity, sampling methods, application and design (Wright, 2005). The aim at the first stage was to obtain a representative sample of 15- to 18-year-old students in Adana in order to create generalisations from the questionnaire results. According to Krejcie and Morgan's widely used table, 379 randomly selected students would be sufficient to represent 30,000 students (Krejcie and Morgan, 1970). There were 15,144 male and 14,960 female students (30,104 in total) who studied in 1,159 divisions in 259 schools (Ministry of National Education, 2014) in the city, and 443 of them studied in villages. In total, there were 381 responses from the 15 state schools.

A purposive sample was selected for interviews and reading sessions in order to obtain detailed data, as is recommended for qualitative approaches (Yin, 2011). Ten students aged between 16 and 17 years old were selected from two successful schools according to their responses to the questionnaire. The intention was to focus on academically successful adolescents who were also keen readers. Therefore, two schools that accepted students with the highest scores, according to a nationwide examination conducted just before starting high school, were selected. The criteria below were considered when choosing students from the questionnaire for reading sessions and interviews:

- studying in a successful school;
- showing an interest in the reading activities;
- showing an interest in, and love of, reading;
- giving consistent responses to the questionnaire;
- reading at least 30 books in one year.

All the participants were Muslim and came from working-class or middle-class families. In order to provide a detailed account of their responses, the rest of the chapter will focus on the case studies of three of the participants: MagicBook[1] (an outgoing, talkative girl who liked listening to her friends' problems), Isfendiyar (a quiet but witty boy) and Leonardo (a strong-minded, intellectual boy). I will also refer to some of the responses from other participants: Kdr (a serious but friendly boy and a wise school representative), BookMonster (a lively, smiling and critical girl) and BoiceLove (an emotional and quiet girl). Their choice of pseudonym gives an idea about their character: BoiceLove, for example, was a kind of girl whose heart seemed to be full of love.

Due to the mixed methods, both quantitative and qualitative analytical approaches (Creswell and Clark, 2007) were employed. I chose an inductive approach for the data analysis because it enables researchers to generate themes and theories according to results and helps to avoid excluding themes that might emerge (Bryman, 2015). Triangulation of the data, through the questionnaire, interviews and focus groups, also helped to increase the credibility, validity and reliability of research (Cohen et al., 2013; Erzberger and Prein, 1997). For the quantitative analysis, I used Statistical Package for the Social Sciences (SPSS), which streamlined the complicated quantitative analysis process (Green and Salkind, 2010). The qualitative data was categorised and coded using the NVivo analysis program.

What the reading fiction questionnaire revealed

The questionnaire data showed that more than half of the students had a positive attitude towards reading and they read books as a daily activity. According to Pearson's r data analysis, which shows the relationship between two results, there was a positive correlation between the amount of reading fiction and non-fiction, meaning that participants who read more fiction books also tended to read more information books. However, the amount of reading fiction was significantly higher than the amount of non-fiction reading. The amount of reading they did, as expected, was related to the time they spent on reading and on other activities. More than half of the participants indicated that they spent more than two hours a day on telephone usage, with less time spent each day on other activities such as studying, reading books, watching TV and computer usage. 10% of adolescents did not usually spend time on reading and 23% read books for less than one hour a day. The reason for spending less time on reading than some other activities could be associated with the extent of their enthusiasm for reading books: 41.3% percent of respondents indicated that they were very enthusiastic about reading, while only 5.5% were not. Approximately a third of the participants had an 'average' amount of enthusiasm for reading and 16.7% had only 'a little'.

In terms of gender differences, in general, the number of fiction books read and the time spent on reading by females was almost twice as much as the number of books read and the time spent on reading by males: 41.7% of female respondents read more than 15 fiction books in one year, while only 14.2% males read the same amount. There was no significant difference between male students' fiction and non-fiction reading choices, but females preferred fiction to non-fiction. One significant finding was that the percentage of male students who did not read books was 16.7%, approximately three times more than their female peers where the percentage was only 5.8%.

E-reading habits were also investigated in the study and this revealed a surprising finding. Slightly fewer than half of the respondents read e-books, but a significantly higher number of girls preferred to read e-books than boys (57% and 35% respectively). While only one out of five boys read e-books from online sites, four out of five girls preferred this type of reading, in particular, from Wattpad, a site where teenagers write-publish-read-review their own books. Wattpad is available in 30 different languages and has become popular among adolescents in Turkey in recent years. The majority of users in Turkey are adolescents, particularly girls. More than 30 Wattpad stories have been published in Turkey by recognised publishers after they became popular on Wattpad and young readers have created many fan pages for some of the characters in the Wattpad stories (Coban, 2015).

Reading activities within the research project

The participating students were offered 15 books from both contemporary Turkish and world young adult (YA) fiction as well as some classic texts in different genres including crime, fantasy, romance, historical, adventure and science fiction. The books were selected from among the list of bestseller books in Turkey. The participants were asked to select one, read it and choose the chapter or pages they liked most, then offer the chapter to their peers in the group to read. I also informed them that apart from the titles I suggested to them, they could read any other fiction book they wanted. After everyone had read a book, we discussed the books as a group.

We managed to discuss chapters from ten books in the reading sessions, including four of the titles suggested by the students. In addition, we did an activity that we named 'three words one book' (3Words) in which they drew a book cover of a book they enjoyed reading and added three words related to that book. Then everyone tried to guess the title. Afterwards, we talked about the book and the influence of the book on the reader who had recommended it. The books they read included international YA bestsellers (all read in Turkish translations) such as *The Fault in Our Stars* by John Green, *The Hunger Games* by Suzanne Collins and *The Curious Incident of the Dog in the Night-Time* by Mark Haddon; adult novels, *The Little Prince* by Antoine de Saint-Exupéry, *The White Ship* by Cengiz Aytmatov and *The Sinner* by Tess Gerritsen; Turkish novels, both adult and YA, *Dance with Heroin* by Canan Tan, *My Brother's Story* by Zülfü Livaneli, *Peace Street* by Şule Yüksel Şenler and *The Disconnected* by Oğuz Atay. In this chapter, I focus mainly on the discussion related to one book, *The Curious Incident of the Dog in the Night-Time* (*The Curious Incident*) and on one response that emerged from the 3Words activity.

Fiction in the memory

In the reading discussions with the young people in my study, participants tended to refer to their previous life and text experiences. Sometimes, they recalled a life experience that was related to the discussion; sometimes they referred to a quote from a book and/or an emotional moment that became memorable for them. This finding overlaps with Hayakawa's (1990) idea mentioned earlier that reading enables one to live and experience other people's lives. When a reader enters the story world, they discover an opportunity to not only explore the lives presented in the text but also to be part of those lives by emotionally responding to them (Nikolajeva, 2014) and by adopting some of these perspectives (Kaufman and Libby, 2012; Gallese and Goldman, 1998).

MagicBook's feelings while she was reading a fictional book highlight this close relationship between the fictional life and the reader:

MAGICBOOK: It is not like you are watching cinema on a screen. Imagine a cartoon. There are eyes that don't have body or head that always wander around.

OC: Yes.

MAGICBOOK: They watch everything; I am like that. It is different. I am not inside the events, my body is not there, but it is as if I am living there. It is always like I am travelling in different universes.

The metaphor of eyes or a fly on the wall observing and sometimes acting like a character is mentioned in previous research on adolescent response (Arizpe, 1994; Thomson, 1987) when the reader describes where they feel they are in relation to the characters. MagicBook's metaphor of 'eyes that don't have body' is a literary and visual example of this idea. Although she was not physically living with the fictional characters, she felt 'as if [she were] living there'. This experience of seeming to live inside the events gives the reader the chance to interact with the characters. Even though the eyes were not visible to the characters, they were among them and 'travelling' with them. Having the opportunity to watch them from such a close distance and being a witness to the detailed account of their lives/emotions requires the owner of these imaginary eyes to take a position with or against them. This is where sympathy and empathy step in. If the fictional character meets the expectations of the reader (e.g., the character is represented as experiencing events similar to those that the reader does), the reader may start adopting some thoughts and experiences from the character (Kaufman and Libby, 2012) and building beliefs upon the story events (Appel and Richter, 2007). In the discussions of *The Curious Incident*, for example, they identified themselves with a fictional character and referred to their childhoods. *The Curious Incident* is the story of a 15-year-old autistic teenager, Christopher, who tries to solve the mystery of a dog's death. As he deals with this mystery, he discovers that his mother is still alive and his father has been lying to him. His unique approach to everyday events makes the story attractive. In the reading session, we discussed Chapter 71, in which Christopher criticises people's perception of people with special needs. MagicBook articulated her identification with Christopher, the protagonist of *The Curious Incident*, several times: 'I would also imagine. If everyone dies, I will go into ice-cream shops. I remember well. But then I would sit and cry because you are scared at some point because you have no one, nothing to do.' She recalled this scene upon reading the chapter where Christopher, narrates his dream. Due to his condition, Christopher does not like being touched. He has a dream where everyone dies because of an illness that spreads to people who can understand what others feel and think. Given that only other autistic people survive, he can now go anywhere without being anxious about being touched. He can do anything he wants and this makes him happy (Haddon, 2004). Here MagicBook's recollection of her daydream was connected to Christopher's: both present the desire to control their world without the influence of others. Reading about a scene that was similar to a daydream from her childhood enabled her to remember her experience, which might otherwise have not been recalled or expressed. This recollection was a way for her to connect herself to her childhood, enabling her to understand her childhood desires and ultimately herself. The example shows how the residue of fiction acts in the inner world of the self and also how it enables readers to explore things that may not be possible to experience in real-life situations.

Similarly, other participants revealed their identification with fictional characters on several occasions and this often led to holding up these characters as models for behaviour, as can be appreciated in Leonardo's self-observation below:

OC: Do you ever act like a character?

LEONARDO: I do. For example, I read Sherlock Holmes a lot. I mean I want to follow and look for something if I read a murder [news] something like that. Or when I face a bad situation, firstly sit, keep calm and think what to do.

OC: Is this Sherlock Holmes's characteristic?

LEONARDO: No, Holmes was the first example. Dan Brown's characters are like that. Then helping good people ... The little books are like that.

OC: Yes.

LEONARDO: There is a character that helps some people.

OC: You think it comes from that character.
LEONARDO: Yes probably. I read comics as well, from old times. My father kept them.
[…]
I always wanted to have a group, and we help some people.
OC: You're like a superhero.
LEONARDO: Exactly.

Leonardo mentioned Dan Brown and comic book characters and tried to show the similarities between them and himself. He stressed that he learned a virtue from those characters by repeating the phrase 'helping people' three times, and this is an indicator of how he was influenced by the characters and wanted to adopt their behaviours. From this conversation, it is not possible to claim that his intention to help people by establishing a supportive peer group was a result of the influence of the books. However, it shows that he was thinking, or was pretending to be thinking, that he wanted to act the way that the characters did. Either way, it is evident that he found similarities between himself and the three different book characters. His description of what he did when he 'face[d] a bad situation' revealed his self-awareness. His reference to the Dan Brown characters then showed his analytic approach to the characters. In this way, as far as he saw it, he was trying to model himself on the fictional characters.

The 3Words activity also revealed how reading functions as a tool for readers to travel through their reading memories. Two of these drawings created for this activity are used as examples. Isfendiyar drew the book called *Metal Fırtına* (*Metal Storm*) (Figure 2.1), which is a fantasy and tells the story of the Turkish soldiers who are going to Africa to help people who try to save their lands against the USA (Uçar and Turna, 2005). At the centre of the picture, there was a 'blood lake' that shows people died because of a 'nuclear bomb' dropped by America. Isfendiyar was 'filled with so much hate and anger' towards 'external powers', especially 'America' (3Words). 'People who died just for the sake of their homeland' attracted his attention, and he became 'upset' to read this. His choice of the aeroplane in black symbolises the evil that causes bleedings and destroys the green tree. The three phrases he chose to describe the book were, 'love of homeland', 'love of duty' and 'external powers'. The indicators of the first two phrases in the picture were people who were 'killed by nuclear bomb', which was the black coloured material under the flight (3Words).

He explained that the book 'increased the value of soldiers and police' in his view and he 'started to respect these jobs and joining the army became [his] dream job'.

OC: You mean you could have been a soldier and this meant it could have changed your life. But you could still become a soldier.
ISFENDIYAR: I won't be able to (*indistinct*) (3Words).

After the reading session, we had a chance to discuss this matter with Isfendiyar, and he said because of a certain problem, he would not be allowed to be a soldier.

FIGURE 2.1 Isfendiyar's drawing for *Metal Storm*

His sadness was visible while he was revealing this information. Isfendiyar referred to several fantastic books he read when he was in middle school, but he said he did not read that kind of book at the time of our conversation because 'they look absurd now'. *Metal Storm* was one of the books that became rooted in Isfendiyar's memory:

OC: Have you ever dreamed about the characters of a book after reading the book?
ISFENDIYAR: Yes. I found myself inside *Metal Storm*.
OC: Ha ha!
ISFENDIYAR: A nuclear bomb is dropping your head, run brother!
OC: Ha ha! This must be just after reading the book.
ISFENDIYAR: I think it wasn't just after reading it. I still have dreams about them.

As in the case of MagicBook and Isfendiyar, there were several instances of the link between books and dreams. In Isfendiyar's case, although he did not reveal the details of his dreams, he seemed to find himself inside the events. According to him, these dreams were not just after reading the book. Although he had read the book when he was in the sixth grade, he said 'he still has dreams' about this book. If, as some psychoanalysts believe (e.g., Freud, 2013), dreams are connected to the subconscious of the dreamer and if Isfendiyar's dream was one of these particular

FIGURE 2.2 Leonardo's drawing for *Confessions of a Sociopath*

dreams, then the book might have found a place in his subconscious. As discussed above, he indicated his sadness about the death of soldiers because of the nuclear bomb. Given his aspiration to become a soldier, he seems to have found a close connection between himself and the soldiers who were killed by the nuclear bomb.

Leonardo drew a thought-provoking cover (Figure 2.2) of *Confessions of a Sociopath: A Life Spent Hiding in Plain Sight* by M. E. Thomas, an autobiography of the author who described herself as a sociopath (Thomas, 2013; DrPhil, 2003; Ronson, 2013). Even if it is not fiction, Leonardo's attraction to the story was so strong that I decided to include this example.

Leonardo's cover was similar to the original book cover in that it portrayed the 'mask' that sociopaths wear to hide their real faces. However, Leonardo used different colours for the eyes and mouths (as he drew two shapes of a mouth in his mask) which, in his words, showed the 'dual personality' of sociopaths (3Words). He added two different faces of one person because, as he explained, sociopaths could be both 'successful and aggressive or anarchist' (3Words).

In comparison to the discussions of the other activities, when confronted by Leonardo's drawing and by the researcher's questions, everyone was quiet as if they were hesitating to say something until, finally, Kdr made a wisecrack that helped the participants to release their thoughts:

OC: What kind of problem did the sociopath have?
KDR: Teacher, you mean Leonardo or the sociopath?

(*laughter*)

LEONARDO: No not me! Ay! I might be like that, but! (*laughter*) OK. I have got inclination to behave like a sociopath and something [like that]. I might be anarchic too! But not to the public. I don't think I am anarchic that much.

OC: How did you feel [when you read this book]?

LEONARDO: Alas! I'm finished! I said.

MAGICBOOK: 'I'm sociopath', ha ha.

LEONARDO: No. I didn't want to think as such. I mean I am prone to violence, but I can at least stop myself. I thought at least I can prevent myself from the things at the end of the book to be calm.

OC: So, you thought it is something about you.

LEONARDO: At some point. You find something from yourself in every book.

OC: How do you think the book affected your friends?

KDR: I think he found himself in the book: a picture of a sociopath.

MAGICBOOK: I think it is like looking at the mirror. There was a Mirror of Erised at Harry Potter; you would look at it and see things that you wanted to do so. It is like that. He looked and saw himself. It is like awareness. Not exactly. I don't think he is a sociopath.

LEONARDO: Then, make sure you are not alone with me!

MAGICBOOK: We won't leave you alone then.

MagicBook refers to the Mirror of Erised, the mirror where Harry Potter sees his dead parents. After his conversation with Albus Dumbledore Harry thinks that the mirror 'shows us what we want … whatever we want' (Rowling 1998: 171). However according to Dumbledore, 'It shows us nothing more or less than the deepest, most desperate desire of our hearts' (171). Interestingly, MagicBook recalled the function of the mirror according to Harry's interpretation, rather than that of Dumbledore, the adult. According to MagicBook, Leonardo wanted to see himself in the book and therefore, he did. Nevertheless, she adds 'I don't think he is a sociopath'. Another aspect that makes her comment significant is that, noticeably, she was still able to recall the Mirror of Erised and its function and to relate it to her friend's experience even though she had read the book several years ago.

Presumably, Leonardo's self-awareness developed after reading this book, drawing a book cover for it and talking about it. His peers also had the chance to learn about this 'condition' from someone who thinks he has got 'some' of its characteristics. BookMonster found his drawings 'too scary' and BoiceLove did not say a single word during the discussion. She only joined her peers when everyone laughed. Kdr was Leonardo's classmate, and MagicBook was one of his friends. Arguably, their comments about him, 'finding' and 'mirroring' himself at the book, could be referring to some of his personality traits given that he himself admitted having them. He put the name of this book as his favourite book in the questionnaire. This was because he 'found himself' in the book; 'he felt good' and he thought he 'developed' himself when he read it. Even if all the things he admitted may not be taken as a true self-portrait, the book presumably added to his awareness about sociopaths as someone who might have some sociopathic characteristics. This example shows how reading enables one to develop self-awareness and awareness of others.

The stories behind the residue of fiction

The analysis of the data obtained through the various activities in this study provided insights into how the adolescent participants deepened and savoured their lived-through experience through verbal, written and drawn responses. These young Turkish readers became self-aware and self-critical as they captured the links between their drawing and 'both the text and their earlier experience and assumptions' (Rosenblatt, 1986: 126). They also learned about different ways of interpreting text and image through listening and responding to each other's drawings and responses. Asking readers to draw the cover for their favourite book and giving them the opportunity to discuss it with their peers, fostered creativity and assisted them to be more critical of themselves and others. At the same time, their responses suggest they developed self-awareness and awareness of others.

The analysis also showed the strong influence of the fiction on the young readers' memory. Accessing the residues of fiction in the adolescents' memory helped uncover glimpses of what they kept in their mind and heart about fictional characters and events and why they did this. This included their childhood desires as MagicBook's recollection of her childhood daydream shows. They also linked their purposes and expectations to stories they drew, as was seen in Isfendiyar's dream job. Although they had read the books a long time ago, they were able to capture the emotional scenes from the books, showing how an emotional moment can become a residual emotion for the reader.

Returning to my original research question, 'Does reading fiction affect the reader and if so in what way?', the discussions showed how a book held a place in their memories and how these books gained a new meaning for the readers when they became owners of the texts by reading and storing some particular scenes from them. Due to sample and method limitations, as well as to the deeply personal and almost ethereal nature of affect and memory, there is no presumption that these the results can generalised. Nevertheless, the findings are consistent with the findings of other studies that have explored the effects of reading fiction on adolescents and which I mentioned at the beginning of this chapter. Whether the readers actually transformed their attitudes and behaviours by modelling them on their reading, and in what way, are important questions but they cannot be addressed without a further, more expanded and interdisciplinary study that combines cognitive psychology, sociology and literary theory. However, what my study showed is that the reading discussions and activities worked as a kind of bridge that connected different fictional times, characters and places together. These young readers, as active agents in the meaning-making process of the fiction, travelled back to their childhood and made connections between these fictional spaces and their real-world times and places. If there is a possibility that these connections act as models that lead to a better (or worse) change in young people's lives, then the importance of engaging with, and exploring, young people's reading is further highlighted and it has significant implications regarding the responsibilities of researchers, educators, publishers and policymakers.

Finally, it is important to note that the residues mentioned in this chapter all occurred from adolescents' own reading choices, not from their obligatory readings. In other words, they chose to read those books for pleasure. However, curricula in various countries often fail to consider adolescents' changing reading interests, especially contemporary fiction and online reading. Therefore, there is a significant gap between what schools offer and what young readers choose to read, suggesting the need for a more student-centred curriculum policy in order to increase the chance of benefiting from the residue that derives from reading fiction for pleasure.

Note

1 MagicBook chose Büyülü Ayraç (Magical Book Mark) as a pseudonym but it was shortened to make it easier to read. BookMonster's pseudonym was also a translation, while the others were the participants' original choices.

References

Adana Governorship. (2015a). Nüfus. Retrieved 1 April 2016 from: www.adana.gov.tr/nufus

Adana Governorship. (2015b). Eğitim. Retrieved 1 April 2016 from: www.adana.gov.tr/egitim

Adana Governorship. (2015c). Kültür. Retrieved 1 April 2016 from: www.adana.gov.tr/kultur

Appel, M., and Richter, T. (2007). Persuasive effects of fictional narratives increase over time. *Media Psychology*, 10 (1), 113–134.

Arizpe, E. (1994). *Reading Response: The Reading Processes of Adolescent Reluctant Readers*. PhD dissertation, University of Cambridge, United Kingdom.

Atay, O. (1972). *Tutunamayanlar (The Disconnected)*. Istanbul: İletişim.

Aytmatov, C. (1970). *Beyaz Gemi (The White Ship)*. Istanbul: Cem Publishing.

Balcı, A. (2009). *Research on Elementary 8th Grade Students' Reading Habits and Interests*. PhD dissertation, Gazi University, Ankara, Turkey.

Barriball, K.L. and While, A. (1994). Collecting data using a semi-structured interview: A discussion paper. *Journal of Advanced Nursing*, 19 (2), 328–335.

Board of National Education in Turkey (BNET). (2011a). Ortaöğretim Türk Edebiyatı Dersi 9, 10, 11 ve 12. Sınıf Öğretim Programı. Retrieved 7 October 2016 from: http://ttkb.meb.gov.tr/program2.aspx/, but no longer available.

Board of National Education in Turkey (BNET). (2011b). Dil ve Anlatım Dersi 9, 10, 11 ve 12. Sınıf Öğretim Programı. Retrieved 7 October 2016 from: http://ttkb.meb.gov.tr/program2.aspx/, but no longer available.

Bryman, A. (2015). *Social Research Methods*. Oxford: Oxford University Press.

Çevre ve Şehircilik Bakanlığı. (2011). İl Çevre Durum Raporu. Retrieved 1 April 2016 from: www.csb.gov.tr/db/ced/editordosya/adana_icdr2011.pdf

Coban O. (2015). Have you not read yet? Wattpad as an online reading platform and the virtual reading culture in the adolescents of virtual world. Presentation at the 2nd International Children's and Youth Literature Symposium, İstanbul.

Cohen, L., Manion, L. and Morrison, K. (2011). *Research Methods in Education* (7th ed.). Oxfordshire: Routledge.

Collins, S. (2009). *The Hunger Games*. London: Scholastic.

Çotuksöken, Y. (2007). *'100 Temel Eser' listeleri üzerine: '100 Temel Eser' tartışması*. Istanbul: Çağdaş Yaşamı Destekleme Derneği Publication.

Creswell, J. W. and Clark, V. L. P. (2007). *Designing and Conducting Mixed Methods Research*. London: Sage.

Currie, G. (1995). The moral psychology of fiction. *Australasian Journal of Philosophy*, 73(2), 250–259.

de Saint-Exupéry, A. (1945). *The Little Prince*. London: Heinemann.

Dilidüzgün, S. (2006). Eğitim Gerçeği Açısından '100 Temel Eser' Tartışmaları. Varlık Dergisi, 1189.

Djikic, M., Oatley, K., Zoeterman, S. and Peterson, J. B. (2009). On being moved by art: How reading fiction transforms the self. *Creativity Research Journal*, 21(1), 24–29.

DrPhil (2003). I abducted a baby/*Confessions of a Sociopath*. Retrieved 25 December 2016 from: www.drphil.com/shows/2035/

Erzberger, C. and Prein, G. (1997). Triangulation: Validity and empirically-based hypothesis construction. *Quality and Quantity*, 31 (2), 141–54.

Freud, S. (2013). *The Interpretation of Dreams*. Evesham, Worcestershire: Read Books Ltd.

Gallese, V. and Goldman, A. (1998). Mirror neurons and the simulation theory of mind-reading. *Trends in Cognitive Sciences*, 2 (12), 493–501.

Gerritsen, T. (2003). *The Sinner*. New York: Ballantine Books.

Gordon, R.L. (1975). *Interviewing: Strategy, Techniques and Tactics*. Homewood, IL: Dorsey Press.

Green, J. (2012). *The Fault in Our Stars*. London: Penguin.

Green, S. B. and Salkind, N. J. (2010). *Using SPSS for Windows and Macintosh: Analyzing and Understanding Data*. New Jersey: Prentice Hall Press.

Haddon, M. (2004). *The Curious Incident of the Dog in the Night-Time*. London: Vintage.

Hayakawa, S. I. (1990). *Language in Thought and Action*. New York, NY: Harcourt Brace.

Jick, T. D. (1979). Mixing qualitative and quantitative methods: Triangulation in action. *Administrative Science Quarterly*, 24 (4), 602–611.

Kaufman, G. F. and Libby, L. K. (2012). Changing beliefs and behaviour through experience-taking. *Journal of Personality and Social Psychology*, 103 (1), 1–19.

Konuşan Kitap. (June, 2008). Konuşan Kitap Şenliği Başladı, Yeni Şafak. Retrieved 19 October 2017 from: www.yenisafak.com

Krejcie, R. V. and Morgan, D. W. (1970). Determining sample size for research activities. *Educational and Psychological Measurement*, 30 (3), 607–610.

Livaneli, Z. (2013). *Kardeşimin Hikayesi (My Brother's Story)*. Istanbul: Doğan Kitap.

Lodico, M. G., Spaulding, D.T. and Voegtle, K. H. (2010). *Methods in Educational Research: From Theory to Practice*. San Francisco: John Wiley.

Mar, R. and Oatley, K. (2008). The function of fiction is the abstraction and simulation of social experience. *Perspectives on Psychological Science*, 3 (3), 173–192.

Marsh, E. J. and Fazio, L. K. (2006). Learning errors from fiction: Difficulties in reducing reliance on fictional stories. *Memory & Cognition*, 34 (5), 1140–1149.

Ministry of Culture and Tourism. (2011). Turkey Reading Culture Map. Retrieved 1 April 2016 from: www.kygm.gov.tr/Eklenti/56,yonetici-ozeti-engpdf.pdf?0

Ministry of National Education (2014). National Education Statistics Formal Education. Retrieved 30 January 2017 from: http://sgb.meb.gov.tr/www/milli-egitim-istatistikleri-orgun-egitim-2013–2014/icerik/95

Neyi ile Meşhur (2013). Adana'da bulunan kütüphaneler. Retrieved 1 April 2016 from: www.neyiilemeshur.com/adana/adanada-bulunan-kutuphaneler-3570.html

Nikolajeva, M. (2014). *Reading for Learning: Cognitive Approaches to Children's Literature*. Amsterdam: John Benjamins Publishing Company.

Ronson, J. (2013). Review: *Confessions of a Sociopath, New York Times*. Retrieved 25 December 2016 from: www.nytimes.com/2013/06/16/books/review/confessions-of-a-sociopath-by-m-e-thomas.html

Rosenblatt, L. M. (1978/1994). *The Reader, the Text, the Poem: The Transactional Theory of the Literary Work*. Carbondale and Edwardsville: Southern Illinois University Press.

Rosenblatt, L. M. (1986). The aesthetic transaction. *Journal of Aesthetic Education*, 20 (4), 122–128.

Rowling, J. K. (1998). *Harry Potter and the Sorcerer's Stone*. New York: Scholastic.

Şenler, S.Y. (1977). *Huzur Sokağı (Peace Street)*. Istanbul: Timaş.

Tan, C. (2012). *Alevden Küle Eroinle Dans (Dance with Heroin)*. Istanbul: Altın Kitaplar.

Thomas, M. E. (2013). *Confessions of a Sociopath: A Life Spent Hiding in Plain Sight*. New York: Broadway Books.

Thomson, J. (1987). *Understanding Teenagers' Reading: Reading Processes and the Teaching of Literature*. Iowa: Nichols Publishing Company.

Turkish Statistical Institute. (2013). Turkey in Statistics 2013. Retrieved 19 May 2015 from: www.tuik.gov.tr/IcerikGetir.do?istab_id=5

Türkiye'nin Okuma. (April, 2011). Turkiye'nin okuma kültürü haritasi, Milliyet. Retrieved 1 April 2016 from: www.milliyet.com.tr

Türkiye Okuyor Kampanyası. (2008). Türkiye Okuyor Kampanyası Martta Başlıyor, CNN Türk. Retrieved 19 October 2017 from: www.cnnturk.com

Uçar, O. and Turna, B. (2005). *Metal Fırtına (Metal Storm)*. Istanbul: Timaş.

Ünal, M. (2013). Konuşan Kitap Okumayı Artırdı. Retrieved 14 December 2013 from: www.zaman.com.tr

Wright, K. B. (2005). Researching internet-based populations: Advantages and disadvantages of online survey research, online questionnaire authoring software packages, and web survey services. *Journal of Computer-Mediated Communication*, 10 (3). Online at: doi: 10.1111/j.1083–6101.2005.tb00259.x

Yin, R.K. (2011). *Case Study Research: Design and Methods*. Beverly Hills: Sage.

3

RIVERS OF READING

A research method to explore young adults' personal reading histories

Gabrielle Cliff Hodges

MAP 3

The original study

As part of my doctoral study of young adult readers between 2006 and 2011, I designed a research project that focused on young people who habitually read for a variety of purposes and pleasures and who counted reading as a worthwhile pursuit among the other activities in which they were involved, such as playing sport, listening to music or spending time with friends (Cliff Hodges, 2010, 2012, 2016).

I was interested to know what an integrated focus on social, cultural, historical and spatial aspects of their reading might add to our understanding of adolescent readers and readership, rather than discovering merely what texts they were currently reading, how often or how many. The project involved an English class of 31 12- to 13-year-old students as they moved with Rosa, their English teacher, from Year 8 into Year 9 in Cornford School, a rural state-maintained school in the east of England.

The 'rivers of reading' activity that originated with that study (and which I am going to revisit in this chapter) proved valuable as one of my four research methods. To make their rivers of reading, the students created collages of their personal reading histories, thereby generating data that made a significant contribution to the rich descriptions of diverse readers developing out of the project. Since then, the same rivers of reading activity has been adapted for use by other teachers and researchers working with a range of readers from young children and their families (Winchester, 2008; McAdam et al., 2014; Williams, 2017) to student-teachers entering the teaching profession (Kelly, 2009). The activity has changed somewhat from the original purpose for which Rosa and I designed it, so I am interested in looking not only at the original rivers of reading once again, but also some of the activity's subsequent uses. It seems timely to reconsider how it worked in the original study, as well as new ways in which it might inform teachers' and researchers' understanding. In particular, I will add some different theoretical perspectives from those I brought to bear originally in order to explore how they can further teachers' and researchers' thinking about the activity's potential value.

Critical incident technique

The rivers of reading were, in my initial project, loosely designed as critical incident collages. However, at that time, my understanding of the critical incident technique as a research method was confined to what I knew about it from colleagues working on image-based methods with students as researchers. It turns out that the critical incident technique stems back more than six decades to the mid-twentieth century. Even then it was not entirely new, but was developed in ways that are worth dwelling on briefly here. In particular, John Flanagan, a flying pilot in the Second World War and later an academic psychologist, used the critical incident technique to help those responsible for recruiting or teaching pilots to understand what made good pilots effective (Flanagan, 1954). Through triangulating perceptions by trainee pilots, observers of experienced pilots and instructors, Flanagan was able to categorise some of the things good pilots actually did and to suggest what, therefore, the critical requirements for a novice becoming a good pilot might be. Reading about this early approach to the technique recently, I found myself wondering whether there were, in fact, any parallels with the requirements for becoming a habitual reader that might be brought to bear.

In social science research, the critical incident method has since been further adapted (Butterfield et al., 2005). However, in the context in which I first encountered it, in an Economic and Social Research Council (ESRC) Project Newsletter (Burnard, 2002), it was not being linked to literacy in any way; nor was the activity referred to as rivers of reading. Instead, the critical incident technique was being used in a much more general way, especially one that could be valuable when consulting young people about their own perspectives on their lives. Pam Burnard describes the activity as drawing the outline of a winding river on a sheet of paper and asking students to plot critical incidents in their lives which they feel have been important onto each bend of the river. Making critical incidents visible in this way prompts students to reflect on their lives thus far and is often a powerful stimulus for dialogue between students and researchers. It therefore works well as a way to generate potentially rich data.

Similar image-based approaches have been used and discussed elsewhere, for example by Ruth Leitch (2008). Here, too, a version of the critical incident technique has proved to be effective, as Leitch suggests, for exploring particularly sensitive topics such as anger or bereavement. In terms of image-based techniques, Leitch also stresses the value to the students of creating collages as distinct from doing drawings, for example in the context of young people reflecting on their experiences of growing up in the social and political troubles of Northern Ireland in the United Kingdom. Her argument is that whereas drawing is often directly linked with judgements about artistic ability, that is not the case with collages. Instead, such judgements tend not to be made about collages and, moreover, the manipulation of different materials for creating them can be both appealing and liberating.

The metaphor of the river

Before embarking on my research, I had already gained experience of using the critical incident technique with teachers who were mentoring student-teachers within the Cambridge Postgraduate Certificate of Education (PGCE). For them, the task was to plot onto the winding river critical moments in the student-teachers' PGCE year when mentors needed to support them through particularly challenging experiences. The critical incident technique was designed to make explicit what the mentors did and how their actions might have proved valuable. The illuminating nature of the activity remained with me, so when I designed the opening stage of my reading research I decided to adapt the critical incident technique to encourage students to reflect on their personal reading histories and be better prepared to talk with me in small group interviews than if they came to the activity without advance warning.

Rosa, the English teacher whose class I was working with, responded very enthusiastically to the idea of the critical incident technique to stimulate dialogue about reading. It was also she who suggested that the students make collages rather than drawing. We therefore asked the students to create a collage of what we described as their reading journeys from their earliest memories to the present day. As necessary, and if they wanted to, students could ask older members of their families to fill in any gaps there might be, for example because they were looking back to a time before they could actually remember. Later, because of the river metaphor, the phrase 'reading journeys' turned into the more alliterative 'rivers of reading', which is the term now most often used for this kind of work (e.g., Arizpe, 2014). As the rivers of reading activity became more widely known, other teachers and researchers began to adopt the idea in their own practice (e.g., those working on the teachers as researchers project recorded by Winchester, 2008). In the first article I published about it, 'Rivers of reading: Using critical incident collages to learn about adolescent readers and their readership' (Cliff Hodges, 2010), I wanted not only to share and discuss some of the students' rivers of reading, but also consider the theoretical perspectives informing the activity. In this current chapter, I argue – with the benefit of hindsight, of course – that there are several reasons for the popularity and ongoing success of the rivers of reading activity over the past ten years or so, both those I cited in my original article and some that are new.

One of the particular appeals of the rivers of reading activity is the choice of the river as a metaphor. Rivers are, as Tom Fort writes in his book *Downstream: Across England in a Punt*,

> more than just fresh water on the move. There is awareness of past, present and future – that the water was somewhere else the day before and will be a different somewhere else the next day; that it connects people and places across space and time; that it is both of itself, self-contained, and integral to its landscape.
>
> (Fort, 2008: 1)

Rivers may also be complex, not straightforward, as Philip Gross writes in his poem, 'Severn Song', which begins like this:

> The Severn was brown and the Severn was blue –
> not this-then-that, not either-or,
> no mixture. Two things can be true.
> The hills were clouds and the mist was a shore.
>
> (Gross, 2009: 64)

The same ideas arguably describe reading. When reading, two things can be true, for example the world of the reader and the world of the text. Reading, likewise, connects the present with the past and the future in terms of what has already been read, which might not only be informing the reader's present understanding but also what might be read in the future. Reading, like rivers, has the potential to connect people and places across space and time, creating encounters between writers from the past and readers in the present or future, across local or global spaces. Because of the different ways in which each reader reads any text (Rosenblatt, 1938/1995, 1978/1994), a reader's reading history is – like a river – integral to their personal life and its landscape, although both may well adjoin and overlap with many other people's. Its source may be infinitesimal and difficult to locate; its destination may be – like a vast open sea – the limitless expanse of what has already been written and what is yet to come. The river metaphor, therefore, offers a particularly apt way of conceptualising reading, one that emphasises momentum, diversity, duality and transformation as it makes its way from small beginnings towards the unbounded future.

Theorists, for example Professor Daniel Schwarz in the United States, have used related metaphors in similar ways. In his book *In Defense of Reading: Teaching Literature in the Twenty-First Century* (2008), Schwarz selects the metaphor of the journey (or odyssey) as an analogy for reading. He describes two kinds of journeying. First, there is the journey that readers make across a lifetime of reading. 'What exactly', he asks, 'is reading but the journey of the mind to understand a world beyond itself?' (1). 'Reading is a kind of travel, an imaginative voyage' (3). But reading over a lifetime is made up of a second kind of journeying, namely separate reading engagements or, rather, a multitude of shorter journeys through individual texts. Each text may either immerse us, or cause us to halt and face the challenge of a quest for meaning through interpretation, or engage us in critical reflection – or, as is most likely, a mixture of all three. Instructing students to draw a river as an outline for their personal reading histories is an invitation for them to chart their whole life's reading journey thus far; the critical incidents plotted onto it mark some of the most memorable individual experiences along the way which contribute to the whole. However, individual readings of particular authors, or novels or series may not be merely isolated incidents; instead they can form incipient patterns which then contribute to the overall configuration of a reader's readership. If that is the case, how each reader creates a design from those patterns, rather than seeing them as a series of unconnected experiences, may be what lies at the heart of becoming a habitual reader. Using the rivers of reading for viewing reading trajectories overall may therefore be a valuable way to characterise a reader's progress, but because each reader's trajectory will be different, we should – perhaps – be hesitant about using the collages simply to list requirements for becoming a habitual reader.

Reviewing the gap between home and school reading

The rivers of reading activity has also proven to be valuable because it invites students to reflect on and value the reading knowledge they have already accumulated (what González et al., 2005, call their funds of knowledge), and begins to close the gap there might be between home and school reading, making it relatively easy for teachers to know what young people have read in the past and are now reading outside school as well as what they are reading in school. The activity makes their reading visible to, and important for, young readers themselves. In the research report, *Journeys from Images to Words*, Child A says: 'when we got to the *Rivers of Reading* ... everybody was saying that we don't really read anything, but then we ended up with a river full of stuff ... that we didn't even know that we actually read' (McAdam et al., 2014: 22). It also helps teachers to understand students' reading better, as is attested by two teachers, Katy and Charlotte, who participated in the *Building Communities: Researching Literacy Lives* project led by Teresa Cremin and colleagues:

> [A]fter developing Literacy Rivers with their classes (collages of their reading and writing over a weekend), Katy and Charlotte were astonished by the diversity reflected in them. Both were completely unaware that particular children had access to and enjoyed Polish comics and magazines, and were surprised by the number of websites, drawing and computer work depicted. They were also encouraged by the enthusiasm that the children showed when talking about their everyday practices which were more diverse, more demanding and more complex than either of the teachers had appreciated.
>
> (Cremin et al., 2015: 85)

Because making rivers of reading collages often involves readers conferring not only with one another but also other people beyond the classroom with whom they have shared their reading over time, the social nature of reading is very much in evidence. Furthermore, the activity requires readers to think historically when applied to lifelong reading histories rather than just reading over the course of one weekend: the rivers of reading plot not just what each student considers to be critical reading patterns in the present, but in the past as well. Making critical incidents explicit in this way potentially enables students not only to recognise that they have reading trajectories, but also to view them in relation to other people's and to see them as dynamic, not static. Each reading river is different, but if such differences make judgements about students as readers harder, not easier, they deepen our understanding of the complexity of young people's reading.

In my research project, I found myself using the rivers of reading in several ways. The first was to encourage students to reflect explicitly on their personal reading histories so that they came to their subsequent small group interviews with me already prepared to think and talk about reading. The small group interviews took place over several weeks, by which time I had read and begun to analyse some of the key features of the collages. The rivers of reading were not a central focus for the interviews; what they often did do, however, was act as a prompt for, or reference point within, the small group interview discussions. For example, many of the rivers of reading suggested several different but very important roles students' parents may have played in their children's development as habitual readers. One critical incident, for example, was the students' memories of adults reading aloud to their children (or grandchildren):

XAVIER: My parents read [Judith Kerr's *The Tiger Who Came to Tea*] to me when I was young and read it to me so many times that they knew it off by heart.

JADE: When I was a little girl my mum and dad used to read to me all the time … Because these [books] were read to me so regually,[1] I learnt the text by heart and so was able to 'read' them to my mum and dad.

Lily wrote at a point quite far along in her river of reading that *The Time Witches* by Michael Molloy was 'the first book I read out loud to my mum'. In the interview, Lily explained that what she was doing was not reading aloud like a young child, but a more mature form of companionable reading aloud:

LILY: I sometimes read to her like out loud at night ... She sometimes asks me to do it so she can hear what's happening next.

GCH: So does she just sit and listen, or does she do something else while you're reading?

LILY: It's usually when she's cooking or something like that

The rivers showed that fathers' reading aloud could be just as memorable as mothers':

JADE: Jeremy James [Wilson, 1977] was a favourite for me and my Dad!

The students recalled grandparents, too, whenever possible reading aloud with their grandchildren. Floella, for example, remembered the Milly-Molly-Mandy series (Brisley, 1928): 'Grandma read this to me and my sister in the mornings.'

Equally memorable, however, appeared to be the students' recollections about developing as more independent readers. Freya's collage showed a stage in her river of reading of which she said: 'This is around the time I started to read alone in my head, but I can't remember exactly when it was.' Zara seemed able to be a bit more precise, but noted an overlap between reading aloud and reading to herself. Between the ages of eight to ten, she wrote: 'I read quite allot to myself and read to my mum still, I stopped when I was 9.' Floella stated that the Disney version of *Snow White* was 'the first book I ever read in my head', while Lily identified that her sister used *Mr Birthday* (Hargreaves, 2006) from the Mr Men series to teach her to read silently to herself: 'My sister taught me to read in my head – this is the first book to read in my head.' How, precisely, her sister might have done that remains a mystery!

As the rivers of reading flowed onwards in the students' lives, some of them realised that they were now adopting the role their parents played for them, reading to younger children. Xavier, for example, positioned *Bill Bird's New Boots* by Vivian French and Alison Bartlett almost at the extreme right-hand end of his river of reading, writing 'I read this to my baby cousin'. Andie, too, seemed surprised to realise that she appeared to have gained an adult role: 'Now believe it or not I am reading to my Aunt Jo's three children who are four, five and seven.'

The rivers of reading did, of course, provide copious information about what students had enjoyed reading (and still do). There are effusive comments about authors such as Jacqueline Wilson, Malorie Blackman, Roald Dahl and Michael Morpurgo. There is also huge enthusiasm for series fiction – everything from Enid Blyton to J. K. Rowling, Anthony Horowitz and Stephanie Meyer. Individual titles were noted, too, especially those that appeared to have proven memorable because – as Freya explained – they had a visceral effect: *Elsewhere* by Gabrielle Zevin 'was a really good book. It certainly made me wonder. It's almost like this book carried on after I finished it. I thought about it a lot more than any other book.' *Finding Grace* by Alyssa Brugman 'was very powerful. It made me nearly cry, it made me smile, and it surprised me. I loved it.' Christine Hall and Martin Coles' *Children's Reading Choices* (1999) suggests that young readers' memories about what books are called and who they were by can be very unreliable. As researchers, Hall and Coles had to do some intricate detective work to try and establish what the young readers were sometimes referring to in their questionnaire. With the rivers of reading collages, the students I worked with used book covers they either cut out from discarded book catalogues or accessed via the internet. It was therefore clear which books they were referring to and there was less room to misconstrue what they meant.

The rivers of reading revealed quite a bit about the social patterning involved in the students' reading although this was an area that I followed up in greater depth by means of other research methods. Nevertheless, there were plenty of indications in the collages that other people – as readers – were significant in these young readers' development. Floella remembered how her mother used Michael Rosen and Helen Oxenbury's *We're Going on a Bear Hunt* (1989) 'to encourage me to walk home'. Louisa noted: 'My mum bought me Sheltie books + I ♥ them! I read them over and over again! For my 9th birthday my best friend Leah bought me [Lauren Child's (2003) *Utterly Me, Clarice Bean*].' Abigail, meanwhile, saw books as a way of bonding with her friends: 'The books I am currently reading are the "Georgia Nicholson" collection. They are fab. Really can relate to them and have brought me closer to my best friend.' Together with the interviews, then, the rivers of reading collages established a strong sense that in these particular students' reading lives, not only books and authors, but relationships with friends and families as well as childhood routines were all critical. Adults were not only providers of reading material; those who also read aloud were acting as role models, which might have supported children's developing the habit of reading, not least because the children saw the adults appearing to enjoy the reading themselves rather than merely doing it to please the children's teacher or in the hope of gaining higher assessment levels in class.

Data analysis

I adopted several theoretical perspectives from which to analyse the rivers of reading data. For the collages, I found Gunther Kress and Theo van Leeuwen's (2006) grammar of visual design helpful, especially its attention to the verbal as a narrative form of data integrated simultaneously with attention to the visual as spatial. These twin approaches chimed not only with theories of textual and narrative power advocated by Robert Scholes (1985) and Jerome Bruner (1986) by which my thinking had already been strongly influenced; they also complemented the spatial theory of Doreen Massey (2005), which I was bringing to bear, representing the students' reading trajectories as coming into contact with other people's, and the historical perspective of Jonathan Rose. Rose, in *The Intellectual Life of the British Working Classes* (2001), insists that we pay close attention to nineteenth- and twentieth-century readers' autobiographies if we want to know more about not just what people read in the past but how they read texts as well. I wanted the twenty-first-century students with whom I was working to generate similarly rich autobiographical data which would make visible what their personal reading histories were like. The rivers of reading did just that. Most stretched back to the beginning of students' reading lives across the years to the present day. A few even looked ahead explicitly to predict future progression. They therefore had a distinctly historical flavour, but one that was clearly visible on the page.

Lest the above makes it sound as if the data could readily be transformed into requirements for becoming a habitual reader, however, it is important to point out that I realised, even then, that no two readers were the same; nor had they been influenced in the same way by other readers, even if there were patterns emerging. Instead, the patterns seemed to be organising themselves into different shapes altogether rather than overlaying one another neatly. It may be more like what J. O. Morgan describes, in his poem sequence, *Interference Pattern* (2016), as a Venn diagram where two circles overlap but:

> that minor overlap is not
> what we share, it represents our differences
> colliding.
>
> (46)

Although at the end of the research I concluded that all readers' reading is different, I now want to consider another possible way to analyse the rivers of reading data, in the light of the critical incident technique specifically and the ever-increasing emphasis on visual research methods more generally, but without losing sight of the complex web of theoretical perspectives that were originally brought to bear in my doctoral project.

In addition to Flanagan's research mentioned earlier in the chapter, I have reflected again on the data from my research in the light of two other pieces of critical literature. One is an ESRC report by Jon Prosser and Andrew Loxley (2008) called *Introducing Visual Methods*; the other is an article by Douglas Harper (1997) called 'Visualising structure: Reading surfaces of social life', which I discovered via Prosser and Loxley's report. Harper's article is about using aerial photography, specifically as a research method, in the context of researching dairy farming. Aerial photography – to my mind – has definite connections with looking at the rivers of reading, as I will attempt to explain below.

Analysing data generated by visual research methods

In *Introducing Visual Methods*, Prosser and Loxley (2008) suggest many different ways to analyse image-based data generated by visual research methods. Prompted by their discussion, I have reflected again on how to do so with the rivers of reading, for example by temporarily separating the visual from the verbal. That involves reading the visual elements – for example drawings, coloured lines, cut-out and stuck-on pictures of popular texts, or book-like features that open out to reveal further images or text or both – without simultaneously attending to the words that may accompany them. Likewise, it is also possible to type up and print out all the verbal elements of a river of reading without attending to the images that accompany them. Looked at as divorced from one another in these ways, both words and images appear bleak, reductionist or even meaningless. Reading the two together, therefore, is a salutary reminder of how much they illuminate one another and how much richer the data is when the visual and the verbal are analysed in conjunction with one another rather than separately. What I did originally, however, prompted by Kress and van Leeuwen, was read the verbal from a narrative perspective and the visual from a spatial perspective. Now, however, I see their combined potential even more powerfully. Reading Harper's article (1997) about aerial photography as a research method is what has influenced my thinking here. I will therefore outline it briefly before going on to explain its possible relevance for the rivers of reading.

As already mentioned above, Prosser and Loxley (2008) refer to Harper (1997) who researched two different types of dairy farming in the US. First, there was the type he calls craft farming (on small, family-run, low-yield farms) and, second, there was factory farming (on farms that were much larger and technology-driven). Harper embedded himself as a researcher into both types of farm for long periods of time, so that he could gain a very finely grained view of their differences on the ground. In the end, however, he realised that simply being embedded – however rich and illuminating that might be – was also limited because it generated close-up rather than long-shot evidence. To acquire a broader picture, therefore, he went up in a small aircraft on numerous occasions and took hundreds of aerial photographs of the different types of farms below. As in archaeology, what became visible through aerial photography were things it would be impossible to see on the ground, for example the overarching layout of the farms, the patterning of their historical development, and sometimes even their recreational affordances such as spaces for skating and ice-hockey when the water-holes freeze over in the winter.

Similarly, the rivers of reading afford an aerial perspective of students' reading over time – for teachers and researchers as well as for the students themselves – which is not feasible if you are looking at single instances of reading at specific moments in time. Single instances, for example when recorded in reading journals, as I have explored elsewhere (Cliff Hodges, 2016), can provide wonderfully rich accounts of what it is like to read a single novel at a single moment in time. Looking down on a page that shows a river of reading winding along from birth to the present day, with critical reading incidents plotted onto it, provides a completely different perspective on each student's reading that it is impossible to gain close-up on the ground. It gives an ecological view that shows how vital different aspects of reading are to the river and the landscape through which it flows. Harper (1997) suggests that one reason aerial photography may not have been used very much in small-scale qualitative social studies research is that sociologists with an interest in the visual have typically been inclined to 'focus on the "micro" dimensions of social life' (62) whereas aerial photographs, by contrast, may be thought of as 'sociological "macroscopes"' which enable researchers to 'distinguish relationships between material elements that have social structural meaning' (63). In a note on the method, at the very end of the article, Harper acknowledges a disadvantage of the process, as it was then, which might have since been overcome by developments in digital technology. At the time, though, Harper noted that because the plane in which you are travelling is flying fast, it is easy to become disorientated: 'It is hard to recognize your location; it is impossible to stand still; and you are covering ground quickly' (76).

The rivers of reading are still images, not moving images. Their affinity with aerial photography, however, lies in the height of their viewpoint. Bearing that in mind, I have returned to some of my original rivers of reading to see what more, if anything, might be learnt from analysing them from this particular viewpoint. I have also looked at a few other rivers of reading that have been created since then, to see what else they might yield (e.g., Williams, 2017).

Rivers of reading as seen from above: What an aerial perspective reveals

The river not the water

When seen from above, we gain a metaphorically heightened perspective of a reader's journey being like a river from its source to the sea. We see the river, not the water. This perspective can be beneficial not only for researchers but for teachers, parents and young readers. Claire Williams, in her account of her Year 4 class's rivers of reading, shows how using them with young readers – some of whom are far from enthusiastic or even habitual readers – developed her own understanding of her class as readers, enthused those who were initially reluctant and won the praise of parents. The long-shot view, however, was what helped her as the teacher to gain particular insight. As an example, she cites Will:

> As a child that is keen to please, it might seem to somebody that didn't know much about his reading practices that he is a keen reader; he always seems engaged when he is reading. However, it became clear from his 'River of Reading' that reading was something he found 'boring' and with this in mind – how he might seem engaged [with] reading even if he isn't enjoying it – it has been important to make the most of opportunities for informal booktalk about reading and texts with him.
>
> (Williams, 2017)

The social nature of reading

Almost without exception, the children in Williams' Year 4 class can not only be viewed reading with, and supported by, more experienced readers such as parents, grandparents and teachers like Williams, but also moving towards ever-greater independence. Reading by themselves is a technique they acquire but it is, nonetheless, a social transaction with the text, not a solitary activity. In my own research, the involvement of parents emerged from the different research methods but was flagged up early in many of the rivers of reading. It was there, too, however, in the rivers of reading made by postgraduate student-teachers who often mentioned early and companionable reading with the adults in their lives. Since my initial research project and writing my original article about the method, I have also undertaken the rivers of reading activity each year with secondary PGCE English student-teachers with whom I have worked. Time has usually precluded making collages rather than drawing. However, it has still been salutary to note some of the additions they have brought to their rivers of reading.

The student-teachers were, for the most part, English graduates who had undertaken a three-year honours degree, usually in English literature, with often a Master's degree in literature afterwards as well. Their rivers of reading provided fascinating data, not least because of the way they variously represented the reading they had done for their undergraduate studies. It was not uncommon to find them taking a less enthusiastic stance towards reading as undergraduates than was the case before or since. Something about the high pressure requirements of their studies had left them feeling as if they had been on a forced march rather than a voluntary journey. Training to become teachers, however, often gave them renewed enthusiasm for reading, something – perhaps – to do with it being more of an applied activity because they were reading with double vision: not just for themselves but for the young people they were working with in school. On the other hand, some student-teachers flourished during their university degree courses and their drawings showed the many ways in which they developed further as critical readers under those conditions and what they brought with them to their teaching. Certainly, like the participants in my doctoral research, these student-teachers acknowledged the social nature of their early reading, especially their reading aloud together with adults as it sealed certain family bonds:

LORRAINE: We nagged [mum] to read old favourites [like *We're Going on a Bear Hunt*] again and again. We still recite them as a family with the same intonation … My brother and I used to read comics [which] … used to belong to dad.

CLARE: My grandma used to read aloud 'the sweet shop' to me [from Roald Dahl's *Boy* (1984)] when she stayed. She was brilliant at voices: Thwaites especially stood out. We did this for ages, till I was about 13/14, a bit old but it was our bond.

LANCE: The adapted version of [Dickens's] *Bleak House* was sooooo good! I remember feeling very grown up reading it as this was my Grandfather's favourite novel. We also lived near Bleak House so it had special local relevance.

What these postgraduate readers often showed as well is the rush and excitement as their rivers gathered pace towards the reading they enjoyed at Advanced level and university. Occasionally, however, their rivers turned into a steep decline at university level, possibly brought about by fierce reading pressures or excessive assessment regimes. What, however, always emerged along the next stage of the rivers of reading – the ones they were currently experiencing as student-teachers – was a revitalised sense of reading as they found themselves intellectually stretched by reading within new genres (educational writing as distinct from English literature, for example) or enjoyed the wealth of texts young people might also have been reading, whether for pleasure or within the classroom.

Progression in reading

The rivers of reading always, however, over their entire course, reveal progression in relation to some of the many types of books and authors that readers feel have helped them develop the habit of reading. Writing by favourite authors features over and over again. Their works are sometimes, but not often, attributed to recommendations by teachers or librarians. But they nevertheless loom large, as if the author or their characters (or both) are more important than the adult in real life who might have recommended them. In addition, there are numerous mentions of reading series fiction, another staging post for many young people in the process of becoming a habitual reader. There is no shortage from which young readers can choose. As Victor Watson has so memorably remarked, reading series fiction is not something that you do by chance; it is a deliberate choice (Watson, 2000). The Harry Potter, Stormbreaker or Twilight series were very visible in the students' rivers of reading when I undertook my initial research, the lie of the land in the collages showing them spaced out along the rivers.

Applying the critical incident technique to rivers of reading

If we are also to apply some of the processes adopted in the early critical incident technique approach to the rivers of reading, what might that tell us? First, it might be helpful to remind ourselves of Flanagan's definition:

> By an incident is meant any observable human activity that is sufficiently complete in itself to permit inferences and predictions to be made about the person performing the act. To be critical, an incident must occur in a situation where the purpose or intent of the act seems fairly clear to the observer and where its consequences are sufficiently definite to leave little doubt concerning its effects.
>
> (Flanagan, 1954: 327)

I have reread the data from the original collages to ask what they suggested about what the students as readers actually did, or what reading events they actually experienced, either of which might be construed as a requirement for habitual reading. A difference between Flanagan's approach and the rivers of reading is that the latter suggest critical incidents that were memorable enough to figure in the collages, but that would need to be repeated frequently over time to be later defined (again, in Flanagan's terms) as a 'critical requirement' (329) for becoming a habitual reader. One such incident is the students' recollection of a very particular emotional response to their reading. Several students recalled that a certain book was the first book that made them cry, for example Malorie Blackman's *Noughts and Crosses*. Louise Rennison's Georgia Nicolson series was very popular with some of the girls and they enjoyed the way the books made them laugh. Whatever the emotional outcome, what the comments appear to suggest more broadly is that to form a critical requirement, readers need to realise and, indeed, repeatedly experience the expectation that reading imaginative literature can have an emotional response.

From here, habitual readers may progress to an awareness that reading more broadly can affect the way in which fellow human beings and their progress through space and time are viewed (Lodge, 2002; Schwarz, 2008; Boxall, 2015). There is often a move, for example, from reading individual texts and authors to reading more thematically to learn more about the civil rights movement and slavery, or love, or powerful women, or views of the world and humanity.

Bringing all the methods to bear

The visual and verbal language of the collages together give a sense of progression generated by the positioning of words and pictures on the winding rivers. Discourse analysis of the words, for example, often highlights phrases such as 'always' or 'used to', which are a reminder that for the most part the readers' experiences were not single critical incidents but habitual procedures, repeated over time. The students also noted how their favourite reading had often changed but said, in passing, that it often chimed with being a favourite of a parent, too. Repeated readings of the same text meant that the students, as very young children, had often learnt a story off by heart and were therefore able to appear to tell it back (as if reading) to their parents. Such recollections were, in the rivers of reading, not seen as mere nostalgia; instead, they provided evidence of each reader's forward momentum. Moreover, some students offered an even more finely grained recollection, for example referring to learning to read in their heads, as already mentioned earlier. In instances such as these, there was a perceived progression from being read aloud to routinely, to reading silently to oneself.

So, what – if anything – do different ways of analysing the data suggest about the requirements for becoming a habitual reader, someone who knows what reading can and does do and who reads in order to journey constantly onwards? I sense that analysing the same data differently has served to underscore the original findings rather than discovering much that is new. However, what I do feel is that the different ways of analysing data – for example, the deliberate attempt to read the rivers of reading from above rather than from a ground-level perspective – persuade us of the value of looking at an activity like reading from both a distance and close-up. Doing so reminds us about the shape formed by lifelong reading journeys as well as the multitude of individual reading experiences from which the shape is created. Both matter.

Note

1 Spelling, punctuation and grammar from the rivers of reading collages have been left as they were written by the students.

References

Arizpe, E. (2014). How much water does your 'river of reading' carry? Retrieved from: http://readingchanges.blogspot.co.uk/2014/12/how-much-water-does-your-river-of.html

Boxall, P. (2015). *The Value of the Novel*. Cambridge: Cambridge University Press.

Brisley, J. L. (1928). Milly-Molly-Mandy series. London: Harrap.

Brugman, A. (2001). *Finding Grace*. London: Allen and Unwin.

Bruner, J. (1986). *Actual Minds, Possible Worlds*. Cambridge, MA: Harvard University Press.

Burnard, P. (2002). Using image-based techniques in researching pupil perspectives. *The ESRC Network Project Newsletter* (5), 2–3 (no longer accessible online).

Butterfield, L. D., Borgen, W. A., Amundson, N. E. and Asa-Sophia, T. M. (2005). Fifty years of the critical incident technique: 1954–2004 and beyond. *Qualitative Research*, 5(4), 475–497.

Child, L. (2003). *Utterly Me, Clarice Bean*. London: Orchard Books.

Cliff Hodges, G. (2010). Rivers of reading: Using critical incident collages to learn about adolescent readers and their readership. *English in Education*, 44 (3), 181–200.

Cliff Hodges, G. (2012). Research and the teaching of English: Spaces where reading histories meet. *English Teaching: Practice and Critique*, 11 (1), 7–25.

Cliff Hodges, G. (2016). *Researching and Teaching Reading: Developing Pedagogy through Critical Enquiry*. London: Routledge.

Cremin, T., Mottram, M., Collins, F. M., Powell, S., and Drury, R. (2015). *Researching Literacy Lives: Building Communities between Home and School*. London: Routledge.

Dahl, R. (1984). *Boy*. London: Jonathan Cape.

Dickens, C. (1852/1996). *Bleak House*. Oxford: Oxford University Press.

Flanagan, J. C. (1954). The critical incident technique. *Psychological Bulletin*, 51 (4), 327–358.

Fort, T. (2008). *Downstream: Across England in a Punt*. London: Random House.

French, V. and Bartlett, A. (2004). *Bill Bird's New Boots*. London: Egmont.

González, N., Moll, L. and Amanti, C. (Eds.), (2005). *Funds of Knowledge: Theorizing Practices in Households, Communities and Classrooms*. Mahwah, New Jersey: Lawrence Erlbaum Associates.

Gross, P. (2009). *The Water Table*. Tarset, Northumberland: Bloodaxe Books.

Hall, C. and Coles, M. (1999). *Children's Reading Choices*. London: Routledge.

Hargreaves, R. (2006). *Mr Birthday*. Los Angeles: Price Stern Sloan.

Harper, D. (1997). Visualising structure: Reading surfaces of social life. *Qualitative Sociology*, 20 (1), 57–77.

Kelly, A. (2009). Forum: Helping the teachers of reading. *Books for Keeps*, 177, 12.

Kerr, J. (1968). *The Tiger Who Came to Tea*. London: William Collins and Son Ltd.

Kress, G. and van Leeuwen, T. (2006). *Reading Images: The Grammar of Visual Design* (2nd ed.). London: Routledge.

Leitch, R. (2008). Creatively researching children's narratives through images and drawings. In P. Thomson (Ed.), *Doing Visual Research with Children and Young People*. London: Routledge, pp. 37–58.
Lodge, D. (2002). *Consciousness and the Novel*. London: Secker and Warburg.
Massey, D. (2005). *For Space*. London: Sage.
McAdam, J. E., Arizpe, E., Devlin, A. M., Farrell, M. and Farrar, J. (2014). *Journeys from Images to Words*. London: Esmée Fairbairn Foundation.
Molloy, M. (2003). *The Time Witches*. Frome, Somerset: Chicken House.
Morgan, J. O. (2016). *Interference Pattern*. London: Jonathan Cape.
Prosser, J. and Loxley, A. (2008). *Introducing Visual Methods*. London: ESRC National Centre for Research Methods.
Rose, J. (2001). *The Intellectual Life of the British Working Classes*. New Haven: Yale University Press.
Rosen, M. and Oxenbury, H. (1989). *We're Going on a Bear Hunt*. London: Walker Books Ltd.
Rosenblatt, L. M. (1938/1995). *Literature as Exploration* (5th ed.). New York: Modern Language Association of America.
Rosenblatt, L. M. (1978/1994). *The Reader, the Text, the Poem: The Transactional Theory of the Literary Work*. Carbondale and Edwardsville: Southern Illinois University Press.
Scholes, R. (1985). *Textual Power: Literary Theory and the Teaching of English*. New Haven: Yale University Press.
Schwarz, D. R. (2008). *In Defense of Reading: Teaching Literature in the Twenty-First Century*. Chichester: Wiley-Blackwell.
Watson, V. (2000). *Reading Series Fiction: From Arthur Ransome to Gene Kemp*. London: RoutledgeFalmer.
Williams, C. (2017). Personal reading journeys: Developing my knowledge of children's reading practices. Retrieved from: https://researchrichpedagogies.org/_downloads/_eop/Personal_Reading_Journeys_FINAL1.pdf
Wilson, D. H. (1977). Jeremy James series. London: Pan Macmillan.
Winchester, D. (2008). Rivers of reading. *English Four to Eleven*, 33, 19–21.
Zevin, G. (2005) *Elsewhere*. London: Bloomsbury.

SECTION 2

Adolescent reading in times of crisis

4

READING FEARS AND OPPORTUNITIES

Researching changes over 25 years in the literacy practices of Mexican adolescents

Evelyn Arizpe and Laura Guerrero Guadarrama

MAP 4

This chapter is based on an investigation that sought to identify the changes in reading and other literacy practices of adolescents living in central Mexico over the past 25 years.[1] It explored some of the possible reasons for these changes, such as the increase in publications for young adults and the presence of digital and social media, and looked at how schools and the curriculum have responded to them. The study included young people's perceptions of these changes, along with their views on reading and books. In addition, it analysed readers' responses to three contemporary texts, selected for their appeal to young adults through their themes, language, visual modes and, in one case, links to online related sites. Humour, romance and fantasy as well as references to poverty, political corruption and violence were among the most noticeable features of these texts. This chapter combines educational and literacy data sources with personal response to literature, within a framework that brings literary hermeneutics together with a consideration of the social, political and economic precarity and vulnerability of adolescents. Despite the fact that young people are usually the largest faction of the population in developing countries such as Mexico, there are still relatively few studies that address their situation as readers within societies that have experienced swift and often unexpected changes, from the technological to the political, in the past 25 years.

The project took place in 2014, in similar contexts and followed similar methods to those of a study conducted by Evelyn Arizpe for her doctoral thesis between 1990 and 1994, in the central state of Morelos, and for a postdoctoral study in 1996 in Mexico City (Arizpe 1994, 2001). The original generation of participants would, roughly, be the same age as the parents of the new group of students in 2014. The existence of earlier data offered a rare opportunity for tracking some of the changes and comparing some of responses with those of a different generation. While the aim of the 2014 project was not to replicate the 1992 study, it did look at similar themes and issues related to adolescent reading, mainly reading in and out of school and the place of young adult (YA) literature. Our premise was that major changes affecting publications (e.g., new authors of YA literature, including Mexican authors), marketing (e.g., globalisation and the Harry Potter phenomenon), transmedia (films, videos, games stemming from books) and digital technology (the emergence and widespread use of the internet and social media) during those 25 years would have had some effect on what and how adolescents read as well as on how they perceive reading books and other literacy practices.

The findings are significant in that they highlight not only the challenges around reading that have been present for decades in the educational and social systems in Mexico but also new challenges and opportunities arising from the affordances of new technologies. The ambiguity of the word 'fears' in the title of this chapter is intentional and refers to the two issues that will be discussed: the first refers to the fears around the decrease in reading, especially books, and also around new multimodal reading practices; the second refers to the anxieties and fears that emerged as the young people in this study responded to the three selected contemporary texts that are a result of the precarity and insecurity in twenty-first-century Mexico. As we will argue in this chapter, these fears are having an impact on the ways in which young people interact with and respond to texts and therefore need to be acknowledged in any further research involving adolescents in that country or in any other similarly challenging contexts. However, we will also argue that drawing young people into creatively responding to and reflecting on words and images in narratives that appeal to them, offers opportunities to reimagine and reconstruct their own more hopeful life narratives.

The context: Progress or stagnation?

The past 25 years in Mexico have witnessed a boom in publishing children's and YA literature influenced by a rapidly expanding global market that includes films and media targeted specifically at this age group. In theory, young people born in the 1990s and 2000s have grown up with access to the widest range of publications intended for their age group, including complex, multimodal texts that demand active readers. In addition to international authors, there is now a generation of national authors who grew up reading YA authors from Spain and other countries and who have successfully entered the Spanish publishing market for this age group. In the past 25 years there has also been a steady increase in events such as book awards, book fairs and other reading promotion activities, both within and outside the school context. However, various factors continue to limit access to books, some of which are noted in other chapters in this book, for example the lack of bookshops and well-stocked libraries, especially in rural areas (Talavera, 2016) and the relatively high price of books (either because they are imported or because they contain high-quality images). Digital technology has offered some advantages by helping to advertise books, promote reading via social media such as book trailers or 'booktubers' (young people who recommend books on their YouTube channels, some of whom have followers in their thousands) and providing access (downloading the text – legally or illegally), but the greater part of the adolescent population in Mexico at the beginning of the twenty-first century still does not have access to the internet or to a device through which to acquire it: in a survey from 2013, the year before our study, only 23.6% of the population between 12 and 17 years old used the internet (Islas, 2015).

As in the case of other contexts mentioned in this book, government-funded national reading programmes have been implemented over the years to provide government schools with libraries and new books. Again, however, these spasmodic initiatives, along with a traditional curriculum structure, poor funding, lack of properly trained school librarians, and a narrow view of what constitutes literacy and literature, persist within the system, particularly in secondary education. Deeply rooted beliefs around a book-centric culture, held by parents, teachers and students themselves, constrain official policies and programmes, both at school and in the home. (For example, boxes of new books sent to school libraries by the government often lie unopened because of fears that the books may be lost or mistreated by readers.) Some of these beliefs stem from an historical rejection of 'books as a hostile, colonizing authority and a means of exclusion' (Petit, 2008). In addition, the changes in adolescents' social and digital literacies have been largely ignored or misunderstood, meaning that the types of texts and practices that adolescents may engage with on a daily basis are rarely included or even discussed within the school context. Finally, in terms of actual reading comprehension and attainment, there has been little change between approximately 1980 and 2016 as revealed by international studies/evaluations such as the Programme for International Student Assessment (PISA, 2015), where Mexico remains among the lowest-performing countries. A recent national study by the Consejo Nacional para la Cultura y las Artes in Mexico (2015), *Encuesta Nacional de Lectura y Escritura* 2015–2018 (ENLE),[2] also revealed disappointing results, although, like other surveys of this type, it focused on the number of books read and ignored any other type of texts (Newman, 2014), resulting in an unhelpful dichotomy between 'readers' and 'non-readers' (Igarza, 2015: 13).

The first survey on digital reading conducted by the International Board on Books for Young People (IBBY) and the Banco Nacional de México (BANAMEX) (IBBY/ BANAMEX, 2015) did consider a broader definition of 'text' and this aligns it more closely with some international studies that attempt to understand adolescent reading within a wider consideration of young people's literacies (Moje et al., 2008; Detrez, 2011; Cliff Hodges, 2012; Manresa, 2013). The survey highlighted a preference for reading novels and other longer literary texts in printed form, and informational or colloquial texts on digital devices (especially smartphones). Another wide-ranging study of readers in Mexico City also sought to view literacies within contexts of cultural and social practices, from book fairs to universities, and to answer the question of what reading might mean to young people in precarious employment that does not call for any literary training (García Canclini, 2015). Despite contextual differences and staggering between periods of progress and stagnation, the findings from both studies mentioned above bring the literacy practices of young people in Mexico closer to those of their counterparts in Anglophone countries.

Research design and methodology

With the larger studies and surveys mentioned above as a background, we decided to seek more detailed and current data from two specific communities of adolescents from government secondary schools in the central state of Morelos. A survey of 209 students from both schools provided quantitative data around literacy practices (including lists of books read) and helped to create a wider picture, which was then used in workshops for a smaller group. The workshops involved a series of questions and prompts as well as creative response strategies. They were designed to combine literary hermeneutics (Ricoeur, 1974) with reader-response theory, which explores readers' transaction with the text (Rosenblatt, 1978/1994) in terms of their meaning and lived experience (van Manen, 1990). At the same time, they were inscribed within a sociology of reading framework that considers the social production of literature for young people as well as the social and cultural implications of literary reading (Lahire, 2004). In addition, wider social issues had to be taken into account for both contexts, but especially the urban one, given that serious problems such as crime and violence (particularly violence against women but also assault and kidnapping) had been on a steep rise since 2005 when the Mexican government launched its 'war' on the drug cartels.[3] These threats not only created a climate of fear among the students but also had implications for the researchers. A risk assessment of the field, in consultation with the school authorities, was carried out before the study[4] but the situation also raised issues in terms of ethics and the positionality of the researchers as well as in terms of the group discussions and the interpretation of the readers' responses to the texts.

The project took place during the first semester of the school year 2014–2015 in two schools. General Borda Secondary School (GBSS) is in the capital of the state, a city of approximately 1,000,000 inhabitants, in a lower socioeconomic neighbourhood that is often described as deprived and dangerous due to gangs and drugs. A small minority of students come from Indigenous families who have migrated from more rural areas. Some of their parents are street-sellers but most work as teachers, secretaries, hair stylists, taxi drivers, waiters or accountants. Calmecac Secondary School (CSS) is located on the rural outskirts of a market town that has attracted tourists for many years because of its history and natural beauty, and has a population of approximately 50,000 residents. The catchment comprises part of this town plus five rural villages in the area and students come from lower-middle to lower socioeconomic semi-urban and rural populations. (Parents are peasant-farmers, builders, craftsmen, market sellers.) A small minority speak an Indigenous language (mainly Nahuatl or Zapotec); some of those speakers are from local and some from migrant Indigenous families.

CSS has large class sizes (of around 40 students each), with five groups per year, while GBSS has classes of 25 students but has two daily intakes (morning and evening). At secondary level (12–15 year olds), education is still obligatory and for many it becomes a final educational stage before abandoning studies for work (only 19.9% of young people continue to higher education). Both schools follow the Official Programme guidelines (Educación Secundaria Básica, Español) for the teaching of Spanish, which includes language and literature (SEP, 2011). Neither school had any data on reading outside school, so an overview of literacy practices was acquired by a survey on reading carried out with randomly selected groups from the second- and third-year classes. Using purposive sampling (Palys, 2008), we invited some of the students who described themselves as 'good readers' or whose practices showed they were regular readers (via the survey) to participate in a workshop series.

The two workshop groups each consisted of five boys and five girls between 13 and 15 years of age (20 students in total), although not all of them attended every session and by the end of the workshop series, four had dropped out. They attended the workshops voluntarily: in GBSS, students came to the small and cramped school library during lunchtime, while in the rural school, CSS, students came to a large classroom that held the school library along one of its walls. The researchers explained to the participants that they wanted to obtain a better picture, not only of what was going on with literacy at home and at school but also of what young people thought about how reading is changing.[5] The three texts they were given (all in Spanish) included different formats and genres: a picturebook (*The Girl in Red* by Aaron Frisch, illustrated by Roberto Innocenti, 2013, translated into Spanish); a graphic novel (*Justicia Divina* by Francisco Haghenbeck, 2013) and the first volume in a fantasy series (*Memorias de Idhún, La Resistencia* by Laura Gallego

García, 2005). All of them reflected issues that the researchers felt would engage adolescent readers: relationships, love, violence and political corruption, as well as the ethical choices involved in these issues.

The qualitative data collection methods were based on response activities successfully used in previous research and which also work as pedagogic strategies:

- small group literature discussions around each of the three texts using open-ended questions and prompts such as 'Tell me…' (Chambers, 1993; Arizpe and Styles, 2003);
- 'rivers of reading' collages, where students draw or paste references to every kind of text they (or members of their family) read over a weekend (Cliff Hodges, 2012);
- visual narratives that consider the interaction between images and words, based on creating a comics frame and drawings and photographs to create a photo-story (McAdam et al., 2014; Arizpe et al., 2014);
- young people as researchers where participants were supported to investigate literacy practices among family members and friends through developing interview questions, carrying out an interview and doing a basic analysis of the results (Alderson, 2001).

At the end of the project, students presented their work to their peers and members of staff during a special assembly in which they talked about the books and showed some of their creative work. Finally, six interviews with publishers, teachers and librarians provided a variety of perspectives and triangulation with results from both quantitative and qualitative methods. In addition, the involvement of multiple texts and the use of interdisciplinary theories and methods (from literature and education) helped to map out the complexity of the topic and at the same time avoid any intrinsic bias (Cohen et al., 2000).

The student group discussions and interviews with adults were transcribed and analysed using NVivo as an organisational tool, and grounded theory (Glaser and Strauss, 2012) to generate themes arising out of the data. This data was cross-referenced with the researchers' memos to complete the thematic analysis. The critical interpretative and iterative process (Erickson, 1986; Atkinson and Delamont, 2005) considered all this data (including the visuals produced), aligning with our hermeneutic phenomenological reflection (Prado, 2013; van Manen, 1990). While we cannot generalise from such a small sample, our results were consistent with recent project and news reports[6] and with the surveys and studies mentioned above. The analysis not only offered insights into the life and literacy experiences of the participants in the study but also into what these experiences might mean more widely for contemporary youth in Mexico in relation to the changes brought about by the presence of the new YA market, transmedia and digital technologies. Although we acknowledge that every context is different, we are confident that these methods can be replicable when exploring adolescent reading and response in other contexts.

Current adolescent reading practices in Mexico

The findings in this section offer some answers to the anxieties around recent changes in reading and other literacy practices among young people in Mexico. They refer to reading preferences; reading in and out of school and digital practices. Where relevant and available, the results are compared to those obtained in the early studies mentioned above.

Preferred and indiscriminate reading

Findings from the IBBY/BANAMEX survey revealed that young people in Mexico engage in some form of self-selected reading every day (2015). One reason for this is that there is a wider selection of texts available in Spanish than there has been in the past and that readers have more agency to choose those that align with their interests. This was reflected in the 130 different titles that had been read in the two months prior to our own survey (results from 1992 only yielded 30 titles). In 1992 and 1996, the titles that stood out were 'problem' novels (sex, drugs, abuse, relationships) with young protagonists, for example, *Born Innocent* (Brown Burnham, 1958), *Go Ask Alice* (Anonymous, 1971) and the bestseller self-help novels by Mexican author Carlos Cuauhtémoc Sánchez. In 2014, many titles continued to fall into these non-fiction and/or self-help categories, but the number of those that could be described as children's or YA literature prevailed. The list of the most popular books (read in Spanish) included both YA and adult novels: *The Fault in our Stars* (Green, 2012) (29), The Hunger Games series (16), *Around the World in Eighty Days* (Verne, 1873) (12), the Harry Potter series (7), *Fifty Shades of Grey* (James, 2011) (6) and the Twilight series (6). Overall, like Manresa and Durán (2009), we found that 'It is the operation of the market that marks the reading tendencies of young people' (109) and 'therefore, the principal characteristic of adolescent reading behaviour is the mix of products in an indistinct and almost unconscious manner' (112).

The IBBY/BANAMEX survey conclusions noted that most of these texts read by young people tend to be brief and their contents ephemeral. The results of the rivers of reading activity not surprisingly included many of this type of texts, both entertaining (e.g., magazine articles or pictures) and functional (e.g., labels on beauty products) as well as those related to films and song lyrics or digital social media communication (Facebook, WhatsApp, Instagram). As in the 1990s, the young people's access to books was limited due to lack of libraries, bookshops and purchasing power, and their selection was often the result of random recommendations, resulting in reading that was eclectic and sometimes inappropriate for their age. Lucio (GBSS), for example, had picked up a copy of *Justine* by the Marquis de Sade (1791/2012) from a second-hand book street-seller without knowing what it was about. It became clear from his need to describe it in detail (a description which the researcher was forced to cut short) that the book had deeply impressed him in a way that did not seem helpful to resolving the tension between his religious beliefs and his sexual identity, an issue that emerged several times in his responses.

The disconnection between reading in and out of school

The findings from the survey and the rivers of reading allowed an insight into literacy practices in the home or the street that were considered distinct from the idea of reading and books in school. The open comments in the survey from 2014 were almost identical to opinions from 1992: adolescents recognised reading as 'useful' and equated books with school activities and boredom. For the majority, reading is important mainly as a tool to 'read better', 'learn', 'obtain knowledge/information', 'develop comprehension', 'write correctly', 'help with spelling' or with 'cultural benefits'. There were only a few who mentioned that it was 'fun' or whose answers reflected a sense of enjoyment or pleasure. Replies indicated adolescents did not 'have time' to spend with books; the only difference here was that in 2014 this was attributed to time spent on screens; for example, 'I would read more if I didn't have a cell phone'.

The message about the functional benefits of reading that is constantly repeated by educational institutions had been absorbed by the students who did not see any connection between the reading done in school and their literacy practices outside it. The study confirmed that, despite national government initiatives to promote reading, as in other countries, the school has failed to keep up with the actual reading and the range of sociocultural practices that are linked to this activity (Cliff Hodges, 2012; Moje et al., 2008, among others). In fact, rather than schools providing advice and encouraging reading for pleasure, school literacies are more likely to be excluding young people from, rather than expanding, cultural capital (Hernandez-Zamora, 2010) and they have not succeeded in addressing inequalities in terms of reading.

Conflicting views/myths and facts about digital practices

Our fieldwork coincided with the first survey on digital reading and digital media from 2015 (IBBY/BANAMEX, 2015) where it was revealed that although young people enjoyed reading online, few of them regarded themselves as 'readers'. In our study, we found that while a few of the participants were sophisticated users of technology in terms of finding and making reading choices, the majority were either not aware of the possible links to fiction texts or had little or no access to apps or digital devices. We found that these teenagers' 'acquired baggage as analogue readers' (Manresa, 2013: 116) led to conflicting ideas around reading online and reflected both excitement and distrust of digital media. Their relationship with reading continues to be mainly through the printed word, leading us to speculate that the 14- to 15-year-olds we worked with are actually still part of a 'generation at the crossroads': they know about the digital world and have some access to it but it is not yet an integral part of their daily lives or reading experiences.

Precarity and vulnerability in literary engagement

As the fieldwork progressed and the participants began to engage more fully in the workshops, we realised that, in addition to the data that was emerging about reading practices, data was also emerging about these young people's anxieties and fears due to the conditions of instability and insecurity in which they were living and studying. These emotions were having an impact on the way they constructed meaning from the selected texts as well as on the way they responded through the creative methods employed. While the researchers did not encourage morbid discussion, they were aware that an individual living in a violent context often 'finds meaning in, and appreciates the felt experience offered by [violent] fiction' (Sarland, 1991: 47). One reason that novels and other YA literature, whether realistic or fantastic, may appeal to adolescents is because they often deal with the fears that emerge in the transition between childhood and adulthood, ranging from the fear of social exclusion to the fear of death. The fears and violence that appeared in all three texts selected for the workshops were reflected through the lens of the readers' personal experience, particularly their anxieties about being victims of crime or violence. The researchers also subscribed to the view that reading literature can have a supportive role in spaces where there is continuous and generalised violence, both as a personal means of understanding and reflection, and as shared activity that can create a 'safe space' to voice individual as well as collective anxieties (Petit, 2008).

To start with, we identified the main categories of literary engagement, most of which align with those frequently highlighted in other studies of adolescent reading response (especially Thomson, 1987) and were similar to those found in the data from 1992:

- life to text and/or text to life analogies, e.g. narratives of life;
- intertextuality; for example, references to other books, film and media but also to current events;
- affective reactions and empathy with characters (Heath and Wolf, 2012; Nikolajeva, 2014); for example, imagining themselves within the story/in the characters' situation;
- 'relating and re-lating' (or re-storying) (Heath and Wolf, 2012: 147); for example, the creating of social relationships and the sharing of life narratives;
- ethical and moral choice (judgements based on the message of the story and the choices made by the characters).

Fear was one of the main themes that ran throughout these categories and we felt that to understand its significance for these readers, and perhaps more widely for other adolescents, as well as the ethical implications in discussing this theme, we required a lens that went beyond literary theory into social and political theories of precarity and vulnerability.

It is beyond this chapter to discuss the historical and political causes that have heightened the current social and economic crisis in Mexico. However, the result of this crisis is that life had become precarious for this group of students in ways that heightened their vulnerability at a time of life when it was already particularly acute, i.e., adolescence. Precarity is normally defined in terms of job, health and other insecurities linked to social class but here we understand it as a general state of insecurity (albeit still rooted in inequality) that 'inhabits the microspaces of everyday life' (Ettlinger, 2007: 319). As for 'vulnerability', we refer to the existential vulnerability of childhood or adolescence as viewed by Andresen and Ben-Arieh, which does not 'rule out potentiality' (Andresen and Ben-Arieh, 2016: 22) or deny resilience and agency but is closely linked to the search for identity and the general emotional 'turmoil' experienced at this life stage. Both precarity and vulnerability are sociopolitical issues and while all human beings are affected by them to some extent (Ettlinger, 2007), they are also contingent on specific geopolitical and socio-economic conditions. Petit is one of the few scholars who has investigated initiatives based on storytelling and reading, particularly in contexts where inequality and displacement are on the rise because of war, violence or economic crisis (such as Argentina and Colombia) and she also links these conditions to an accelerated transformation of traditional frameworks (Petit, 2009). This is the same for the young Mexican participants in our study and it meant that their experience at that specific time and space was immersed in instability and unpredictability.

Thinking about these two concepts, precarity and vulnerability, allows a deeper understanding of how fear is connected to readers' transaction with texts and, thus, to their construction of meaning. The following examples refer to the main fear expressed by the readers, namely violence or the threat of violence that results from precarity because it 'lies in the unpredictability of terror, which can emanate from a wide range of contexts: the household via domestic violence; urban ghettos via gang violence' (Ettlinger, 2007: 321) and that seizes on the vulnerability of these young people.

In *Justicia Divina*, a trio of legendary Mexican ghosts, 'La Llorona', 'El Monje Loco' and 'El Coco',[7] complain that they can no longer frighten anybody so they decide to help a psychic young man, Victor (who describes himself as a 'nobody'), in his quest for justice. The readers enjoyed the humour in this graphic novel; they were behind Victor's moral choices and understood the metaphor of the spectres; as Ernesto (GBSS) said, 'people now have new fears, they are not afraid of ghosts … they are more afraid of the assaults, the narco-traffic and the police'. Fernanda (CSS), made it more personal: 'we now worry about other things, we don't worry about meeting La Llorona, well, we'd just say hi, but if we encounter bad people, that can be ugly'.

The encounter between Sofia, the 'Red Riding Hood' character in *The Girl in Red*, and the stranger/wolf also resulted in many comments about the potential violence that confronts young people, and especially women, in certain environments. The underlying threat of violence permeates this urban version of the traditional tale, particularly through the commercial, sexualised images of women that form the background to Sofia's journey. The picturebook has alternative endings (both tragic and happy) but most readers assumed that the first ending in which Sofia does not return was the most realistic, with comments such as 'she was obviously raped and killed' (Marcos, CSS). However, a surprising response from Mariela (CSS) shows an awareness of the possible cause of violent crime that led the others to consider yet another alternative: 'here we don't know if the villain has a family and he only did this because he like just wanted to kidnap her and sell her because his family didn't have anything to eat'.

In all three texts, as in real life, the social structures that should have acted as a support (parents, community, police) were not always there or could not be relied upon: the main characters are very much on their own, either because they are different, lost or orphaned. Empathetic comments about the combined anger, sadness and fear that Jack, the male protagonist of *Memorias de Idhún*, must have felt when he finds his parents have been killed, allowed readers to express their own fears of the death of loved ones and to make links to other deaths in fiction they had read previously but that still had the power to affect them (e.g., Dobby, the house elf from the Harry Potter series), as seen in this example from the CSS group:

MARCOS: Because maybe, like now that we are adolescents, we may have felt what he did or maybe you haven't but you know you will feel it.

YOLANDA: I understand what he felt because if I found my parents like that, I'd be like that too.

[...]

MARIO: Like when Dobby died, it was the worst [he is interrupted by the rest of the group]

EVERYONE [SIGHING]: Dobby!

The threatening atmosphere of *The Girl in Red* was creatively reflected in the photo-stories put together by the participants to narrate a walk across their neighbourhood or town. Lucio's (GBSS) powerful and disturbing oral version of his story began with a photograph of houses on a hill and then the streets on the way to the centre of his city. He borrowed from his reading of the three texts and mixed his experience of reality and the symbolic to enhance the 'unpredictable terror' (Ettlinger, 2007: 321):

> And this is a city like any other one, where no one knows what can happen to them in each house they see. We can look at it but we can't know what is happening inside each home. Perhaps in one a woman can be suffering blows from her husband or someone can be committing suicide ... And in this road few people walk by because they say that 'La Llorona' goes by a lot and also there it's the same, there are a lot of kids that go out to get drugged and no one wants to walk by because they are afraid of seeing them ... and this street is near the Cathedral where perhaps one is safe from dangers but perhaps not, perhaps we walk past and find an evil wolf about to hurt us ... we go out without knowing who we will find ... perhaps a hungry vampire, thirsty for blood.

Yolanda (CSS) spoke about the way fears change when one grows up, from the fear of ghosts to fears of not getting a job or having a child who gets ill. Her photo-story, however, reflected a change with a more positive note:

> The protagonist is myself and I'm also the narrator. The story starts in the same way … but as she goes through the streets she then finds a [street] mural that attracts her attention, then she starts to imagine different worlds and she realises that it is not only at home and with her mother that she feels safe, she begins to discover confidence in herself.

Yolanda's story illustrates the title of this chapter because it provides evidence of how reading and creative response offers an opportunity for expression, but can go further and support a reworking of the original story into something more personal. It is her reflections on an artwork that are the source of her imagining alternative narratives and her self-realisations. She places herself as both the protagonist and the narrator, and this synthesis puts her more firmly in control of the story, one that begins to make a life with insecurity and unpredictability more manageable.

Research and reading in times of crisis

Petit found evidence of the value that literature and reading have in precarious contexts and that, in fact, people tend to turn to books, book fairs and libraries when there is chaos; she concludes that:

> A crisis is like a rupture, a time which reactivates all the anxieties of separation, abandonment and produces the loss of that feeling of continuity that is so important for the human being. Narratives, among other things, reactivate that feeling [of continuity] in ourselves, not only because they have a beginning and an end, but also because of the secret order that emanates from good literature. It is as if the internal chaos becomes placated (and) takes shape.
>
> (Petit, 2009: 141, *EA translation*)

This aligns with the comments that many of the students in our study made about how they take refuge from problems or fears in books and reading. They told us that they escape from reality but that at the same time, in that 'intersection of the world of the text and the world of the hearer or reader' (Ricoeur, 1988: 71), they apply what they learn to their own situation. Thus, the transformative power of fictional narratives, described by Ricoeur as 'refiguration' or 'mimesis' (ibid.), helped students to shape their own experiences of rupture and tension and although there is no assurance of a happy ending, according to Ricoeur, reading and reflection at least offer them the opportunity to re-create a more coherent sense of self and life and to imagine a more hopeful future (Valdés, 1991).

From another perspective, studies on Theory of Mind and literature are also pointing to the positive cognitive effects of fiction as readers enter the minds of characters and gain a deeper understanding of others and themselves (Zunshine, 2006; Kidd and Castano, 2013; Nikolajeva, 2014). Heath and Wolf (2012) argue that this is particularly true for YA literature and adolescent readers, as it offers them 'practice in fundamental cognitive behaviours: envisioning and embodying for positive emotional fuelling' (146). This brings us back to importance of young people being able to access YA literature and other types of fiction that respond to both their social and cognitive needs, encourage 'relating and re-lating' (ibid.: 147) and can offer support when vulnerability is heightened during a critical situation.

The presence of metaphor, humour, irony and other literary and visual features in the texts read during our study, encouraged the students to construct meaning and to imagine alternative ways of confronting emotions such as fear. For ethical reasons, it was important that the researchers steered some of the response away from personal disclosures that might involve risk to the speaker (e.g., one girl in GBSS was dating a gang member) but overall the group conversations created a supportive community where sharing and making connections between fiction and students' own life experiences was enabled. The creative responses, especially the photo-stories, invited readers to use some of those literary and visual features to address their fears in a symbolic or alternative manner. Finally, the participatory aspect of the research – which involved asking the young people to act as researchers and find out about literacy practices among their families and friends – encouraged a reflection on how reading and texts have changed but it also gave them the opportunity to become experts and develop self-confidence. As in the case of other projects that included young people as researchers, this one also challenged 'traditional under-estimations' (Alderson, 2001: 150) of what they were able to contribute to a complex study.

In terms of fears and anxieties about young people reading less than the previous generation, this was not confirmed by our findings; in fact, the list of titles was longer and included many YA titles. Our initial premise is that these new publications, along with marketing, transmedia and digital technology, have had a major impact on literacy practices, including reading, over the past 25 years in Mexico. However, we also found that these young people are at the crossroads between the accelerated global and technological changes that are affecting texts, and that traditional educational structures are not keeping up with these changes. Our study showed that creating a safe space through the workshops, reading and discussing fiction provided opportunities to discuss these changes but also to deal with the impact of wider socioeconomic factors. It is important to focus on these opportunities to counteract not only vulnerability and despair but also a deficit view of these young people's literacy (and education in general) in circumstances of precarity.

Our findings have implications not only for reading research but also for educational practice. They illustrate van Manen's argument that 'pedagogic situations are always unique' and that to address this uniqueness we need to 'strengthen the intimacy of the relation between research and life' by valuing 'lived experiences' as well as literary novels and art forms, among other research sources, to determine what the best pedagogy is for that unique situation (van Manen, 1990: 155).

In the case of the young people described above, their learning would benefit from an encouragement to read that included their interests, literary reading, digital knowledge and skills that can be developed to participate as critical observers (or researchers) themselves. It would also benefit from a pedagogy around reading and other literacies that acknowledges the precarity and vulnerability in their lives and which can therefore promote the opportunities rather than dwell on the fears. Finally, further research in this and other similar contexts of crisis should employ participatory and creative research methods that provide a space for investigating the transformation of literacy practices but also offer opportunities for participants to express and share their thoughts and emotions, to create connections and enable changes that could help envision alternative, more positive futures.

Notes

1 The research project, *Transformaciones lectoras/ Young adult (YA) literature and the changing reading practices of adolescents in Mexico*, was supported by a Children's Literature Assembly Award, by the University of Glasgow and by the Universidad Iberoamericana.
2 A national survey on reading and writing in Mexico.
3 The disappearance and massacre of 43 student teachers from the Ayotzinapa Rural Teachers' College on 26 September 2014 took place in the neighbouring state of Guerrero at the beginning of the fieldwork period. There is strong evidence it was carried out by corrupt police involved in the drug trade, something the government denies but refuses to investigate.
4 School authorities in one school had made an unofficial agreement with the local gang of non-interference in the immediate area surrounding the school.
5 The translation of the word 'literacy' into Spanish poses a problem and there is still no agreed common term which goes beyond *alfabetizacion* (the teaching of reading and writing). Rather than confuse the students by using alternatives such as *literacidad* or *practicas letradas*, we decided to stick to the simpler, although not ideal, term 'reading' (*lectura*).
6 For example, the young people's reading project at the Biblioteca Vasconcelos, 'Linternas y bosques': https://linternasybosques.wordpress.com/2017/01/31/los-jovenes-hablan-manifiesto-soy-joven-soy-lector/
7 The Wailing Woman, the Mad Monk and the Bogeyman.

References

Alderson, P. (2001). Research by children. *International Journal of Social Research Methodology*, 4 (2), 139–153.

Andresen, S. and Ben-Arieh, A. (2016). Can we compare children's well-being across countries? Lessons from the children's worlds study. In C. Hunner-Kreisel and S. Bohne (Eds.), *Childhood, Youth and Migration*. Springer International Publishing: Switzerland.

Anonymous (1971). *Go Ask Alice*. New Jersey: Prentice Hall.

Arizpe, E. (1994). Whose Spanish? Language and literature in the secondary school in Mexico. In M. Hayhoe and S. Parker (Eds.), *Who Owns English?* Buckingham: Open University Press, pp. 53–61.

Arizpe, E. (2001). Responding to a 'Conquistadora': Readers talk about gender in Mexican secondary schools. *Gender and Education*, 13 (1), 25–37.

Arizpe, E. and Styles, M. (2003). Picturebooks and metaliteracy: How children describe the processes of creation and reception. In M. Styles and E. Bearne (Eds.), *Art, Narrative and Childhood.* Stoke on Trent: Trentham, pp. 115–126.

Arizpe, E., Colomer, T. and Martínez-Roldán, C. with Bagelman, C., Bellorín, B., Farrell, M., Fittipaldi, M., Grilli, G., Manresa, M., Margallo, A.M., McAdam, J., Real, N. and Terrusi, M. (2014). *Visual Journeys through Wordless Narratives: An International Inquiry with Immigrant Children and* The Arrival. London: Bloomsbury Academic.

Atkinson, P. and Delamont, S. (2005). Analytic perspectives. In N. Denzin and Y. Lincoln (Eds.), *The Sage Handbook of Qualitative Research.* Thousand Oaks: Sage, pp. 821–840.

Brown Burnham, C. (1958). *Born Innocent.* New York: Prentice Hall.

Chambers, A. (1993). *Tell Me: Children, Reading and Talk.* Exeter: Thimble Press.

Cliff Hodges, G. (2012). Research and the teaching of English: Spaces where reading histories meet. *English Teaching: Practice and Critique*, 11 (1), 7–25.

Cohen, L., Manion, L. and Morrison, K. (2000). *Research Methods in Education* (5th ed.). London: Routledge.

Consejo Nacional para la Cultura y las Artes (CNCA). (2015). *Encuesta Nacional de Lectura y Escritura 2015–2018* (ENLE). Mexico: CNCA.

de Sade, D. A. F. (1791/2012). *Justine.* Oxford: Oxford World Classics.

Detrez, C. (2011). Les adolescents et la lecture, quinze ans après. *Bulletin des bibliothèques de France*, 5, 32–35.

Erickson, F. (1986). Qualitative methods in research on teaching. In M. C. Wittrock (Ed.), *Handbook of Research on Teaching* (3rd ed.). New York: Macmillan, pp. 119–161.

Ettlinger, N. (2007). Precarity unbound. *Alternatives*, 32, 319–340.

Frisch, A. (illustrated by R. Innocenti). (2013). *La Niña de Rojo.* Sevilla: Kalandraka.

Gallego García, L. (2005). *Memorias de Idhún, La Resistencia.* Madrid: SM.

García Canclini, N. (2015). Leer en papel y en pantallas: el giro antropológico. In *Hacia una antropología de los lectores.* México: Ediciones Culturales Paidós, Fundación Telefónica y Universidad Autónoma Metropolitana, pp. 1–38. Retrieved on 8 October 2017 from: www.fundaciontelefonica.com/arte_cultura/publicaciones-listado/pagina-item-publicaciones/itempubli/469/

Glaser, B. G. and Strauss, A. L. (2012), *The Discovery of Grounded Theory: Strategies for Qualitative Research.* London: Transaction Publishers.

Green. J. (2012). *The Fault in Our Stars.* London: Penguin Books.

Haghenbeck, F. (2013). *Justicia Divina.* Mexico: Universidad Iberoamericana.

Heath, S. B. and Wolf, J. L. (2012). Brain and behavior: The coherence of teenage response to Young Adult literature. In M. Hilton and M. Nikolajeva (Eds.), *Contemporary Adolescent Literature and Culture: The Emergent Adult.* Farnham, Surrey: Ashgate, pp. 139–154.

Hernandez-Zamora, G. (2010). *Decolonizing Literacy. Mexican Lives in the Era of Global Capitalism.* Bristol: Multilingual Matters.

IBBY/BANAMEX. (2015). *Primera encuesta nacional sobre consumo de medios digitales y lectura.* Retrieved on 8 October 2017 from: www.ibbymexico.org.mx/images/ENCUESTA_DIGITAL_LECTURA.pdf

Igarza, R. (2015). El desafío de poner en perspectiva el comportamiento de los lectores en México. In *Informe Encuesta Nacional de Lectura 2015.* Retrieved on 8 October 2017 from: https://observatorio.librosmexico.mx/encuesta.html, pp. 4–15.

Islas, O. (2015). Cifras sobre jóvenes y redes sociales en México. *Entretextos*, 7 (19), 1–16.

James, E. L. (2011). *Fifty Shades of Grey.* London: Vintage.

Kidd, D. and Castano, E. (2013). Reading literary fiction improves Theory of Mind. *Science*, 342, 377–380.

Lahire, B. (2004). Del consumo cultural a las formas de la experiencia literaria. In B. Lahire (Ed.), *Sociología de la Lectura*. Barcelona: Gedisa, pp. 179–197.

Manresa, M. (2013). *L'univers Lector Adolescent. Dels Hàbits de Lectura a la Intervenció Educativa*. Barcelona: Rosa Sensat.

Manresa, M. and Durán, C. (2009). Entre países: La acción educativa en nuestro entorno. In T. Colomer (coord.) *Lecturas adolescentes*. Barcelona: Graó.

McAdam, J. E., Arizpe, E., Devlin, A. M., Farrell, M. and Farrar, J. (2014). *Journeys from Images to Words*. London: Esmée Fairbairn Foundation.

Moje, E., Overby, M., Tysvaer, N. and Morris, K. (2008). The complex world of adolescent literacy: Myths, motivations and mysteries. *Harvard Educational Review*, 78 (1), 1–35.

Newman, B. (2014) En México sí se lee. *Reforma*, 14 June 2014. Retrieved on 8 October from: www.reforma.com/aplicacioneslibre/editoriales/editorial.aspx?id=28927&md5=e119daab76a00482689eae82fa7915df&ta=0dfdbac11765226904c16cb9ad1b2efe

Nikolajeva, M. (2014) *Reading for Learning: Cognitive Approaches to Children's Literature*. Amsterdam: John Benjamins.

Palys, T. (2008). Purposive sampling. In L. M. Given (Ed.), *The Sage Encyclopaedia of Qualitative Research Methods* (Vol. 2). Sage: Los Angeles, pp. 697–698.

Petit, M. (2008) Reading in crisis areas. IBBY Congress Archive. Retrieved on 8 October from: www.ibby.org/subnavigation/archives/ibby-congresses/congress-2008/plenary-speeches/michele-petit-france/

Petit, M. (2009) *El arte de la lectura en tiempos de crisis*. Barcelona: Océano.

Programme for International Student Assessment (PISA). (2015). Excellence and equality in education. Retrieved 28 October from: www.oecd.org/pisa/pisa-2015-results-in-focus.pdf

Prado, G. (2013). *Creación, Recepción y Efecto*. Mexico: Universidad Iberoamericana.

Ricoeur, P. (1974). *The Conflict of Interpretation: Essays in Hermeneutics*. Evanston: Northwestern University Press.

Ricoeur, P. (1988). *Time and Narrative, Volume 1*. Chicago: University of Chicago Press.

Rosenblatt, L. M. (1978/1994). *The Reader, the Text, the Poem: The Transactional Theory of the Literary Work*. Carbondale and Edwardsville: Southern Illinois University Press.

Sarland, C. (1991). Young People Reading: Culture and Response. Milton Keynes: Open University Press.

Secretaría de Educación Pública (SEP). (2011). *Programas de Estudio 2011 Guía para el maestro. Educación Secundaria Básica, Español*. Mexico Distrito Federal: Secretaría de Educación Pública.

Talavera, J. C. (2016). Enfrentan falta de librerías en el país. *Excelsior*, 31 October. Retrieved on 8 October 2017 from: www.excelsior.com.mx/expresiones/2016/05/31/1095825

Thomson, J. (1987). *Understanding Teenagers' Reading: Reading Processes and the Teaching of Literature*. North Ryde, New South Wales: Methuen Australia.

Valdés, M. (1991). Narrated time. In *A Ricoeur Reader: Reflection and Imagination*. Toronto: University of Toronto Press, pp. 338–354. Retrieved on 8 October 2017 from: www.jstor.org/stable/10.3138/9781442664883

van Manen, M. (1990). *Researching Lived Experience: Human Science for an Action Sensitive Pedagogy*. Ontario and London: Althouse Press.

Verne, J. (1873). *Around the World in Eighty Days*. London: Sampson Low, Marston, Low & Searle.

Zunshine, L. (2006). *Why We Read Fiction: Theory of Mind and The Novel*. Ohio: Ohio State University Press.

5

YOUNG ADULTS' ATTITUDES TOWARDS READING IN LEBANON

Nayla Aramouni

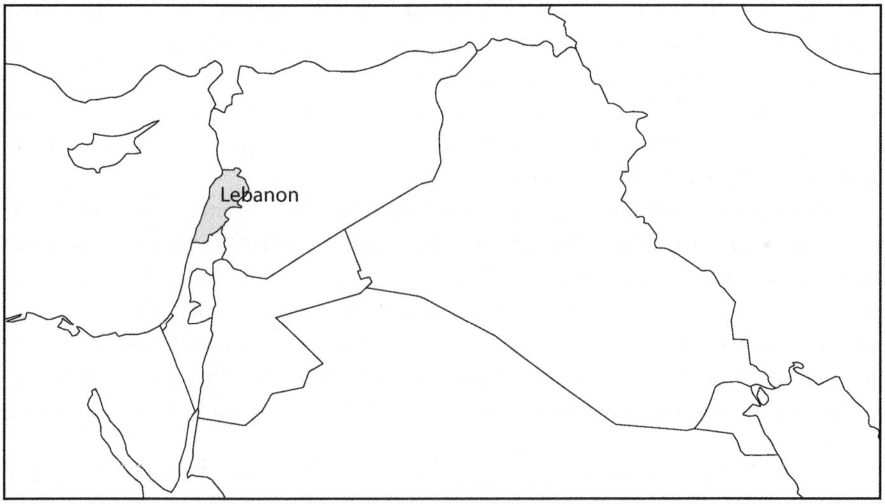

MAP 5

The 15-year-long civil war in Lebanon that started in the 1970s often takes centre-stage in discussions about the country. I did not want the war to be a starting point for my own doctoral study fieldwork which I began in 2011 but, rather, having worked in the educational field for five years, I wanted to understand why and how the people who read for pleasure in Lebanon did so, given that it was not a common occurrence, despite how highly valued the idea of reading seemed to be. However, the war was not something I could simply put to one side during my investigation. I was born in the middle of it and spent the majority of my life in its aftermath. Everyone I knew while I was growing up was living the same reality.

For example, it was not unusual to anyone that my grandmother had a collection of shrapnel picked up from her garden, carefully dated, labelled and stored in my grandfather's empty cigar boxes. Daily power cuts were normal, as was queuing for bread or at natural springs to fill large plastic tanks of drinking water.

What did seem to make me stand out from most of my peers was my love of reading. At the age of ten, I spent my recess time carefully stocking and labelling books for a makeshift classroom library out of my own and one other classmate's books. Like the participants in my study, what I read for pleasure was in English, even though my native language was Arabic. I devoured any text I could find, flipping ahead in my textbooks, reading the back of every product in our bathroom (learning the meaning of 'exfoliate' and 'lather' in the process) and reading all the novels and comic books in the house several times over. I tried to re-enact scenes inspired by the books I read, even though the cool forests of Virginia and the rolling moorlands of England were a far cry from the pine forests and rubble that made up my stage in the late 1980s. Although I could understand the language I was reading, and eventually learned to appreciate the nuances, cultural references and jokes, some things remained a fantasy. A mown front lawn surrounded by a picket fence belonged to the same world as a hobbit hole; the world where people waited at a bus stop was the same one where you climbed into a wardrobe and ended up in Narnia. I wanted to understand how people in Lebanon's prior experiences with stories and books might have shaped them as readers. To what extent, and why, did they enjoy reading? What difference did it make if the settings and cultural contexts of their reading were not their own?

Although the civil war officially ended in 1990, the country continues (even at the time of writing this chapter) to deal with a myriad of issues concerning corruption, the environment, society and politics, to name just a few. Years of these problems have come together to create what the Lebanese call 'The Situation', which is still an all-encompassing term in Lebanese discourse. Conducting my doctoral study as both an insider and outsider helped to crystallise this concept and see how it affected the way that the young people I met read and perceived reading for pleasure.

As a researcher investigating reading attitudes in Lebanon, I was faced at that time with two different reactions. Locally, people wondered why I was bothering, that surely there were more important things to worry about; they were not wrong. But, in the United Kingdom, on the other hand, people were interested. They were interested to hear that young adults in Lebanon read mostly in French and English, that a network of public libraries did not exist until 1997, and that even in 2011 I had yet to meet a single person in Lebanon who had been in a public library to read or borrow a book. So, given these very diverse reactions, I set out on my study in order to explore for myself what was driving young people in Lebanon to read.

My investigation into reading attitudes of young adults in Lebanon provided a small-scale but in-depth look into the habits and perceptions of some of the readers in the country. Previous studies were rare and were mostly surveys with little insight into a reader's individual history or motivation. Some of my findings were comparable to their counterparts elsewhere in the world, but some seemed to be more unusual. This chapter presents some of the findings from my study, as well as a glimpse into the process of data collection and the experiences from six months of fieldwork.

Setting up the context: Lebanon, learning, language and literacy

Lebanon is a small country on the Mediterranean Sea, with an area of 10,452 square kilometres. It is bordered by the sea to the west, Syria to the north and east, and Israel to the south. Because the last census was in 1932, there are no official figures to tell us about population size or make-up (Faour, 2007). However, at the time of my study, the population was around 4.6 million (UN, 2017), in addition to around 400,000 Palestinian refugees (UNRWA, n.d.). Today, there are also an estimated 1.5 million Syrian refugees (UNHCR, 2017). The influx of people has put additional strain on the country, both in terms of resources and political tensions. This was not the case at the time when my study was conducted and the Syrian war had only just begun. It is an example, however, of the volatile environment in the country, in part due to its geopolitical location. Within and despite (or perhaps as a result of) The Situation described earlier in this chapter, Lebanon is a complex country, full of contradictions and complicated intricacies.

Schools in Lebanon today and at the time of the study can be broadly categorised into two types: private schools and government-run schools. Government schools are, in general, poorly funded and often, as a result, poorly run. Students are typically enrolled in them only when the option of private school is not viable, usually for socioeconomic reasons. Although a National Curriculum exists, which all schools must follow, private, fee-paying schools vary greatly in all aspects, from funding and resources to curriculum subject matter and language of instruction. Some schools are secular, others are Christian or Muslim. Most private schools use English and/or French as a language of instruction in addition to Arabic. Some also use Armenian. Thus, most young adults who attend them are fluent in English and/or French. It is important to note that spoken Arabic is different to Modern Standard Arabic (MSA), which is the written form of the language (and spoken only in formal settings: newscasters, for example, read the news in MSA). Therefore, literate Lebanese speakers are all functionally bilingual in any case, since the language they learn to read and write once they arrive in school varies so greatly from what they learn to speak from infancy and use in their daily lives.

While preparing for my study, it was very difficult to find reliable figures on the production and sales of books in Lebanon and the Arab world. Information was pieced together from several scattered sources and was almost impossible to verify. However, indicators such as those provided by the United Nations Development Programme (UNDP) suggested a severe shortage of writing, especially when it came to books that can be read for pleasure in Arabic (UNDP, 2002). Translated works were similarly scarce. The Arab world translated approximately 330 books into Arabic annually, only a fifth of what nearby Greece translated into Greek (ibid.). In addition to the relative scarcity of books, the quality of books available in Arabic is not of the same standard as English or French books on the market. The Situation has been blamed for the lack of creative and original high-quality production (Alqudsi-Ghabra, 2004). In Lebanon, books published in English and French are more numerous than books published in Arabic. However, despite many Lebanese people's ability to read these books, readership in all languages remains low. A question may be raised about whether or not this might be due to a cultural rejection of Western or foreign material. However, other foreign media have proven to be highly successful and popular, even preferred by Lebanese youth. English is by far the most popular language among young adults in Lebanon for all entertainment-related media activities such as watching television or surfing the internet (Melki, 2010). Because of this, my reading interests in Lebanon, including those of my participants, are sometimes very closely aligned with those of their counterparts elsewhere in the world.

It may be suggested that low readership in Lebanon is due to sociocultural reasons like the ones described by Shirley Brice Heath (1982), Brian Street (1984) and others. This may be so. However, it cannot be denied that access to books, in any language, is not easy in Lebanon. Public libraries are badly stocked, very rarely frequented, and seen and described as more of a study space (El-Rouss and Kalache, 2006) than one associated with borrowing books or reading for pleasure. Bookstores are rare and usually do not stock a large selection or variety of books, but tend to supply only what is at the very top of the sales lists abroad. This makes their collections limited and very geared towards a Western audience. Most schools do not have libraries on site.

The structure and state of the education system, the languages spoken, and the ways in which people access books were the main factors taken into consideration when selecting the schools I chose to work with. I selected from private schools that used both Arabic and English as languages of instruction. It was also a main criterion that the school have a library on site. I describe my choices more thoroughly in the following section.

Selection of participating schools

At the outset, my study sought to focus on how young adults in Lebanon at that time felt about reading for pleasure: whether they engaged in it, and why or why not. From my own experience growing up, living, and working in Lebanon, I had the impression that although reading was valued and literacy rates were relatively high, very few people read for pleasure. This impression was confirmed by the conversations I had and interviews I conducted with teachers, parents, academics, bookstore managers, book suppliers, publishers and members of the Ministry of Culture. The two schools that I selected for the investigation were in the most densely populated regions of Beirut and Mount Lebanon. I named one Cedar Woods School (CWS) and the other Pine Hill School (PHS). They were mixed-sex, secular, fee-paying schools. Although it would have been ideal to work with a wider variety of schools (particularly to include government schools), I was conducting a relatively small study for my doctoral work, so choices had to be made to narrow down the scope and size of it. Therefore, a purposive decision was made to approach fee-paying schools with libraries on site and English as their language of instruction to maximise the participants' access to books. This access was made possible not only through the physical presence of reading material, but also through the students' ability to read in a language in which more books are published. Given the lack of public libraries in the country, this measure was taken to ensure that the lack of access to books was not a central factor influencing participants' attitudes to reading for pleasure. The socioeconomic influence was minimised by choosing schools that have relatively affluent families who are less exposed to the hardships many of their counterparts in the country face on a regular basis.

Theoretical framework

The reason I decided these factors were central to my investigation was a result of the theories that informed my study as a whole. These theories and previous studies also shaped the way I chose to conduct my investigation and analyse the generated data. Arab countries have some of the lowest levels of research funding in the world (UNESCO, 2013). Therefore, at the time of my investigation, only a handful of prior studies had been conducted in Lebanon, the Middle East or the Arab world, most of them surveys, and the majority did not address reading directly. However, many touched on the subject and the results flagged up some key findings relevant to my study. For example, although Lebanon had (and still has) a very high literacy rate (UNESCO, 2017), children rarely read for pleasure and adults even less so (Al Amine and Faour, 1998; Next Page Foundation, 2007; Melki, 2010; Hachem and Beidoun, 2011). Even more significant for my investigation, however, were the studies that signalled a mismatch between attitude and behaviour related to reading.

Al Amine and Faour's report of their survey of Lebanese university students in the late 1990s (although lacking a precise definition of terms and any indication of the contents of the survey questionnaire) still showed that although almost 80% of the respondents claimed they had a high level of attachment to books, more than half of all the participants had not read a single book (besides textbooks) during the past two years (Al Amine and Faour, 1998). This result suggests that although students might have been aware of the importance of books and valued reading, their claimed attitude rarely translated into habit. Similarly, Hachem and Beidoun's (2011) survey of first-year university students (which asked about reading habits, number of books read, visits to bookstores and types of text) found that the percentage of students who were inclined to read was dismal in all categories, across all regions and sects, as well as across all socioeconomic and sociocultural levels.

Thus, in designing my own study, I devoted much thought to the experiences that shape us as readers and the reading instances that influence our attitudes and perceptions of reading as a pleasurable activity. My thinking brought together theories of attitude acquisition, reading culture, reading development and reader response, all of which formed the framework of the study. These theories attempted to answer questions such as how my participants' attitudes towards reading might have been formed, what reading for pleasure meant to them, how it affected the reader and different levels of engagement with a text. They were also concerned with the impact of culture and context on reading behaviour, the notion of what Frank Smith (1988) calls a 'literacy club' and what it might have meant to be a part of one.

The idea of the literacy club stems from the notion that we learn from people around us whom we are like or wish to be like. It implies that we learn the skills required for reading by being admitted to a community of keen readers. Smith's conversations with such readers brought to the foreground this concept of a literacy club, helping to tease out the intricacies of how reading is perceived and how it is influenced by the social context of the reader. (Based on the analysis of the data from my study, however, I suggest an amendment to the concept, which I describe later in the chapter.)

The participants in my study were investigated as readers from different angles. The first angle concerned the relationship between reader and text, looking inward at the reading experiences that shaped attitude. Rosenblatt's (1978/1994) theory of reader transaction provided the framework for that approach. I was interested in reading taking place from an aesthetic stance, in which the text is approached to enjoy an emotional, aesthetic, or intellectual experience.

Another angle concerned the relationship between reader and context, particularly the reader's social context, for which theories of reading culture were important. Heath's ethnographic study of literacy and language in advantaged and disadvantaged communities in the United States (Heath, 1982, 2012) shows how cultural differences, even within the same county, can have an impact on reading attitude and practices. Similarly, Evelyn Arizpe's work with young adult readers in Mexico (2001) illustrates how a reader's context and culture may have a powerful influence on response.

It was also important to ground the study in theories that help to illustrate why reading can be a pleasurable experience. I looked at the feeling of being lost in a book and reading as a state of flow (Csikszentmihalyi, 1990), as well as Nell's (1988) work on ludic reading and its conditions. These texts developed my understanding of why some people find reading pleasurable while others do not. For example, a pleasurable reading experience according to these theorists depends on the right balance between the reader's reading ability and the challenge the text presents, positive expectations of the outcome of the reading experience, and a sense of choice or control over it.

At a broader level, an understanding of attitude acquisition and motivation was needed to frame the ways in which the external world influences how participants perceive reading and, importantly, the link between attitude and behaviour. This was particularly important because of the apparent disconnect whereby the way people seemed to feel about reading (positive) did not translate into action (reading for pleasure). For that purpose, I drew on theories of attitude acquisition, mainly on the model of reading development by McKenna, Kear and Ellsworth (1995). Bringing together these theories and studies guided the decision-making process as I designed and conducted my own research, which I outline briefly below.

Research design framework and selection of participants

The design of the study and the methods used drew on the theories mentioned and on previous studies of young people's reading habits and attitudes. In putting together the tools and methods for my own study, I looked at large-scale surveys of reading attitudes (McKenna and Kear, 1990; Gambrell et al., 1996; Hall and Coles, 1999) and studies that involved deeper conversations with readers (Cliff Hodges, 2009; Sarland, 1991; Fry, 1985).

The survey questionnaire that I developed was a redesign of two different questionnaires (McKenna and Kear, 1990; Gambrell et al., 1996), which were synthesised and modified to accommodate the age of participants and the nature of the reading I was investigating. The resultant short questionnaire of 30 items using a four-point Likert scale produced three separate scores measuring: attitudes towards recreational reading; attitudes towards academic reading; and self-perceptions of the participants as readers. The results of the survey had two functions. The first function was to select my participants. After considering the sums of the scores, 12 participants were selected, all with positive self-perceptions as readers but with attitudes towards reading varying between what I called positive, negative or neutral. A closer look at the separate scores and individual responses sometimes helped inform my selection when scores were tied. When visiting the schools, and in my conversations with teachers about their students, my choices seemed to align with what they knew of their students. I tried to balance my choices between male and female participants, and initially enlisted more participants than I needed in case any opted out later or in case of any unforeseen circumstances. Following participant selection, the second function of the survey questionnaire was to help contextualise the participants' experiences and perceptions relative to their peers' and to form a general understanding of the milieu I was working in.

The 12 participants I selected, based on their responses to the survey questionnaire, were between the ages of 16 and 18, all in their last year of school before going on to university. They consisted of seven males and five females. They were all at least bilingual (in Arabic and English); some were trilingual (in Arabic, English and French). More than half came from homes where both parents worked and at least one parent was educated to university level. More than half the participants had been at their current school since kindergarten. Three grew up in nearby Arab countries, but the remaining nine had all spent most of their lives in Lebanon. Five respondents were identified as having positive attitudes to reading, four had negative attitudes and three had neutral attitudes.

Some participants were immediately engaged and talkative and seemed to enjoy answering questions and reflecting on their reading. Examples were Rami, Maria, Laura, Diane and Mia, all with positive attitudes towards reading. Others, like Dima and Thomas, with negative and neutral attitudes respectively, were quiet and reserved, and took a few minutes before opening up and trusting that our conversation was an exploration rather than an assessment. Mark, whom I identified from the survey as having neutral attitudes towards reading, had even thought I had made a mistake in selecting him, asking 'Why me? I'm not special.' He later answered questions thoughtfully and said he very much enjoyed speaking with me. The most challenging participant to reach was Mohammad who would repeatedly agree to a time for an interview but not turn up. I realised soon after, however, that he was under the impression that participation was mandatory, due to the well-intentioned insistence of one of his teachers. As soon as I explained the purpose of the interview to him once more and stressed the fact that he was by no means obligated to participate or continue once he had agreed to, he became more enthusiastic and came to the next scheduled interview.

The style of interviews and indeed the decision to place in-depth interviews at the heart of the study was mainly influenced by preceding studies such as Cliff Hodges' (2009), which highlight the importance of engaging with readers to form a deeper understanding of their perspective. Each of the selected participants was interviewed for about an hour. The interviews were semi-structured, so each student was asked the same questions, in addition to any natural or interesting deviations the conversation took. The conversations were captured on an audio-recording device and transcribed as soon as possible. The first set of interviews and the responses to the survey questionnaire were then carefully thematically analysed and coded, which generated a new list of questions to be used in a follow-up interview. Once the first round of analysis was complete, I returned to the field for the second interviews, this time with pairs or small groups depending on availability of the participants. These interviews were also recorded (this time using video to help identify speakers and capture any non-verbal communication), transcribed, coded and thematically analysed. A second round of discourse analysis was then carried out on all transcripts. Alongside these main methods of data collection, I kept a detailed field notes journal through all stages of the study, from planning and piloting, through to execution and analysis.

Advice from experience with hindsight

Because I was from the region and had had some years of work experience with and within schools, I was able to pre-empt some problems and avoid them, particularly any to do with communication and scheduling. I contacted people who had spoken at conferences for their articles, I met with an academic in the field who put me in touch with a contact within the Ministry of Culture and I visited booksellers and met with bookstore managers to understand the market. At the schools, I also tried to make friends with the secretaries, the gatemen, librarians, and the staff in general so that I became a familiar face. I was invited into classrooms and to school events, giving me the opportunity to familiarise myself with the context I was studying. I had deeply revealing conversations with librarians about the ways in which the library was used and perceived by the staff, students and librarians themselves. Once the data was collected and all the interviews transcribed, I began the first round of analysis, which involved reading the interview transcripts repeatedly, identifying overarching or recurring themes and coding them.

Other matters, I can see with hindsight, could have been improved and optimised. For example, one piece of practical advice I received on commencing work with older students was to consider their workload and academic pressure. This affected not only the time they had to spare for interviews, but also their mental availability during the course of the investigation. In their last year of school, students were juggling local and international examinations and college applications, in addition to their usual schoolwork. Many were preparing to travel abroad, as far away as Canada and Australia, to pursue their undergraduate degrees. Choosing to work with students a year younger or older might have made arranging an interview schedule more straightforward. However, I found that students at this critical stage of their academic life were especially eager to look back and reflect on their experiences.

Popular and unpopular texts

Although all the participants spoke Arabic and could read MSA, all of them read almost exclusively in English, apart from an occasional French text for the two trilingual students. None of the texts mentioned in any of the interviews were in Arabic. It is important to note that the participants were aware that I had grown up in Lebanon and spoke fluent Arabic, otherwise it would have been assumed that the reason Arabic books were not brought up was because they did not think I would be familiar with them. However, I started every interview in Lebanese dialect and made it clear that we could speak in any language they were comfortable with, and could equally switch between them (which is common in conversation). The reasons why these young people did not read in Arabic requires further research. I speculated, however, that it was due to two main reasons: the lack of high-quality original young adult fiction in Arabic discussed in the beginning of this chapter, and the predicament of the language. The young people I interviewed tended to think in spoken Arabic, but were still more likely to think in English than in MSA. It feels unnatural to think or speak in MSA. Thus, it was understandable that MSA was not the language of choice when it came to reading for pleasure. Although technically possible if written phonetically, publishers were probably reluctant to publish in Lebanese dialect because it would have limited the market tremendously.

In terms of where they got their reading material, none of the participants mentioned borrowing books from public libraries. Only Laura, as it transpired in a group interview, had been to one with Maria who had not even realized they were in a public library. This illustrates the state of public libraries in the country at that time. The school libraries were also not a very popular resource for books. Participants said that the titles stocked were not what they wanted to be reading. Thus, all my participants obtained their books from the same three stores (with the exception of those lent to them by friends, or purchased from abroad by friends or relatives). Two were bookstores that stocked books and magazines (in English, French and Arabic), one of which also specialised in printing, copying, electronics and gadgets. The third was Virgin Megastore, which sold CDs, DVDs, video games, electronics and novelty items in addition to books and magazines in Arabic, English and French. Maria and Laura had discovered the unpublicised willingness of one of the bookstores to place book orders on request. Digital reading was mostly utilised as a last resort when the participants were unable to access or afford books in physical form. None of them owned a Kindle or similar e-reader, but some borrowed their parents'.

The keen readers read a wide variety of genres and, because all the participants read in English, many of the titles mentioned were those popular among their counterparts in other countries. These included the Twilight and Harry Potter series. Other titles mentioned included *Life of Pi* by Yann Martel (2001), *The Help* by Kathryn Stockett (2010), *Looking for Alaska* by John Green (2006), *Sense and Sensibility* by Jane Austen (1811/2004), The Chronicles of Narnia by C. S. Lewis (1950), *The Knife of Never Letting Go* by Patrick Ness (2008), *The Truth About Forever* by Sarah Dessen (2008), *Holes* by Louis Sachar (2000), and Millennium, the Swedish crime novel series by Stieg Larsson.

There was more mention of philosophy books than I had expected, with *Sophie's World* by Jostein Gaarder (1995) coming up repeatedly as a favourite, especially among those who had said they did not enjoy reading. Paulo Coelho, author of *The Alchemist* (1995), also came up frequently. Rami, who enjoyed reading, mentioned he liked reading *Towards the Third Modernity* by sociologist and political scientist Alain de Vulpian (2008). Tarek (identified as having a neutral attitude) enjoyed *The Origin of Species* by Charles Darwin (1859/2012). Their choice of texts seemed to be driven by a desire to understand the world around them, to make sense of their own and others' behaviour, and also to find a more universal understanding that could reflect upon their own, thus connecting them with what they were reading through a means that was independent of their country or context. Mohammad, the participant at PHS who was reluctant to take part initially and identified as having very negative attitudes towards reading said he enjoyed *Sophie's World* for the ideas it put forward: 'I took it more to the philosophy side of it, I didn't take it as a novel.'

Mark enjoyed reading biographies of his favourite musicians. Ali, although identified as having negative attitudes towards reading, talked at length about *Assassin's Creed* (Bowden, 2009) that he had read as an extension of the videogame it is based on. The storyline was a complex one, but it had captured his interest and he spoke about it at length. Only one participant mentioned a magazine, *Teen Vogue* (2004).

Many of those with positive attitudes towards reading stated that they actively avoided reading stories that took place in, or involved, a war or a violent context, particularly if they were set in the Middle East, Africa and Asia.

LAURA: I find one depressing thing: that all the books written by African, Lebanese, Afghan writers, are all about war and sadness. It's just like their inspiration and muse is the war. They don't really go and write about something else, something … there are a lot of other creative ideas floating around. This is why we're inclined to read American or British books more. Because they have this wider horizon.

MARIA: I don't think it's the wider horizon. I think we want to escape the idea of all these ideas of war because we live in a state of war.

It was interesting to hear Maria refer to the state of war she felt she was living in, given that at the time of the interview, the country was not experiencing any armed conflict. Rather, she was referring to a more permanent, constant state of turmoil the country as a whole was experiencing: The Situation.

Different literacy clubs

Once I began to analyse the data I had gathered from different sources (bookstores, libraries, schools, teachers, participants, academics, ministry officials), I began to notice a duality in the ways in which people spoke about reading. Initially, I identified it as a discrepancy between reading attitude and reading behaviour. In my study, it seemed that some people read for pleasure alone. Other readers, however, although still experiencing reading as a pleasurable activity, read in order to become a member of a club. I therefore felt that because there might be several factors that influence or motivate people to read, there might also be different types of literacy clubs. Perhaps Smith's definition could be adjusted to accommodate the different kinds of literacy clubs within any given society. For example, there seemed to be a culture in one of the schools, CWS, where those who said they liked to read, and saw themselves as readers, nevertheless very intentionally played the part of a reader. The divide in that school between readers and non-readers was very pronounced and all the participants at CWS referred to those two categories of people. Being a reader was very much to do with the kind of person you are, with traits extending far beyond reading such as being part of an elite group of insiders who read. Thomas, who identified as a non-reader and had been selected as a participant with neutral attitudes towards reading, said:

> There are people that love to read, but the non-readers hang out with the non-readers, you know, and the readers hang out with the readers. But it's a problem for the non-readers to move to the readers, but it's not a problem for the readers to talk to the non-readers.

Mia illustrated how this was extended into society outside her school, reinforcing the idea that the literacy club she was aware of had a particular type of member. She referred to them as Café Younesites, which is to say people who frequented Café Younes, a café in Beirut that on occasion hosted cultural activities such as poetry readings or art exhibitions, for example. It was popular with university students, but was frequented by many different types of people. When you walked by you would often see people working on their laptops or chatting and it was almost always busy. Mia said:

> People here, the older people, they're well-read, you can't deny that. Maybe not the younger generation, but the people in universities, the Café Younesites, everybody just – the ones that are on a different level, they're well-read.

These participants seemed to read because they saw themselves as readers, and identified with the image of intellectuals on a different level. Mia's spontaneous explanation helped to illustrate this view: 'You're not smart because you read, you read because you're smart.'

PHS had more blurred lines and the idea or identity of being a non-reader did not seem to exist. Some read more than others, but the club of readers was more inclusive: everyone was a part of it, because everyone was reading *something.* This was an attitude that even the participants themselves felt was unique and unusual in the country.

RAMI: I find a lot of people who read here. In my old school, it was the opposite. No one read. It wasn't something that they would hide. They'd say 'I don't read'.

MARIA: In our class, it's nice to see that even the boys, you know how the boys are always refusing to read. You, Rami, you do read, but you know the guys who are very 'scientific' and stuff they always refuse to read. But in our class, no, they actually discuss books and stuff.

LAURA: And they recommend books.

MARIA: But they're not exactly the same type that we read ... Like Zahi reads a lot about cars and engines and stuff, John reads about politics and science, more documentary. The rest ... Christopher wants to start Stephen Hawking, they talk about books, which is really cool. And it's nice to discuss what they like because it's a different point of view. Laura and I like almost the same books, so we discuss them. But it's nice to see someone else talking and it makes you proud. No, we're not like other people! We read in this class! It's good.

They also spoke about the ways in which their teachers in different subjects often had books to recommend. Indeed, Mohammad, who had enjoyed *Sophie's World*, read it on the recommendation of a non-teaching staff member.

These two different literacy clubs were also in evidence when I was asking my participants about their favourite books. Both those in the more inclusive club, and those who did not identify as a member of the club in the case of CWS, seemed eager to speak about the stories they read, the way the books made them feel, and the writing style that captured them, whereas others, although they perhaps had genuinely enjoyed their reading, used words like 'interesting' without much elaboration or personalisation. Take Dima, for example, who had been identified by the survey (and described herself likewise on many occasions) as having a negative attitude towards reading. Here she is describing one of the first pleasurable reading experiences she had:

> I was reading *The Truth About Forever*, since the girl is my age and everything she's going through I can relate to what I've been through so every time an incident happens I go like, 'No way! You shouldn't have done that!' I interact with the book.

She did not see herself as (what her peers in the school called) a reader, but the way she lit up when she spoke about her book illustrated her enjoyment through deep engagement. By contrast, Diane, who had very positive attitudes towards reading and read often, described reading her favourite book in this way: '[My favourite book is] *The Chronicles of Narnia*, the way it was written, the old English version is really good, it's very detailed, it's rich in language.' I do not doubt that Diane read and enjoyed the book she was telling me about, but I had got to know her as a perceptive and accurate individual (she spotted a typo in the questionnaire and brought it to my attention) and was surprised that she did not refer to an individual book, but rather the series title. She did not speak of any sort of engagement with the story at all, not in any of our interviews, nor in relation to any of the books she mentioned.

Being forced to read

All the participants, even those who claimed to hate reading, had had at least one very positive reading experience. This seemed to be attributed, in many cases, to what they called being forced to read by their school or teacher, but still being given freedom to choose what to read. Consequently, those with negative attitudes towards reading had the opportunity to experience pleasure in reading because they had to read the book they chose long enough to be immersed in it. An illustrative example comes from Dima. She explained that she stopped reading for pleasure when the school started to assign summer reading: 'I stopped reading books when I became like in a … in 6th grade maybe? [At that age] they started giving us summer reading books, so we were forced to read them and that was it.' However, the year my research was conducted, the school had changed its policy and had given the students a list of almost 100 books to choose from as their holiday reading. They had to read three books, but they could choose which three. This created a shift for Dima, and many other participants:

> *The Truth About Forever* [is a book I loved reading]. I had to read it last year in the spring vacation, but I didn't have a lot of time, I had like a couple of days so I was forced to read it in these days, but I actually enjoyed it. I didn't skip a page. Because *I* chose it. So, I chose something interesting I'll like.

International implications

Much of what I found during this investigation has international implications. In particular, this is true for the finding that volatile or unstable environments can have an impact on the reading choices and habits of young adults. The impact is not only on what they are reading, but also upon how, why, how often and how much they are reading. What the participants described was an internal anxiety from which they were unable to escape through the written word. The Situation in Lebanon affected all aspects of life, including reading. It affected what was being read (participants avoided violent, gruesome subjects concerning war and the effects of war, as Laura and Maria explained) and how much was being read (second only to time, participants cited anxiety or unease as the reason why they did not read more):

MIA: You get so anxious all the time. You hear car horns and babies and drills and my parents and the TV. You get really, really anxious and you can't sit still and I'm the type of person, I need to be fully concentrated to be able to read.

Rami even referred to just such a situation specifically when he recounted the time he had made a decision to stop reading over one summer (I strongly suspect that Rami was referring to The Situation that I have already defined, but I did not want to capitalise the word in the transcript because it is not entirely clear):

> Actually, I was angry because it was the coming-of-age part where I started to understand what Lebanon is, the situation, the whole dilemma, and so I became angry and was like, 'what's the point of reading books that had a lot of meanings and messages and images when the situation we live in is not healthy and we could invest this same time in something else'. I don't know what that other thing is. It was like an excuse, I don't know.

Either way, what he was reading about suddenly became pointless as he saw it framed in his environment. What he once might have viewed as an escape, since he loved magic stories (as he called them), had now not only become irrelevant and a waste of time, but also a source of anger. This created the dilemma or tension between what he once loved to do (reading) and what he felt his environment was forcing on him.

Implications of findings for pedagogic strategies

There have been many studies that show the positive role choice plays in the promotion of reading and cultivation of positive reading attitudes (Flowerday et al., 2004; Fry, 1985; Hall and Coles, 1999; Sarland, 1991). My study has also shown the need to balance that choice with a requirement to read regularly because sustained reading can allow for deep engagement with the text.

In addition, talk about books should take place in all contexts in order to create a literacy club that is welcoming and accessible. By surrounding students with references to reading, books and stories, we reinforce the idea that reading is still relevant to all our lives and not just a subject in English classes or only for high-attaining students.

An obvious recommendation that emerges from this research is that the anxiety that students are experiencing related to The Situation should be addressed by educators and writers. Although this may be a sensitive issue, acknowledging the difficulties and recognising how they may impact our lives is essential. This is important not only for the young adults themselves, who need to be aware of their own and others' fears, but also for educators, who must understand how the young people under their care are influenced by the world around them and must adjust their expectations and behaviour accordingly. Because the sheer number and duration of issues within the country have become so large that they have taken on a form of their own, it is only by addressing the effect The Situation has on us that we can begin to take it apart again and, if not resolve it, then at least see it for what it really is.

References

Al Amine, A. and Faour, M. (1998). *University Students in Lebanon: Background and Attitudes, the Heritage of Division*. Beirut: Lebanese Association for Educational Studies.

Alqudsi-Ghabra, T. (2004). Arabic children's literature. In P. Hunt (Ed.), *International Companion Encyclopaedia of Children's Literature* (2nd ed.). New York: Routledge, pp. 954–959.

Arizpe, E. (2001). Responding to a 'Conquistadora': Readers talk about gender in Mexican secondary schools. *Gender and Education*, 13 (1), 25–37.

Austen, J. (1811/2004). *Sense and Sensibility*. London: Penguin Books Ltd.

Bowden, O. (2009) *Assassin's Creed*. London: Penguin Books Ltd.

Cliff Hodges, G. (2009). Children as readers: What we learn from their conversations about reading. *Education 3–13*, 37 (2), 165–176.

Coelho, P. (1995). *The Alchemist*. London: HarperCollins.

Csikszentmihalyi, M. (1990). Literacy and intrinsic motivation. *Daedalus*, 119 (2), 115–140.

Darwin, C. (1859/2012). *The Origin of Species*. London: HarperCollins.

de Vulpian, A. (2008). *Towards the Third Modernity*. Charmouth: Triarchy Press

Dessen, S. (2008). *The Truth About Forever*. New York: Penguin Books Ltd.

El-Rouss, A. and Kalache, S. (2006). *Project of Beirut Municipality Public Libraries. Report 2: Sassine Library*. Beirut.

Faour, M. (2007). Religion, demography, and politics in Lebanon. *Middle Eastern Studies*, 43 (6), 909–921.

Flowerday, T., Schraw, G. and Stevens, J. (2004). The role of choice and interest in reader engagement. *The Journal of Experimental Education*, 72 (2), 93–114.

Fry, D. (1985). *Children Talk about Books*. Milton Keynes: Open University Press.

Gaarder, J. (1995). *Sophie's World*. London: Orion Publishing.

Gambrell, L. B., Palmer, B. M., Codling, R. M. and Mazzoni, S. A. (1996). Assessing motivation to read. *The Reading Teacher*, 49 (7), 518–533.

Green, J. (2006). *Looking for Alaska*. London: HarperCollins.

Hachem, M. S. and Beidoun, A. S. (2011). Bein al-lahou wa el-jed: Al moumarasat al-thaqafiyya l-il-shabab al-loubnani (Dirasa maydaniyya) [Between amusement and seriousness: The cultural practices of Lebanese youth (A field study)] (In Arabic). *Idafat (Arab Journal of Sociology)*, 13.

Hall, C. and Coles, M. (1999). *Children's Reading Choices*. London: Routledge.

Heath, S. B. (1982). What no bedtime story means: Narrative skills at home and school. *Language in Society*, 11 (1), 49–76.

Heath, S. B. (2012). *Words at Work and Play: Three Decades in Family and Community Life*. Cambridge: Cambridge University Press.

Lewis, C. S. (1950). *The Chronicles of Narnia*. London: HarperCollins.

Martel, Y. (2001). *Life of Pi*. London: CannonGate Books Ltd.

McKenna, M. and Kear, D. (1990). Measuring attitude toward reading: A new tool for teachers. *The Reading Teacher*, 43 (9), 626–639.

McKenna, M., Kear, D. and Ellsworth, R. (1995). Children's attitudes toward reading: A national survey. *Reading Research Quarterly*, 30 (4), 934–956.

Melki, J. (2010). Media habits of MENA youth: A three-country survey. *Youth in the Arab World Working Paper Series, 2*. Retrieved on 26 October 2017 from: www.med-media.eu/library/media-habits-mena-youth-three-country-survey/

Nell, V. (1988). The psychology of reading for pleasure: Needs and gratifications. *Reading Research Quarterly*, 23 (1), 6–50.

Ness, P. (2008). *The Knife of Never Letting Go*. London: Walker Books Ltd.

Next Page Foundation. (2007). *What Arabs Read: A Pan-Arab Survey on Readership (Phase One: Egypt, Lebanon, Saudi Arabia, Tunisia, Morocco)*. Retrieved 26 October 2017 from: www.npage.org/IMG/pdf/3._What_Arabs_Read_-_Phase_1_readership_report_in_English.pdf

Rosenblatt, L. M. (1978/1994). *The Reader, the Text, the Poem: The Transactional Theory of the Literary Work*. Carbondale and Edwardsville: Southern Illinois University Press.

Sachar, L. (2000). *Holes*. London: Bloomsbury Childrens.

Sarland, C. (1991). *Young People Reading: Culture and Response*. Milton Keynes: Open University Press.

Smith, F. (1988). *Joining the Literacy Club: Further Essays in Education*. Portsmouth, NH: Heinemann.

Stockett, K. (2010). *The Help*. London: Penguin Books Ltd.

Street, B.V. (1984). *Literacy in Theory and Practice*. Cambridge: University Press.

Teen Vogue. (2004). New York: Condé Nast.

UN, United Nations. (2017). *World Population Prospects: The 2017 Revision*. Retrieved 26 October 2017 from https://esa.un.org/unpd/wpp/

UNDP, United Nations Development Programme. (2002). *The Arab Human Development Report 2002: Creating Opportunities for Future Generations*. New York: United Nations Publications. Retrieved 26 October 2017 from: hdr.undp.org/sites/default/files/rbas_ahdr2002_en.pdf

UNESCO, United Nations Educational, Scientific and Cultural Organization. (2013). *World Social Science Report 2013 – Changing Global Environments*. Retrieved 26 October 2017 from www.unesco.org/new/en/social-and-human-sciences/resources/reports/world-social-science-report-2013/

UNESCO, United Nations Educational, Scientific and Cultural Organization. (2017). *Lebanon: Education and Literacy*, UNESCO, Institute for Statistics. Retrieved on 30 October 2017 from: http://uis.unesco.org/en/country/lb?theme=education-and-literacy

UNHCR, United Nations High Commissioner for Refugees. (2017). *UNHCR Syria Regional Refugee Response. UNHCR Syria Regional Refugee Response.* Retrieved 22 September 2017 from http://data.unhcr.org/syrianrefugees/country.php?id=122

UNRWA, United Nations Relief and Works Agency. (n.d). *Lebanon, UNRWA*. Retrieved 22 September 2017, from www.unrwa.org/where-we-work/lebanon

6

'I THINK I WAS BORN WITH A SUITCASE'

Blackfoot adolescent readers' responses to Sherman Alexie's *The Absolutely True Diary of a Part-Time Indian*

Erin Spring

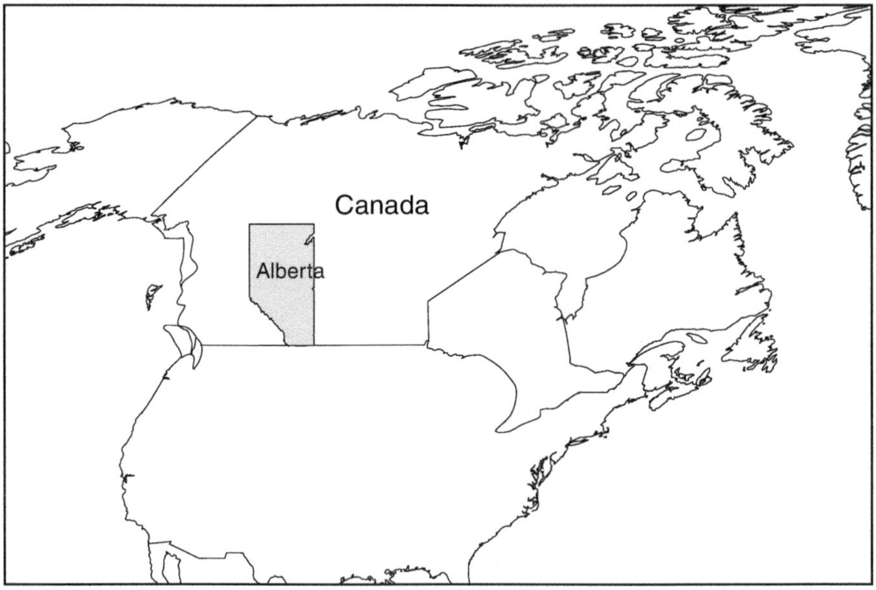

MAP 6

In literary critic Francis Spufford's reading memoir, *The Child that Books Built*, he recalls how the geographies of his childhood shaped his interpretation of fictional settings:

> For a long time, just as I set any wild scene in Keele woods, whenever I read a story set somewhere urban, I borrowed Newcastle in my mind's eye as the

> setting. Newcastle figured as London, as Paris; tweaked with columns, it was Rome, with a few pointy bits on the roof it was Chinese. Later, when I read *To Kill a Mockingbird*, I made it into the Deep South.
>
> (Spufford, 2002: 77)

My interdisciplinary research is concerned with the intersections between place and identity construction in the lives of Canadian young people. I am particularly interested in understanding the ways in which youth make sense of their identities, cultures, and communities through the reading process. Several guiding questions underpin my work, including:

- How do readers conceptualise the role of place and place-identity within their own lives?
- Simultaneously (as Spufford's memoir proposes), how do their memories and experiences of place shape how they interpret and engage with texts?

I begin this chapter with an overview of the ways in which reading can be conceptualised as a spatial event. I then provide a snapshot of the geographical, social and cultural contexts in which I am currently working, or have worked in the past. After outlining the methodological design of my empirical work, I turn to my current participatory project with Indigenous readers of the Blackfoot First Nation in southern Alberta, and share some of their responses to Sherman Alexie's largely autobiographical *The Absolutely True Diary of a Part-Time Indian* (2012).

Reading as a spatial event

In her seminal text *The Case of Peter Pan, or The Impossibility of Children's Fiction*, Jacqueline Rose (1984) argues that there is no awareness of the child reader in children's literature because there is no child to address. Therefore, children's texts replicate the adult author's perceptions of childhood that are inherently governed by the adult's ideas and perceptions of the world. Conversely, reader response scholarship is designed to foreground readers' experiences of texts. Louise Rosenblatt (1938/1995, 1978/1994) and Wolfgang Iser (1978) give the reader agency – an integral role to play – in creating meaning with and from the text. Iser, for example, asserts that there are blanks or gaps in the text that the reader has to actively fill using knowledge from elsewhere. He describes the process as such: 'As the reader passes through the various perspectives offered by the text and relates the different views and patterns to one another he sets the work in motion, and so sets himself in motion, too' (1978: 21).

Similarly, Rosenblatt (1978/1994) argues that the text, 'an object of paper and ink' (23), has no meaning until it meets the reader, who then draws on prior experiences to create a personal evocation of the text. As she perceives reading to be an ecological endeavour, she does not envisage the reader as distinct from their external surroundings. Hence, when discussing the act of reading, the world of the reader cannot and should not be ignored.

An understanding of Rosenblatt's transactional theory is paramount for thinking about reading as spatial. She writes:

> The special meaning … the submerged associations that these words and images have for the individual reader will largely determine what the work communicates to him. The reader brings to the work personality traits, memories of past events, present needs and preoccupations, a particular mood of the moment, and a particular physical condition … in a never-to-be-duplicated combination.
>
> (1938/1995: 30–31)

Every reader interprets a text differently, depending on the experiences they bring to the text, including their knowledge of specific places. More recently, several children's literature and reader response scholars have begun thinking explicitly about the ways in which our place-based experiences shape the interpretive process. In *One Child Reading: My Auto-Bibliography*, Margaret Mackey revisits the texts she read as a child, emphasising the important role that geography played (and continues to play) in the ongoing construction of her reading identity. She writes:

> for me, the where was a given: I learned to read in St. John's Newfoundland … The *why* and *how* of my reading varied from one text to another, but the *when* and *where* conditions were pervasive. They localized my reading. I was not just a generic child learning to make sense of texts; I was a *placed child.*
>
> (2016: 13, emphasis in original)

By recalling and rereading her childhood texts, and sharing the process, Mackey illustrates how, in her experience, the process of becoming literate paralleled her meanderings through the streets of St John's, Newfoundland. The premise of her argument is that, as children develop as readers, their engagement with fiction becomes more complex; simultaneously, with the burgeoning sense of independence that accompanies growing up, their knowledge of place expands. Mackey's emphasis (2010, 2016) has two purposes: not only does she suggest that a knowledge of the physical world is brought to a reading of the text, but also that reading in itself is an active pursuit, resembling the position taken by Rosenblatt.

Canadian author Tim Wynne-Jones has similarly written about the ways in which the places where he lives and thus writes from are embedded in his fictional narratives. Echoing Mackey's emphasis on the role of feet, he articulates that reading involves an engagement with real *and* fictional places, 'the one that we live in and the one that the writer takes us to' (Wynne-Jones, 2011: 122). Wynne-Jones introduces the idea of scaffolding, explaining that readers interpret fictional places by drawing on their personalised knowledge of the world beyond the text. During an author visit to Williams Lake, British Columbia, Wynne-Jones was met by a group of readers who had recently read his novel *The Maestro* (1995). The students were convinced that Burl's adventure was set in their small town, many miles away from its actual setting in Ontario's rocky shield. Wynne-Jones eloquently explains their reading experience as follows:

> The magical thing that had happened … is that those kids read right through my flora and fauna – not ignored it but transcended it – translated it into the language of the world they knew and loved. They had made Ghost Lake their own: replaced the white pine with Douglas fir, the poplars with aspen, the low slung hills with mountains, the smallmouth bass with salmon. Their vicarious adventure in this other world, two thousand miles from their own, had reinforced their own sense of place within a quite different environment. (2011: 123)

This particular reading event – this text, these readers, in this locale – encouraged the readers to reflect on their relationships with place beyond the text; the boundaries between reality and fiction were blurred. I have read *The Maestro*, and unlike the students from Williams Lake, the setting mirrors my reality – northern Ontario is my home. In reading about Burl's adventures on Ghost Lake, my own experiences within this familiar landscape were brought to mind. These connections exemplify Rosenblatt's (1978/1994) transactional process in that, for all of us, it required recalling our prior knowledge of place, and actively using this experience to shape a personalised response. As readers, we use the representations of place provided by the author to scaffold a reflection of our own place-identity, outside of the text. Wynne-Jones' readers from Williams Lake transcended the details of his setting, the information that would have probably led them to recognise Ghost Lake as nothing like Williams Lake. Much like Spufford's ability to transform Keele or Newcastle into Maycomb or Rome, the readers read over the precise details and found glimmers of recognition. Reading made them contemplate their own positions in place.

Rural and urban readers in Ontario, Canada

Drawing on Rosenblatt, Mackey and Wynne-Jones' observations as examples, this chapter similarly seeks to unravel the intersections between reading, place and identity constructions in the lives of Blackfoot youth. Before turning to my current project, I briefly outline the doctoral study that I conducted between 2010 and 2013 with ten 17- and 18-year-olds from geographically diverse Canadian communities. I worked with four female participants and one male in a rural town in northern Ontario (renamed Lakeside) approximately 300 miles from the nearest centre. The participants had never lived elsewhere; some had never even visited a city. My own observations of the town were that it was a primarily lower- to middle-class community. My participants were white and Canadian-born. I also worked in a multicultural neighbourhood of Toronto that I renamed Kirkville. The school's demographic was mixed. In close proximity to the school is one of Toronto's most affluent streets, where, according to census data, 50% of household incomes are above $150,000 (Canadian dollars). But a few blocks away is an area of high-density apartment complexes, where many families receive social assistance. During my visits to the school, I was aware of its multicultural population; I heard numerous languages spoken as I wandered the halls. Of the five female participants that I worked with, two were immigrants to Canada (from Russia and Korea), and one was a first-generation Canadian with British heritage. While my cases were situated in two locations, my study was not comparative in nature; my participants did not see this distinction (urban/rural) as relevant, but rather identified with a range of physical, social and cultural places.

One of the most significant and surprising findings of my study was the diversity with which my participants conceptualised the role of place within their lives. Several of my readers thought about place as a geographical construct, such as a family home, neighbourhood or specific street, while others prioritised a more social engagement with place, such as familial connections or networks of friendship (Spring, 2016a, 2016b, 2016c, 2017).

Lethbridge, Alberta: Why here, why now?

Soon after completing my doctoral degree, I began a postdoctoral fellowship at the University of Lethbridge, in southern Alberta, Canada. Lethbridge is located on the Treaty 7 territory of the Blackfoot (Niitsitapi) Confederacy. While the city has a vibrant urban Indigenous community, it is also in close proximity to the Kainai Blood Reserve. The reserve stretches from the Rocky Mountains in the west, east to Saskatchewan, and south towards Yellowstone, Montana. It is the largest reserve in Canada and the second most populous. The Blood Tribe[1] are considered to be the earliest residents on the western prairies of what is now called Canada. In Lethbridge, the high population of Indigenous people uniquely intersects with issues of shared space. As a settler scholar visiting this territory, and given my research interests in place and its ties with identity construction, it became evident to me that an understanding of this particular location necessitated a consideration of Blackfoot ways of knowing and interpreting place.

In contemporary Canadian communities, including southern Alberta, ongoing colonial practices continue to threaten Indigenous peoples' rights and cultures. During my first spring in Lethbridge, the Truth and Reconciliation Commission (TRC) of Canada (2015) released its final report to the Indian Residential School legacy, naming the experience 'cultural genocide'. Trials had been held across the country to allow Indigenous people to share their experiences of residential schooling. From the 1880s to the mid-1990s, approximately 150,000 Aboriginal children were forced to attend residential schools, funded by the federal government and run by churches (Vowel, 2016). Children were removed from their families and communities, and were stripped of their languages, traditions and cultural identities. Most experienced emotional and physical abuse, and at least 6,000 children died (ibid.). As a result of colonialism and the intergenerational trauma caused by the residential school system, a long legacy of families, cultures, languages and traditions has been disrupted. In an attempt to redress the impacts of residential schooling, the

TRC report outlines 94 recommendations and calls to action that can be adopted by all Canadians. In order to respond to the calls for action addressed in the TRC, particularly the need to develop a culturally appropriate curriculum and to build student capacity for intercultural understanding, the voices of Indigenous youth need to be heard. My overarching research aims are a direct response to these calls for action.

Additionally, my current project is motivated by my concern that Indigenous young people in Canada, generally speaking, do not have opportunities to read culturally relevant fiction, a concern that is also echoed in the TRC (Korteweg et al., 2010; Bradford, 2007, 2010). Perhaps unsurprisingly, I have found a striking omission of the voices of Indigenous youth in our understanding of the ways in which young people respond to and engage with fiction. Numerous children's literature scholars have reflected on the problematic colonial assumptions that are often embedded in Indigenous children's fiction, most commonly through a postcolonial lens (Johnston, 2003; Bradford, 2007). While some texts perpetuate the exclusion of Indigenous voices, other texts *do* offer narratives that feature Indigenous cultures in diverse, multifaceted ways. As I am a settler scholar who is not a member of the cultural community where this research is situated, I have been working closely with a Blackfoot teacher, principal and librarian at the school. They have helped me to select texts that, in their opinion, most closely represent the cultural worldview of their students. Some of the texts that I have selected specifically have Blackfoot readers in mind. I recognize that power imbalances are consistently at play, and that academic research has been used to colonise (Smith, 1999). As a result, I have worked diligently to ensure that my research is child-centred, ethical and focuses on the lives, experiences and values of my participants, their cultures and their community.

Ten participants volunteered to be part of my project (four male, six female). The students are aged between 12 and 14 years old. They are being raised on the reserve. One of the students moved from another community at the age of six, but the remainder of the participants have never lived elsewhere. While some have shared stories with me of visiting family or friends in other places, it is clear to me that their personal, social and cultural identities are strongly rooted in this place.

Methodological design

My understanding of place and identity rests on the idea that places, and our place-identities, have multiple layers of meaning, and are never static (Massey, 1991), necessitating a methodology that is open to multiplicity and dynamism rather than stasis. While I am conscious of the ways in which place has shaped my own identity, my aim as a researcher is to accentuate and focus on my participants' constructions of the world, rather than my own. In order to understand my participants' reflections, I used reading discussion groups, the creation of place-journals and semi-structured interviews. Connections can be drawn between these methodological decisions and the reading theories of Rosenblatt, Wynne-Jones and Mackey, all of whom perceive reading to be an active process. Using a range of qualitative methods has allowed me to position the voices and experiences of young readers at the heart of my work. As a result, I have been able to contribute to an understanding of the ways in which place, broadly speaking, informs the identities of young people in complex, multifaceted ways.

While I asked the participants to read the texts in their spare time, I quickly observed that there were varying literacy levels within the group. I therefore decided to read the texts aloud with my participants during a series of meetings in the school library. These read-aloud sessions helped to create a sense of community within our group, as we often took breaks to chat about other things, or to answer questions. When we had finished reading the Alexie text, we started informal reading discussion groups. During these sessions, my role was minimal. It was important to me that the readers led the conversations. In order to spur the discussion, I offered a list of questions to consider, prior to meeting as a group, such as: What images of place does the text evoke? What is the influence of the setting on your reading of this text? What kind of relationships do the characters have with place? What view of nature is represented?

The purposes of the discussion groups were twofold: first, they were an opportunity for the participants to share their reflections pertaining to the chosen texts; second, the conversations allowed me to interrogate the ways in which the participants used their readings of the text to engage critically with their own place-identities beyond the text. I chose group discussions as a point of departure, agreeing with Gordon Wells (2000) who, drawing on Lev Vygotsky's theory of learning, writes that 'an individual is able to achieve more with assistance than he or she can manage alone' (57). By providing my participants with an opportunity to sort through their thoughts and experiences, and to contribute to what were critical, engaging discussions, they had the chance to consider their perceptions of place, and to 'clarify [their] own minds, in order to communicate [their] thoughts to another person' (Chambers, 1985: 142).

An evident strength of the discussion group format is that close, collaborative talk is an integral part of interpretation. In *Tell Me: Children, Reading and Talk* (1993), Chambers argues that children are capable, critical readers. Rather than reading in a linear fashion, meaning is 'discovered, negotiated, made, arrived at organically' (50). As such, opportunities to discuss texts as part of a group are integral to critical thinking, as they allow for 'shared contemplation' (20) whereby readers recreate ideas, form arguments and gradually arrive at a heightened level of understanding, one that would not be achieved on their own. Gabrielle Cliff Hodges (2009), like Wells, draws on Vygotsky's sociocultural theorising to explore the conversations of a small group of Year 8 students in an English school. Using discourse analysis, she focuses on the conversations that shaped their responses. Through social interaction, her students 'reached a different destination from the place where [they] embarked' (197). The discussion groups offered participants the space and flexibility to negotiate and create an understanding of place and identity by critically interacting with other thinkers.

Alongside the discussion groups in my own study, each participant created a place-journal, containing visual and verbal responses to the texts, but also to the ways in which place was influential within their lives. The journals contained maps, sketches, written narratives, and poems, offering insight into my participants' lives in ways that complemented and sometimes contradicted the information gleaned from the discussion group conversations. Lorraine Young and Hazel Barrett (2001) assert that traditional social science methods 'rarely involve children in the research process' (14). Cliff Hodges (2016) has written about her use of critical incidents collages or 'rivers of reading', where readers visually map out their identities, indicating where 'various trajectories cluster together' (168). The journals, by documenting the voices of my participants, required them to share their trajectories in a way that felt most suitable to their varied experiences.

Lastly, I conducted one-on-one semi-structured interviews with each participant. As with the place-journals, the interviews facilitated an interpretation of my participants' understanding of the world, accessed directly through their point of view, in their chosen words. A semi-structured approach guaranteed a heightened level of understanding, as it left the power of response with the participant. Questions included, for example: Where are you from? What does 'home' mean for you? Where do you consider to be 'your place'? What was the influence of setting on your reading of the texts?

Reading Sherman Alexie from a reserve

To stay or go

One of the first texts that we read aloud together was Sherman Alexie's *The Absolutely True Diary of a Part-Time Indian* (2012). The protagonist, Junior, lives with his family on the Spokane Indian reservation near Washington. In junior high, his teacher encourages him to leave the reservation school to attend the 'all white' school in Rearden, 22 miles to the west. Here, he joins the basketball team, falls in love with the popular Penelope and befriends Gordy, the smartest boy in the school. Junior's future, off the reserve, appears to be filled with hope, but he continues to grapple with poverty, bullying, violence and alcohol abuse at home on the reservation. Junior explains that,

> Reardon was the opposite of the rez. It was the opposite of my family. It was the opposite of me. I didn't deserve to be there. I knew it; all of those kids knew it ... I felt like two different people inside of one body.
>
> (Alexie, 2012: 56)

The theme of identity runs throughout the text, as Junior seeks to define himself while straddling two very different places and cultures. He is aware that there are likely to be more opportunities available to him if he leaves the reserve, but that also means leaving behind his family, friends and direct access to his culture.

Junior's identity struggles are similar to the ones my readers were currently facing, especially as early adolescents. All of them had the choice of attending school off the reserve, which they articulated as being sometimes aligned with the hope of a brighter future. Star, a female participant, connected with Junior's experience of leaving for an education. During one of our discussion groups, she shared her thoughts:

STAR: Last year, I left, too (*pause*). My sister and me [twins] went to St Paul's in the city. Um … so it wasn't as hard for us to get there, because my mom drives in for work … I didn't have to hitchhike or walk (thank God) like Junior (*laughs*), but I remember leaving really early, before the sun even, and getting home in the dark … St Paul's was opposite. It was so big, and they split us up. Even though we are in the same grade (*pause*) they put us in different classrooms. I got lost at lunch just trying to find her. We were back here at home before Christmas. We begged our mom.

Star's narrative differed from Junior's in that she chose to return to the reservation school, rather than staying at the city school. Junior's experience provided Star with a moment of transaction or recognition, prompting her to tell her own version of leaving. Like Junior, Star drew a 'here versus there' distinction between the city and the reserve, which she ultimately referred to as home. Her description of St Paul's being 'in the city' accentuated the distance that Star felt between these two places. She did not name the city, but rather referred to it generically. Travelling to and from the reserve was perceived as being an event ('leaving', 'getting there', coming 'back here'). Her use of the word 'opposite' chimed with Junior's own use of the word, illustrating how she was internalising or borrowing the words of the text to articulate her own experience. Star's language reaffirmed her feelings of isolation, both from the reserve, but also from her sister while at the city school. The importance of community and family came through strongly in Star's reflection. She began by telling us that she left with her sister, but that they were 'split' into different classes. 'Split' conveyed a sense of being broken in half, which reiterated the sense of opposition or alienation that Star felt in her absence.

While themes of isolation and distance emerged through Star's reflection, it was clear that the larger issue was actually being separated from her sister while at the city school not her absence from the reserve. Star explained that it is 'not hard' to get to the city, and that she did not have to hitchhike or walk. While there was a distance between the two places, the process seemed navigable. What prompted her decision to return to the reserve school was not being isolated from her culture or community, but rather the dislocation that she felt from her sister while in the city. Being 'split' from her sister further exacerbated the distance between these places. Star's reflections suggested that a connection with her family was more important than a sense of rootedness in a geographical place. However, place and family appeared to go hand in hand, as Star was unable to feel at home in the city, even with her sister close by.

Picking sides: Here versus there

Jet, a male participant, was more explicit than Star about his reasons for staying or leaving the reserve. His comments were prompted by the following passage in Alexie's book:

> 'The people at home,' I said. 'A lot of them call me an apple.'
>
> 'Do they think you're a fruit or something?' he asked.
>
> 'No, no,' I said. 'They call me an apple because they think I'm red on the outside and white on the inside.'
>
> 'Ah, so they think you're a traitor.'
>
> 'Yep.'
>
> 'Well, life is a constant struggle between being an individual and being a member of the community.'
>
> (Alexie, 2012: 56)

Jet commented:

JET: I want to go to university someday. I think I'd like to be a teacher. And then maybe I could come home. Then some days I want to (*pause*) take over my dad's shop. Or something like that here, and not leave. My parents are here and my grandma always says to me, um, you have to stay. Some days there is not much to stay for, it seems, really. But it would be easier to stay. People would be happier for sure if that was my decision.

Star's motivations for leaving the city school were straightforward: it did not provide her with the proximity that she needed to her family, most importantly her sister. The physical disconnection prompted her decision to return to the reserve. Jet's comments were complicated by his awareness of various tensions pulling him in two directions. He made his individual aspirations known: he had dreams of becoming a teacher. Becoming a teacher would require leaving, to attend university, but it would also give him the option of 'maybe' coming back. His motivation for becoming a teacher was not necessarily dependent on that, however. Jet clarified that there were reasons why he could (and maybe should) stay: his family, primarily. And yet he explained that there was 'not much to stay for', which contradicted Star's motivations for returning to the reserve. Jet's family might not have been enough to convince him of the importance of staying. His comments about it being 'easier to stay' and people being 'happier' if he stayed were tinged with an air of regret. He appeared to want to make his family happy, and to care for them in the future, perhaps financially ('take over my dad's shop'), and yet this did not feel like the decision that Jet imagined himself making, if he had had the freedom to choose. Jet's individual aspirations, his belonging to a culture and his family values appeared to clash; it did not seem possible, at the time, to reconcile the wishes of both.

The seemingly opposing tensions of individual decision-making versus community/cultural expectations came up on numerous occasions. For example, a conversation emerged in response to the following passage:

> My mother and father both lived within two miles of where they were born, and my grandmother lived one mile from where she was born. Ever since the Spokane Indian Reservation was founded back in 1881, nobody in my family had ever lived anywhere else. We Spirits stay in one place.
>
> (Alexie, 2012: 89)

TAYLOR: (*Laughs*)
LEON: I am not sure why you would leave, though.
TAYLOR: I want to leave for basketball. I already go twice a week for practice.
LEON: I leave to visit my family in the city but Junior's leaving is real leaving. He leaves Rowdy with no other friend and his dad drinks too much and he should stay but he goes (*pause*). He just leaves them.
TAYLOR: He comes back though, in the end. He returns.
LEON: But not forever, really. You don't know, I guess. It doesn't say if he comes back. I think he leaves it. His family.

Like Jet, Taylor, a male participant, appeared to understand the appeal of leaving. He 'already goes' for basketball, twice a week, and seemed to find the experience of coming and going relatively straightforward, much like Star. Leon's comments, however, pointed to his disapproval or disconnection with Junior's decision to leave his family, friends and responsibilities behind. He distinguished between 'leaving' and 'real leaving'. While it was appropriate to visit the city, visiting was not the same as 'real' leaving, in that there was always the promise of return. At the end of the novel, Junior's decision of where his future would be (on or off the reserve) is not made clear to the reader. Leon anticipated that Junior would leave 'it', his family. It was not leaving the physical place that Leon could not understand, but rather Junior's ability to disconnect from his family and friends, who appeared to need him more than he needed them. Leon's repetition of the word 'leave' evoked a certain element of finality, as though it denied the possibility of return. Again, in this short excerpt, the focus was on the social or familial elements of place, rather than the geographical, echoing Massey. Leon and Taylor did not comment on the desire of living in another location, or on the physical elements of the reserve that were worth staying for. Rather, the focus remained on the familial responsibilities that were associated with this place.

This land carries all I'll ever need to know

There is a scene in Alexie's text where Junior and his best friend Rowdy climb a pine tree on the reserve:

> The reservation is beautiful. I mean it. Take a look. There are pine trees everywhere. Thousands of ponderosa pine trees. Millions. I guess maybe you can

> take pine trees for granted. They're just pine trees. But they're tall and thin and green and brown and big. … Rowdy and I climbed and climbed and climbed. We made it to the top … From our vantage point, we could see for miles. We could see from one end of the reservation to the other. We could see our entire world. And our entire world, at that moment, was green and golden and perfect.
> (Alexie, 2012: 219)

When I read this scene aloud, two of my participants, Taylor and Jet, had the following discussion:

TAYLOR: (*turning to Jet*) Remember that time we went to Montana? Uncle Tim took a wrong turn on one of those long roads, like up near Milk River, right?

JET: (*laughs*) And then we thought we were really lost, because all you could see were yellow fields and fields.

TAYLOR: (*turning to Erin*) But on the rez there are these houses, and the houses tell you where you are. Like you know where you are because of what house you are near.

JET: You can see forever but then your eyes hit a house and then, like that, you know you have to turn down that road.

ERIN: So you know where you are, because of the house that you are near?

JET: You know who lives there, so yeah. It's not just a yellow (*pause*) mess like those roads on the way home that day. You look up and think, OK, I've been here.

TAYLOR: This land carries all I'll ever need to know.

Similar themes emerge within this discussion: of connections with family, and of community relations. However, the local landscape is brought into focus here for one of the first times. It is described as a flat, open and, at times, isolating space. Rowdy and Junior's perspective of place from up in a pine tree does not look exactly like the expansive prairie that is so familiar to Jet and Taylor. And yet they recognised that feeling of familiarity, of knowing a place well, and translated that into their own experience. It is interesting, here, that Taylor turned to me, as if to let me in on a secret. They were aware that I was an outsider to this place, to this geography. While they were sharing this personal moment of an encounter in place, they welcomed me in; they explained to me their way of navigating the reserve in relation to community, to the houses of friends and family members. Taylor's final comment contradicted his statement about 'wanting to leave for basketball'. Even though this place, particularly 'this land' was all he would ever need to know, he was still tempted by the desire for something more. 'Need to know' suggests, however, that it was not necessary to leave. Everything that he 'needed' could be found here.

Conclusion

As my research shows, using culturally relevant and local, place-based fiction encourages adolescents to have discussions about their cultural, social and place-based identities within and beyond the text. Jet, Taylor, Leon and Star's reflections illustrate how the act of reading has the potential to unravel stories of place, aligning with Rosenblatt's transactional theory of reading. The participants' place-trajectories were not separate from their reading trajectories, bringing to mind Mackey's (2010) assertion that exploring place and interpreting texts work in tandem, and Wynne-Jones' (2011) depiction of reading as an intermediary between two worlds – real and fictional.

Alexie's text afforded opportunities for my participants to critically engage with concepts of place and place-identity. A significant strength of my methodological design were the discussion groups, as they allowed me to confirm that reading texts can be a catalyst for participants to reflect on their experiences of place. Issues such as home, place and family were unsurprisingly at the heart of our conversations. Rosenblatt (1938/1995) asserts that, for a young adult reader, the reading experience is particularly specialised, as they 'have not yet arrived at a consistent view of life or achieved a fully integrated personality' (31). While I do not think that individuals (at any age) ever achieve this, as I construe identity and place to be continually in motion, I do propose that my data is particularly rich because of the life stage of my participants.

Thinking about the intersections between reading, identity and place encouraged me to interpret the discussion groups as a particular type of transaction where the students were sharing, challenging and thereby changing their constructions of place as they met with one another. My participants' reflections not only indicate their ability to think critically about the role of place within their lives, when prompted, but that these concepts have been in their minds for some time. The methods that underpinned my project pushed their thinking forward, reiterating how concepts such as place and place-identity, as part of a transaction, are continually in motion.

Note

1 For more information, see Blood Tribe. Retrieved 21 October 2017 from http://bloodtribe.org.

References

Alexie, S. (2012). *The Absolutely True Diary of a Part-Time Indian*. New York: Hachette Book Group.

Bradford, C. (2007). *Unsettling Narratives: Postcolonial Readings of Children's Literature*. Waterloo, Ontario: Wilfrid Laurier University Press.

Bradford, C. (2010). Reading indigeneity: The ethics of interpretation and representation. In S. Wolf, K. Coats, P. Enciso and C. Jenkins (Eds.), *Handbook of Research on Children's and Young Adult Literature*. New York: Routledge, pp. 331–341.

Chambers, A. (1985). *Booktalk: Occasional Writing on Literature and Children*. London: Bodley Head.

Chambers, A. (1993). *Tell Me: Children, Reading and Talk*. Stroud, Kent: Thimble Press.

Cliff Hodges, G. (2009). Children as readers: What we learn from their conversations about reading. *Education 3–13*, 37 (2), 165–176.

Cliff Hodges, G. (2016). *Researching and Teaching Reading: Developing Pedagogy through Critical Enquiry*. London: Routledge.

Iser, W. (1978). *The Act of Reading: A Theory of Aesthetic Response*. London: John Hopkins University Press.

Johnston, I. (2003). *Re-mapping Literary Worlds: Postcolonial Pedagogy in Practice*. New York: Peter Lang.

Korteweg, L., Gonzalez, I. and Guillet, J. (2010). The stories are the people and the land: Three educators respond to environmental teachings in Indigenous children's literature. *Environmental Education Research*, 16 (3), 331–350.

Mackey, M. (2010). Reading from the feet up: The local work of literacy. *Children's Literature in Education*, 41 (4), 323–339.

Mackey, M. (2016). *One Child Reading: My Auto-Bibliography*. Edmonton: University of Alberta Press.

Massey, D. (1991). A global sense of place. *Marxism Today*, 35 (6), 24–29.

Rose, J. (1984). *The Case of Peter Pan, or The Impossibility of Children's Fiction*. London: Macmillan Press.

Rosenblatt, L. M. (1938/1995). *Literature as Exploration* (5th ed.). New York, NY: The Modern Language Association of America.

Rosenblatt, L. (1978/1994). *The Reader, the Text, the Poem: The Transactional Theory of the Literary Work*. Carbondale, IL: Southern Illinois University Press.

Smith, L. (1999). *Decolonizing Methodologies: Research and Indigenous Peoples*. New York: Zed Books.

Spring, E. (2016a). Where are you from?: Locating the young adult self within and beyond the text. *Journal of Children's Geographies*, 14 (3), 356–371.

Spring, E. (2016b). Place and identity in children's and young adult fiction. In N. Worth, C. Dwyer and T. Skelton (Eds.), *Geographies of Identities and Subjectivities, Volume 4, Geographies of Children and Young People*. Singapore: Springer.

Spring, E. (2016c). The experiences of two migrant readers: Freedom, restriction, and the navigation of adolescent space. *Jeunesse: Young People, Texts, Cultures*, 8 (1), 227–247.

Spring, E. (2017). 'Without Manifest, none of the book would have happened': Place, identity, and the positioning of Canadian adolescent readers as literary critics. *Children's Literature in Education*. Retrieved 26 October 2017 from: https://doi.org/10.1007/s10583-017-9313-y

Spufford, F. (2002). *The Child that Books Built*. London: Faber.

Truth and Reconciliation Commission of Canada (TRC). (2015). *'Honouring the Truth, Reconciling for the Future': Summary of the Final Report of the Truth and Reconciliation Commission of Canada*. Retrieved from: www.trc.ca/websites/trcinstitution/File/2015/Findings/Calls_to_Action_English2.pdf

Vowel, C. (2016). *Indigenous Writes: A Guide to First Nations, Métis, and Inuit Issues in Canada*. Winnipeg: Highwater Press.

Wells, G. (2000). Dialogic inquiry in education: Building on the legacy of Vygotsky. In C. Lee and P. Smagorinsky (Eds.), *Vygotskian Perspectives on Literacy Research: Constructing Meaning through Collaborative Inquiry*. Cambridge: Cambridge University Press, pp. 51–85.

Wynne-Jones, T. (1995). *The Maestro*. Toronto, Ontario: Groundwood Books.

Wynne-Jones, T. (2011). Where is here anymore? A personal reflection on 'Representing the Environment,' Chapter 3 of *The Environmental Imagination* by Lawrence Buell. *The Lion and the Unicorn*, 35, 118–131.

Young, L. and Barrett, H. (2001). Adapting visual methods: Action research with Kampala street children. *Area*, 33 (2), 141–150.

SECTION 3

Young adult readers' experiences within and beyond school and university

7

ADOLESCENT READING HABITS

The effect of school activities on reading practices

Mireia Manresa

MAP 7

Personal reading, school reading

In order to establish the focus of this chapter I will begin with the consensus reflected by many theorists in the field (e.g., Manresa and Durán, 2009; Fittipaldi, 2013) that the reading of literary works in the classroom has two primary objectives. On the one hand, there is the will to create, solidify and extend the reading habits of young people and, on the other, there is the academic aim to improve students' interpretative competence, including within local and universal literary traditions. These two objectives have been embraced more swiftly in some contexts than in others depending on educational traditions, and in some cases they have been dealt with more explicitly than in others. Either way, the combination of these two objectives in the classroom reveals the integration of a private cultural practice, such as the habit of reading, within public cultural practices in the school.

These two objectives also highlight the idea that adolescent reading habits are shaped by a mixture of inputs from different contexts that can influence reading development in different ways. Robine (2005) identifies two reading practices connected with these two objectives – the institutional and the informal – namely directed reading and free, spontaneous reading. This duality places adolescent reading in a space that spans both the personal and the social, and that defines the development of a reading habit as divided between personal, independent reading choices and the obligatory nature of school reading.

Understanding the dynamics between these two types of reading practice is one way to gain better knowledge of how adolescent reading works and to improve the teaching of literature in the classroom. For this to happen, it is essential to have approaches that allow us to distinguish between the texts that students read out of personal choice and those that they read because they were recommended or prescribed by their teachers. Although both sources of reading constitute what we might call the reading universe of each individual, we agree, following Baudelot et al. (1999: 71), that 'only the titles read for oneself or perceived as "personal" allow us to correctly measure interest in reading and its evolution over the years'.[1] We might add that it is only these titles that allow us to discover the scope of the students' intrinsic motivation towards literary reading. In short, it is that intrinsic motivation or genuine interest in reading that should remain the final goal of the school when searching for strategies to promote reading habits that will allow students to attain their educational objectives.

One of the specific reading strategies that has been applied in many countries is to provide independent reading time in the classroom, sometimes known as free voluntary reading (Krashen, 2004a, 2004b); in other words, it is reading that emulates everyday reading practices outside the classroom. This means that individuals are able to choose which texts to read, to stop reading when a book does not meet their expectations, to read in a continuous and sustained manner and to do so without any academic purpose being the main requirement. Even when such reading time is provided in the classroom, it would be naïve to think that it would reproduce the reader's private practices identically, given that the school has a clearly educational agenda. It is therefore appropriate to consider this type of semi-independent reading as being a borderland between personal reading and school reading – a permeable space that combines both.

Selecting literary texts for Catalan schools

Classrooms in Catalonia are governed by the general laws of the Spanish state, which in turn are specified and developed by the Catalan government taking into account sociocultural particularities of context and local pedagogical traditions. It is a bilingual context with Catalan and Spanish as the official languages. A language immersion programme[2] is applied from the first years of primary school, which means that all children in Catalan public schools learn to read and write in the region's language, Catalan, and then switch to learning Catalan and Spanish as two different subjects during the rest of their schooling.

Language immersion is important since educational traditions concerning reading in secondary schools in Catalonia are based on the prescription of a complete literary work per school term in both official languages. In fact, this tradition is a legacy from before 1990 when compulsory secondary education did not yet exist. At that time, these termly readings at the post-compulsory education stage (which was undertaken by only one third of the 14- to 18-year-old population who would continue to university studies) were seen as a means of providing canonical models of local (Catalan and Castilian) and universal literary traditions.

The possibilities of educating this minority of young people who were already interested in studying were much higher than later on when compulsory schooling was extended to 16 in 1990. Even so, the aforementioned termly readings have remained the only school-based literary reading of complete works up to the present day. However, the democratisation of schooling has brought about a change that has converted the function of literature teaching from literary reading to literary promotion. The increasing diversity of students in the classroom has also encouraged teachers to adapt their chosen book titles and educational book-reading practices. This has been possible because in compulsory secondary education in Catalonia there has never been any list of books provided by the educational administration. Once schools assumed the role of the social expansion of reading, it was found that the mandatory termly reading of literary works did not lead to the expected results in adolescent reading levels and were not enough to consolidate reading habits.

My own study was set in a social context with low literacy attainment. School dropout rates were 20% in 2016. Reading rates were also low with only 28.7% of Catalans over 14 years old claiming to read literature every day (Eurostat, 2016). The family environments of the students did not represent a context in which they could naturally develop reading habits. In addition, there was a phenomenon of reading inequality that is still increasing: according to the statistics, 40% of the population never reads. These factors are important because, if we consider the educational system in a broad sense as some theorists do (i.e., formed by school, family and sociocultural subsystems), it seems that schools do not have the support of the other vertices of the triangle to strengthen the reading practices of their students. In contexts of low readership, schools must therefore make a greater effort and be aware of their compensatory responsibility.

An eclectic methodology

My study explores the interrelations between mandatory school reading and voluntary personal reading by adolescents in order to better understand the transaction between both types of reading and the influence that schools have on the shaping of the adolescent reader profile.

The interest of sociology in adolescent reading became prominent when European surveys began to show a decrease in reading in the 1970s and 1980s. The concern caused by these poor results led studies to focus on the adolescent population in schools. It was considered that this population could be influenced since it was still in the process of being educated. Some of the seminal studies looked into the boundaries (or spaces of interrelation) between the school reading and social reading as a focus of relevant interest. In France, for example, Robine (1984) studied the effects of schooling on the reading habits of young workers a few years after leaving school. Her results have been both confirmed and debated in later studies. They include the fact that adolescent reading choices mainly occur via channels of non-institutional sociability and that school reading does not leave a positive mark on young people. In the same country, de Singly (1989, 1993) detects a trend that is confirmed and becomes more acute at the turn of the century (Baudelot et al., 1999; Manresa, 2013) and that determines reading at the present time: reading takes on a new status for new generations because it is no longer a sacred activity for the youth of the 1990s; even those who read very often dissociate themselves from the symbolic representations that literary texts had for the educated elites of earlier generations. This awareness calls upon educational institutions to rethink school reading planning. The democratisation and the expansion of education also emphasise the social and personal dimension of the practice of reading in the classroom. In Germany, for example, Schön (1993) was interested in reading habits beyond the school context and pointed out that it is in secondary school – and not before – that readers perceive there is a borderland between the books they choose themselves and those prescribed or recommended by the school.

Parallel to this intersection between in-school and out-of-school environments there was also a shift in literary studies during the second half of the last century, which no longer focused exclusively on texts but also on the reader. This tendency stems from an increasing interest in the individual reader and his or her reading experience and it aims to discover the perspective of the real reader in contrast to that of the implied reader (Rouxel, 2005). In addition to studies on child and adolescent reading such as Meek (1988, 1990) and Fry (1985), there has been qualitative research based on interviews with specific participants such as that carried out by the anthropologist Petit (1999) in France; those focused on reading life autobiographies and stories such as the investigations of Rouxel (2004) or Munita (2014); or studies based on readers logging critical incidents of reading by means of a reflective instrument such as the 'rivers of reading', a collage with visual and verbal information, discussed by Cliff Hodges (2010).

My investigation acknowledges the progress made in various disciplines and agrees with the interrelationship of some of the aforementioned studies, in particular the interrelationship defined by Robine (2000) between sociological studies and pedagogical intent. It is a case study that lists and analyses the works of fiction read by 80 adolescents enrolled in three classrooms in a high school from a city near Barcelona during a three-year period. These groups had a standard academic and sociocultural student demographic. The methodological design of this research falls within certain parameters:

- It was a longitudinal three-year study (of students aged 12–15) to show personal reading paths, with a framework based on Baudelot et al. (1999).
- The data collection was not based on the self-perception of the subjects but on the specific titles they read during the research period and thus falls into the tradition of studies on reading choices from the United Kingdom (Jenkinson, 1940; Whitehead et al., 1977; Hall and Coles, 1999). Analysing the books read by the students made it possible to take a closer look at their tastes and to have an understanding of what they really chose on their own. The possible limitations of focusing on a specific context with so many variables in hand were compensated for by the study's extended timescale and by the fact that the analysis was based on the identification of recurrent patterns in reading behaviour.
- My research mainly uses the free voluntary reading work of Krashen (2004a, 2004b) as a method. A contrast was established between two sample groups participating in the reading programme, one of which read more than the other, and a control group. The distinction between the two sample groups was established in a natural way, taking advantage of the difference that already existed in these classrooms due to the methods used by the two teachers who taught Catalan language classes to these groups, one of whom (during the first year) was me.
- Unlike most studies on reading habits, mine collected data on the students' assessments of the works they read by registering their arguments about why they liked or disliked them.

The data analysis is therefore based on: a sociological perspective, because it relates reading to sociobiographical variables (for example, age, sex or sociocultural context); literary theory, because it classifies the titles according to genres, subgenres and other literary variables; and on reading responses, because it creates categories to analyse what the adolescents said about the books.

The data provides an overview of the adolescents' reading practices through analysis of three defining dimensions of reading habits established in the study: the number of books read, the diversity of the texts, and the ways in which students assessed their reading. This overview is one of the contributions made by the research, but also one of its limitations. Although the research provided broad, panoramic results of the students' reading habits, the high degree of methodological eclecticism made it difficult to focus on a specific line of analysis. This chapter focuses therefore on the effects that the free voluntary reading programme had on the students' reading habits and looks into some of the relevant data.

The incidence of free voluntary reading in shaping the literary reader at school

The relationships between school reading and personal reading are extremely complex and often contradictory. On the one hand, the boundaries between the two types of reading are blurred because personal reading space is diminished (and in some cases disappears) with the passage of time as students tend to read less; on the other hand, tensions appear between free voluntary reading (or its representation) and institutional reading, creating a profound division between the two.

These tensions are partly caused by the phenomenon of what in Denmark is called *book-dropping*,[3] in other words the gradual abandonment of reading over the years. According to my data 14% of adolescents do not read fiction on their own at the age of 13, a figure which rises to 45% at the age of 15. Without the school's intervention, it appears that a significant number of young people do not read fiction at all or progress any further by themselves. Therefore, young people rely strongly on school reading, which raises questions about whether schools should be even more proactive about developing adolescents' reading.

The first relevant result of my study is confirmation that the existence of a free voluntary reading programme affects personal reading habits: the students in the groups with a free voluntary reading programme in class increased their own personal reading in their free time, as Table 7.1 shows.

Contagion or permeability between school reading and personal reading is possibly caused by two things at the same time: on the one hand, there is the students' progressive adoption of the role of literary readers within the structure of a reading community in the classroom; on the other hand there is the movement towards more personal reading, which indicates that free voluntary reading in school is seen less as an academic activity than other forms of reading. Young people continue to value books as a source of socialisation and leisure, searching for collections such as commercial series, magazines, multimodal texts that provide them with reading pleasure. Schools need to ensure that students do not, at the same time, distance themselves from literature recommended in the classroom because they see it merely as a school requirement. However, we must note the fragility of achieving such a balance if personal reading programmes are not maintained continuously over time. During the second year of my work there was a decrease in the school's proactivity,

TABLE 7.1 Books read outside school as personal reading

	First year	*Average number of books per student*
Groups with free voluntary reading programme		
Most avid reader Group A	79 books	3.1
Least avid reader Group B	68 books	3.2
Group without free voluntary reading programme	60 books	2.4

which clearly had an impact on reading results since the groups included in the free voluntary reading programme significantly decreased their reading activity while a slight increase was seen in the control group. It is also worth underlining the fact that the decrease affected the less avid of the two sample reading groups in particular. Nonetheless, as the rest of this chapter will show, beyond these initial factors, the free voluntary reading time in the school had other repercussions on the genuine reading habits and practices of young people.

Compensating for inequality

The increase in reading in terms of books encountered via the school, in other words dependence on the school for the development of reading habits, is a phenomenon that is closely linked to social variables. Therefore, older students and weaker readers (made up mostly of boys, adolescents from culturally disadvantaged families and readers who already had a weak profile in previous years) are those whose reading is often more school-based because all they read are the texts set by the school.

Social factors are one of the constants in studies on reading that show the correlation between reading literature and living in an environment sensitive to literary culture. In relation to social differences, many studies (e.g., Petit, 1999; Alvermann, 2002; Aliagas, 2009) have already shown that not reading certain canonical or academic texts does not preclude reading other forms of fiction. However, this possibility must be taken very seriously: our research suggested that there are often still cultural inequalities expressed in family attitudes that are disapproving of literary reading, perceiving reading fiction as purely academic or unnecessary. For example, one participant remarks:

> When I was little my parents made me read because I had to learn; now they always tell me that I have to do my homework and pass my exams and they don't make me read like before (13-year-old student from my study).

The fact that secondary school classrooms can provide time for free voluntary reading addresses, albeit only very slightly, one of the greatest challenges of current education: inequalities among students living in different family contexts. It shows that the fact that children do not read outside school does not necessarily impede reading inside the classroom. My data also shows that in the first year of the free voluntary reading programme, any inequality in starting points is already slightly offset. Specifically, 57% of adolescents from precarious sociocultural contexts score the highest in terms of the number of books read in the free voluntary reading programme but not in the control group.

Consolidating emerging habits

Sofia, one of the students in my study, read 15 books in the first year of high school; her interest in reading then decreased until it disappeared completely in her third year. Another of the students, Ana, did the same amount of reading as Sofia in her first year; however, her reading did not stop completely but merely decreased to six books of personal reading during her third year. Both girls participated in the free voluntary reading programme. There were other young people similar to these two participants whose progress I observed and I detected that these two types of behaviour were consistent in the case of the more avid readers. What caused them to stop or keep going over the years? The differential factor emerges from the analysis of the personal reading of these two girls during the first school year: Sofia chose to read 15 books from two realist sagas for young readers that fell outside the list of school set texts. Although Ana also read popular literature for girls, her personal reading world was nourished with much more variety: fantasy titles both for young readers as well as for adults; fiction books for young readers by Catalan authors; classics for adults from the Spanish literary tradition; English authors writing for young people; and classic children's literature authors. This can be seen in Table 7.2.

These behaviour patterns suggest that diversity in reading material is a strength in reading habits. For this reason, even if it seems paradoxical, strong or frequent readers (i.e., those who undertake personal reading of more than ten books per year) need more school attention than one might think. This is especially true for those who remain reading the same types of texts because they are as vulnerable as those who read very little literature at all. According to my data these are the more unstable readers because they stop reading in a more pronounced way than other types of readers and they often tend to abandon reading completely.

I also observed that for those who are stuck, free voluntary reading in school was beneficial in a way that was very difficult to achieve through more academic school reading practices because of the lack of reading time. Free voluntary reading in school allows for what we have labelled 'progressive recurrence', that is to say specialisation but remaining within readers' preferences. Here we refer to variation within the same genre, such as different versions of detective novels at different levels of complexity that would not naturally reach the adolescent circuit outside the classroom. This is

TABLE 7.2 Sofia and Ana's personal reading

Student	*Authors read as personal reading*
Sofia 15 books	• Minte-König, Bianka • Stine, Robert Lawrence
Ana 15 books	• Minte-König, Bianka • Rennison, Louise • Gallego, Laura (Spanish author of adolescent literature) • Delgado, Josep Manuel (Catalan author of adolescent literature) • Cervantes, Miguel de • Allende, Isabel • Kipling, Rudyard • Carroll, Lewis

clearly exemplified in the case of Maria, who read many realistic novels for young readers by authors such as Louise Rennison or Steve Barlow by choice but the free voluntary reading programme lured her into reading other types of realistic books, such as *The Diary of Anne Frank* (1952).

Other sociocultural factors appeared in the analysis, such as the fact that adolescents' reading choices are influenced by social media, confirming that in globalised societies, the specific selection of titles by adolescents is often the same regardless of the reader's country or social status. The titles named by teenagers have equivalents in all countries, with a predominance of bestsellers, fashion genres and the derivatives of audio-visual products. These books adapt well to adolescents' abilities and are usually left out of school selections. Since the path of personal reading does not tend to merge with schooling in most classrooms, its practice remains outside literary learning and there are few activities aimed at helping students to reflect on reading itself or to systematise aspects of what they have learned. However, similarity of reading choices offers positive compensation because it creates a common frame of reference, even for less avid readers, something that can be used in the classroom to create a sense of community.

But with such globalised reading habits, what are the differences between the Catalan adolescents in this study and those in other contexts? The answer lies mainly with the reading that is recommended by the school, because their personal reading choices actually tend to be similar to those of their peers in other places. This leads one to think that it depends on the educational tradition to which a young person is exposed as to whether their reading experiences lack certain types of texts, such as the most canonical or those of certain specific genres. Contrasting data on adolescent preferences in different countries (Hersent, 2000; Baudelot et al., 1999; Hall and Coles, 1999; Manresa, 2013) reflects differences in readers' experiences of texts of varying quality – commercial, popular, canonical, classical, complex – which reminds us that there is a risk in not differentiating the corpus selected by the school from that selected by the students. This statement may seem to contradict my proposal of free voluntary reading programmes that include books which match adolescents' tastes, but what the data tells us is that it is counterproductive to simply imitate or repeat what they already read and that teachers should not give up on the objective of encouraging students to progress towards more complex texts. This is where the mediation of teachers becomes necessary. It helps students identify what they already like to read and enables them to analyse more challenging and sophisticated proposals. Reading lists of popular genres – such as romance or vampire literature – that include both the juvenile books of the moment and their classical counterparts, would be an example of such mediation, which aims to develop literary tastes by suggesting contrasting titles.

Enriching reading habits

Another relevant finding from my research is that when talking about their reading adolescents often do not know how to apply literary metalanguage. Their assessment of reading matter continues to be based on criteria of realism or empathy: as many of their comments confirm, they comment that a text 'seems real' or is 'a real story' or seems 'as if it was happening to you'. This fact reveals a lack of ability to transfer literary learning from school reading to personal reading. Once the student has left school, it seems that their ongoing literary reading does not benefit from what they have learnt during their years of schooling.

Among the typical rituals of literary reading practices are the sharing of one's own love of reading, interaction with what is going on in the world of literature and communication about texts that are read. These rituals have often been associated with the academic task of analysing works but not with extra-curricular reading. However, education regarding conversations about fiction is becoming ever-more important due to increasing reader socialisation on the web. In this regard Rouxel (2005), following Eco (1994), distinguishes between *interpreting* the text, which requires specific skills, and *using* it, which implies a personal appropriation and emotional attachment to the text that develops construction of a discourse about oneself and about the world.

Some studies have investigated this personal use of text in non-mediated reading situations: Leveratto and Leontsini (2008) offer an analysis of social conversation about texts in the virtual environment. They track and interpret internet forums where adult readers talk about the books they have read. They show how literary socialisation through sharing one's own reading experience develops literary competence and thus becomes a means of consolidating participant readers' identities. Sarland (1991), investigating readers' spontaneous responses to the popular texts chosen in their free time, argues that the pleasure experienced by young people who read popular texts is identical to that obtained by educated readers who read great literature.

The students in my study shared their arguments for recommending texts in a natural way, without teaching mediation or intervention of any kind by way of preparation. Analysis of their statements shows that the most sophisticated arguments are almost exclusively from adolescents who have vast and diverse reading experience. We noted, in particular, the use of metalanguage, arguments based on the characteristics of the text, and discussions that avoid generalities such as 'it's boring' or 'it's fun'. The arguments of the students with little reading experience are based exclusively on the relationship between the text and the life of the reader, as these examples show:

> I like this book because it is about young people like me.
>
> I like it because it's about girls my age.
>
> I like it because it talks about a TV show that I used to watch when I was little.

In contrast, young people who have read more books tend to use metalanguage or comment on characteristics of the text:

> I liked it because it's a realistic book.
>
> I liked it because it is intriguing.
>
> The plot is very original.
>
> It's okay because it's a girl writing a personal diary.
>
> I didn't like the ending.
>
> I didn't like it because at first it was very descriptive and you end up getting lost, bored.
>
> I liked it because the story is written in the first person, so I can know what he thinks and how the character acts according to what he observes.

In fact, only 10% of the weaker readers are included in this type of discussion as opposed to 33% of those who read 'quite a lot' or 'a lot'. This confirms theories that affirm that the construction of abstract thought and conceptualisation does not always come from explicit awareness but from frequent return to recurring patterns of observed objects (Bruner, cited by Rouxel, 2005). In other words, interpretive progress can arise from recurring contact with literary fiction through opportunities to compare and contrast, or from emotional attachment to texts that allow readers to pause and reflect on them.

Building reading habits and training literary readers: Two sides of the same coin

We have seen that, despite the fact that reading tends to decrease with age, all students read more when there is school intervention, provided it is not sporadic. It is also clear that if school input decreases, the weakest are most affected, since the decrease in pressure from the school leads to the same effect on personal reading. We have also observed that if both academic reading and free voluntary reading take place, reader rejection decreases and there is an increase in the variation of the corpus and forms of reading. Thus, progress is made towards seeing reading more as a cultural construction rather than simply a form of primary socialisation.

Usually the tension around school reading and the negative attitudes it creates come from the difficulties adolescents have meeting school expectations. First, schools too often provide adolescents with short extracts to read, which affects their reading skills when they are required to read longer texts; that is one of the most important differentiating factors in the prediction of school success and the creation of reading habits. Second, adolescents need to share preferences in order to become a community of readers, hence the success of book forums on the internet, which more fully satisfy aspects of socialisation that are not catered for within normal school reading time. Third, adolescents need more background knowledge and bases for prediction than they often possess, not only to understand the texts recommended by the school, but also those they have already read. It is not a question of schools acting in a demagogic way but of acknowledging personal reading preferences (Rouxel, 2005) and developing more appropriate teaching approaches such as:

- Organising multiple ways of reading within the school and increasing the time for reading to give all adolescents more opportunities to read. The school can then play a compensatory role. Combining multiple ways of reading improves attitudes and provides a wider variety of texts, which enriches the reading horizons of all readers.
- Selecting the corpus by taking into account the personal reading practices of young people. This means including, and knowing how to take advantage of, the various corpuses found on the frontiers of this type of reading, for example works that include text and image in a way that allows for less linear and more fragmented reading; genres that have a strong fictional and audio-visual presence; texts that include artistic demand, popular tastes and the specificity of their times.
- Guiding the evolutionary process of corpus fusion, reading forms and practices. This means: promoting activities of shared reading; attending to the genuine response of readers about the experience of belonging to a reading community; intensifying and improving mediation that leads to more distanced and evaluative reading; articulating learning experiences in sequences that make sense and that teach strategies in an explicit manner.

It is essential to delve into the interrelationship between school reading and personal reading in order to understand better one of the most unknown aspects of this field: the desire to read fiction. We must also continue to investigate how to create links between the reader and the text, links that seem to be the doorway to more sophisticated forms of reading. This necessarily involves expanding the plurality of reading modes to make the boundaries between school reading and personal reading more permeable. Technologies play an important role in this expansion because although we know that reading frequency has not yet been changed by young people in social networks, it is true that new forms of fiction (Manresa and Real, 2015), new ways of reading and new ways of relating to fictional reading and writing have appeared on the internet and they must be taken into account in this line of enquiry regarding the relationship between reading in the school classroom and the cultural uses of reading in society.

Notes

1 '[S]euls les titres lus pour soi ou perçus comme "personnels" permettent de mesurer de manière pertinent cet intérêt pour la lecture et son évolution au fil des ans' (*translated into English by Mireia Manresa*).

2 Language immersion programmes were first implemented in Canada in the late 1970s and are characterised as proposals aimed at an entire population and not just linguistic minorities.
3 An English translation of the Danish term.

References

Aliagas, C. (2009). Adolescents' insights on the academic reading practices in high school: A case study with a school clique. *The International Journal of Reading*, 6 (16), 293–307.

Alvermann, D. (Ed.), (2002). *Adolescents and Literacies in a Digital World*. New York: Peter Lang.

Baudelot, C., Cartier, M. and Detrez, C. (1999). *Et Pourtant Ils Lisent...* Paris: Éditions du Seuil.

Cliff Hodges, G. (2010). Rivers of reading: Using critical incident collages to learn about adolescent readers and their readership. *English in Education*, 3 (44), 181–200.

de Singly, F. (1989). *Lire à 12 Ans. Une Enquête sur les Lectures des Adolescents*. Paris: Nathan.

de Singly, F. (1993). Les jeunes et la lecture. *Les Dossiers Education et Formation*, 24, Ministère de l'Education nationale et de la Culture, Direction de l'Evaluation et de la Prospective.

Eco, U. (1994). *Six Walks in the Fictional Woods*. Cambridge, MA: Harvard University Press.

Eurostat (2016). *Europe 2020 Education Indicators in 2015*. Retrieved on 23 October 2017 from: www.ecestaticos.com/file/69c31da60800a47d9273c73f260806e0/1461753274.pdf

Fittipaldi, M. (2013). *¿Qué han de Saber los Niños sobre Literatura? Conocimientos Literarios y Tipos de Actuaciones que Permiten Progresar en la Competencia Literaria*. PhD dissertation, Universitat Autònoma de Barcelona.

Frank, A. (1952). *Anne Frank: The Diary of a Young Girl*. New York: Doubleday.

Fry, D. (1985). *Children Talk about Books: Seeing Themselves as Readers*. Philadelphia: Open University Press.

Hall, C. and Coles, M. (1999). *Children's Reading Choices*. London: Routledge.

Hersent, J.F. (2000). *Sociologie de la Lecture en France: État des Lieux*. Paris: Direction du livre et de la lecture. Retrieved 27 October 2017 from: www.culture.gouv.fr/culture/dll/sociolog.rtf

Jenkinson, A.J. (1940). *What Do Boys and Girls Read? An Investigation into Reading Habits with Some Suggestions about the Teaching of Literature in Secondary and Senior Schools*. London: Methuen.

Krashen, S. (2004a). Free voluntary reading: New research, applications and controversies. Paper presented at the Regional English Language Centre (RELC) Conference, Singapore, April, 2004. Retrieved on 27 October 2017 from: www.sdkrashen.com/content/articles/singapore.pdf

Krashen, S. (2004b). *The Power of Reading: Insights from the Research*. Westport, CT: Libraries Unlimited.

Leveratto, J. M. and Leontsini, M. (2008). *Internet et la Sociabilité Littéraire*. Paris: Bibliothèque Publique d'Information.

Manresa, M. (2013). *L'Univers Lector Adolescent: Dels Hàbits de Lectura a la Intervenció Educativa*. Barcelona: Rosa Sensat.

Manresa, M. and Durán, C. (2009). Entre países: La acción educativa en nuestro entorno. In T. Colomer (coord.) *Lecturas Adolescentes*. Barcelona: Graó.

Manresa, M. and Real, N. (Eds.), (2015). *Digital Literature for Children: Texts, Readers and Educational Practices*. New York: Peter Lang.

Meek, M. (1988). *How Texts Teach What Readers Learn*. Stroud: Thimble Press.

Meek, M. (1990). Why response? In M. Hayhoe and S. Parker (Eds.), *Reading and Response*. Milton Keynes: Open University Press, pp. 1–12.

Munita, F. (2014). *El Mediador Escolar de Lectura Literaria: Un Estudio del Espacio de Encuentro entre Prácticas Didácticas, Sistemas de Creencias y Trayectorias Personales de Lectura*. PhD dissertation, Universitat Autònoma de Barcelona.

Petit, M. (1999). *Nuevos Acercamientos a los Jóvenes y la Lectura*. Mexico: Fondo de Cultura Económica.

Robine, N. (1984). *Les Jeunes Travailleurs et la Lecture*. Paris: La Documentation Française.

Robine, N. (2000). *Lire des Livres en France des Années 1930 à 2000*. Paris: Electre-Éditions du Cercle de la Librairie.

Robine, N. (2005). Les réseaux de lecture des adolescents. *Lecture Jeune*, 116, 31–39.

Rouxel, A. (2004). Autobiographies de lecteurs à l'entrée au lycée. *Le Français Aujourd'hui*, 147 (4), 57–66.

Rouxel, A. (2005). *Lectures Cursives: Quel Accompagnement?* Paris: Delagrave.

Sarland, C. (1991). *Young People Reading: Culture and Response*. Milton Keynes: Open University Press.

Schön, E. (1993). La fabrication du lecteur. In M. Chaudron and F. de Singly (Eds.), *Identité, Lecture, Écriture*. Paris: Centre Georges Pompidou-Bibliothèque Publique d'Information, pp. 17–44.

Whitehead, F., Capey, A.C. and Maddren, W. (1977). *Children and Their Books*. Basingstoke: Macmillan Education.

8

YOUNG PEOPLE READING IN UGANDA

Making connections between literature and reality

Rebecca Nambi

MAP 8

In 2012–2015, I undertook my doctoral research. It was a case study exploring the challenges and possibilities of using learner-centred pedagogy (LCP) to teach literacy in a secondary school in Uganda. According to UNESCO (2014), the youth literacy rate in sub-Saharan Africa at that time was 69%. In Uganda it was 48.3% (UNEB, 2012). These figures were in sharp contrast to the global youth literacy rate of 89.4% (UNESCO, 2014). Critical literature I had read showed that LCP could enhance literacy proficiency among students. Within my research, I explored LCP in three ways. I wanted to learn more about the teachers' perspectives, the students' perspectives and the impact of the school on this particular form of pedagogy. In this chapter, however, I focus on one small part of the overall study, namely the students' perspectives on reading. I explore how some participants in my study located reading resources, what kinds of reading choices they made and – in particular – the ways in which some young people navigated the gaps between the expectations of the curriculum and their personal experiences when they were studying a literary text. I was interested to know to what extent exploring personal responses might allow them to express ideas they would have normally not raised in the classroom.

Adolescent readers in Uganda

Students join secondary school in Uganda at the age of 12, when they have acquired and mastered certain sub-skills of reading. For example, they can read whole simple books or novels, passages and simple poems. These reading skills however are more influenced by academic needs than personal interests (Jönsson and Olsson, 2008; Kyeyune, 2003; Parry, 2010). Academic needs in turn are guided by the Ugandan National Curriculum and examinations, which are used as yardsticks to determine whether a student proceeds to the next level of education or not. This reading situation, in which students mainly read for academic purposes, suggests that their reading is restricted by the curriculum and hence they hardly read for personal purposes. Although students can gain tremendously from reading competently for academic purposes, it can also be argued that personal reading goes a long way towards enhancing their interpretive skills and academic achievements. Moje, Overby, Tysvaer and Morris (2008), in their study about what motivates adolescents to read, argue that despite curriculum prescriptions, adolescents still choose for themselves to read books related to their own social networks and needs, which means that it is important for teachers to explore their reading interests beyond the school context.

In Ugandan secondary schools, students usually have the opportunity to select specific subjects of interest as they train for future careers. Sports, drama and practical subjects such as woodwork are attractive to many adolescents. Their commitment to and motivation for reading then become subjected to the diverse programmes available at the school. Moje (2002) argues that researchers should examine the different contexts in which adolescents read texts to address some of the challenges they may be facing. In particular, she stresses the need to focus on the impact of the school context, whether that be curriculum, values or teaching approaches.

School curricula in most parts of the world have a singular focus that leads students to passing examinations. In developing countries such as Uganda the curriculum is dominated by a range of subjects, most of which are not related to students' local social experiences (Vavrus et al., 2013; Verspoor, 2008). Curricula and syllabi usually prescribe specific items that the student should master as they prepare to take examinations at the end of a given course. Hence, by implication, the study of literature tends to be limited to specific aspects of a text, in particular those that are perceived as examinable. Reading for examinations affords students opportunities to improve their reading skills as they memorise and interpret key information. However, the risk is that students may fail to make connections between texts and their personal experiences. Part of what this chapter attempts is to establish how the Ugandan students who participated in the study perceived study of a literary text in the classroom in relation to their individual experiences and contexts.

In Uganda, English, which is a core subject, and Literature in English, which is an optional subject, provide major avenues for reading for secondary school students. Local languages such as Luganda and Runyakitara, and international languages such as French and German, are taught as optional subjects but these classes usually have very limited numbers of students. Hence formal reading and the learning of reading skills among adolescents are mainly catered for in English and Literature in English.

The reading materials

Scarcity of reading materials is a major challenge cited in the literature regarding the teaching of reading in developing countries (Vavrus et al., 2013;Verspoor, 2008). Books are costly and the schools often pass on the burden of acquisition to parents. Moreover, in some schools the effective use of books is hindered by the need to safeguard them, perhaps because of accountability to the school, local administrators or even parents. Verspoor (2008) points out that in many schools in sub-Saharan Africa there is usually a lack of variety of books and teachers often resort to the old titles that they used when they were in school themselves. All these challenges are compounded by the fact that most reading materials are imported into developing countries so they rarely reflect the local context of students. In Uganda, in particular, the government makes some effort to provide reading materials especially at the primary school level to support the thematic curriculum (Kyeyune, 2011). However, the adolescent reader in Uganda has to rely mainly on class notes from teachers due to the examination-oriented teaching approaches and limited access to books (Magara and Batambuze, 2005).

The International Reading Association (IRA, 2012), among other indicators of literacy for adolescents, suggested that they should be able to read multiple texts in different forms. In my own study, it was therefore important to me to explore how learners accessed a variety of texts beyond the classroom and the role of the school in providing these texts.

Research design

In my case study, I collected qualitative data for a period of six months to explore the challenges and possibilities of using LCP to teach literacy at a school I have called Bakira Senior School (BSS), an urban secondary school in Uganda. I adopted an interpretivist research design in order to engage with the context using naturalistic research methods (Cohen et al., 2011; Denscombe, 2007). I viewed BSS as a sociocultural context with human beings who participated interactively to make meaning in their specific setting. The research context was a multifaceted space that needed to be explored from different angles using multiple research methods to access participants' perceptions of reading (Simons, 2009). The data and findings presented in this chapter are from the group interviews with students. The groups were composed of five to six students and, although they were a small percentage of the large classes they came from, their role was to provide further embedded insights into students' experiences of reading to enrich data from other research methods such as lesson observations and documentary evidence. The major advantage of interviewing learners in groups was that some of the questions they responded to related back to their lesson content but further enhanced their interaction with texts.

Data was condensed into manageable chunks and then coded according to the key concepts that arose from the reviewed literature (Miles et al., 2014). At this level, the data seemed to address the research questions in general ways but did not reveal the sociocultural nuances that might explain the participants' reading choices. For this reason, I also adopted discourse analysis to examine sections of the data further. Selected categories of data were analysed to establish how the social realities of the participants' reading activities were represented in their use of language (Gee, 2014). The emerging patterns from this examination helped to strengthen the evidence.

The students and the texts

The students, whose reading choices and experiences I present here were aged between 12 and 18 at the time of data collection and they attended Senior One (S1) to Senior Six (S6) respectively.[1] My first acquaintance with them was during the lessons I observed and my impression was that they were respectful of their teachers and usually followed instructions. A large percentage of them seemed eager to give answers to the questions that were asked, volunteered to read aloud or dramatised roles in the classroom.

Several texts were read during the period of data collection by the different classes, but for the current chapter I focus on the play *Lysistrata* by Aristophanes (2011), in order to explore S6 students' personal experiences and responses to a literature text. *Lysistrata* was one of the set texts on the Literature in English syllabus set by the Uganda National Examinations Board for 2009–2013. In the play, Lysistrata is the major character. After decades of endless wars that take away husbands, brothers and sons, Lysistrata persuades her fellow womenfolk to deny their husbands any sexual pleasures until they stop the war. She invites women from different parts of Greece to be part of this plan. After a farcical process where men threaten and beg while the women provoke them and work hard to remain aloof, an agreement is reached and the war is stopped. Lysistrata is triumphant.

Relating *Lysistrata* to modern society

The findings show that while some of these 18-year-old S6 students could relate parts of the text to their personal and community experiences, several of them questioned the relevance of the play to a modern society (given that they knew it had first been performed in 411 BCE). They applied critical skills to analyse the appropriateness of the text to modern society. For instance, the following extract is from the group interview transcript. It is a response to the question about the contemporary relevance of *Lysistrata*. In the examples I use here and below, I identify the students as either female or male mainly because their arguments are strongly drawn along lines of gender identities.

> STUDENT B [MALE]: For example, the act of women refusing to sleep with their husbands would not work in our society today. With things like homosexuality and the changing morality it would be difficult. During the war and at that time people valued sex, they had ceremonies involving sex and some of them were religious. It would work there. But we are living in a generation where some people are gay, where some believe that when you remain celibate you are pleasing God, we have prostitutes, we have people that masturbate it just does not work now. People do not hold sex in such a high esteem today, people do not even have to be married to have sex.

The student above outlines a number of reasons why some of the themes of *Lysistrata* would not be relevant in Uganda, which suggests that he had thought about this systematically and pragmatically in relation to the world around him. The student was clearly aware of alternative avenues for sex, probably from what he had read elsewhere or from what he observed in his society. For instance, when he says that some people would rather practise celibacy he could be echoing the religious beliefs emphasised by the school. However, when he suggests homosexuality as an alternative, one needs to pause and ponder further on this submission. Generally, it can be argued, there is little tolerance of homosexuality in Uganda. For example, homosexuality is still an unwelcome topic in schools and whenever it arises, teachers, learners and parents usually condemn it in the strongest terms possible. Despite this negativity, Student B above still thinks about it as a viable option as opposed to the action taken by the women in the play. In addition, the students in BSS were very committed to the teachings of Christianity as part and parcel of the school ethos. In this instance, however, Student B seems to step out of the moral teachings of religion and the expectations of the curriculum to acknowledge that in his contemporary society, people do not need to be married to be involved in sexual relationships, as is the case in the play. Therefore, it is clear that this student was engaging in some form of critical literacy by questioning the status quo presented in the play (Janks, 2010).

A number of factors could explain the atypical opinion given by the learner above. First, the students' sociocultural backgrounds and personal achievements (at least in the extract from the transcript that follows) seemed to influence their responses to texts. Social beliefs such as gender roles and religious inclination were at the core of most students' responses. Sometimes the content of the texts appeared to contradict their social beliefs; at other times they relied on what their teachers told them and drew a line between their personal experiences and the expectations of the teacher or the curriculum. Below is a part of a discussion during the group interview which illustrates both these positions:

RN: One of the women says: 'But dearest Lysistrata! How can women do a thing so political? We belong at home. Our only armor's our perfumes, our saffron dresses and our little shoes!' Imagine you are twenty-first-century Lysistrata: what would be your personal response to this woman?

STUDENT A [FEMALE]: The modern woman is more confident, she has less self-doubt, she is so sure about her position in modern society and she knows what she is capable of.

STUDENT E [MALE]: Talking about rights, for example women working, I think we need to review because with the modern working woman there are more divorces, the women have neglected their roles, for instance, leaving the children at home with maids. One of the issues leading to divorce is that when women are given the chance to work they challenge men and they stop taking their roles seriously. They go away from their role as stated in the Bible of being submissive.

STUDENT D [FEMALE]: As a modern woman, if this woman said this to me I would be shocked. With the emancipation and all a lot has changed.

STUDENT B [MALE]: When women are given these positions of power they start challenging the men and men do not want to be challenged. Men have to be bosses it is in their nature.

STUDENT A [FEMALE]: I can be a good wife but still continue working. There is no way I would stay at home. Then what is the use of going to school?

RN: Does your sympathy lie with the women or the men in the play?

STUDENT C [MALE]: With the women obviously. But this is because we follow the writer's opinion and what the teacher said.

An analysis of the exchange above shows that each member of the group has strong beliefs about their gender roles. What is particularly outstanding in their exchange is that the girls take the side of emancipation while the boys seem to be reluctant to support them. The girls' experiences and perceptions seem to be informed by what could be referred to as personal achievement in their lives so far. For example, they refer to modernity, the fact that the world has moved on and the role of education as reasons for them not to be submissive. The boys, on the other hand, appear to experience the text through their cultural lenses and one of them cross-references his experience with the Bible. They take a patriarchal stance that men are the givers, bosses and reviewers of situations while women are meant to be submissive, unserious and home carers. Despite the awareness of these possible readings into the text that seem to originate from personal beliefs, the students still recognise the fact that they have to limit their analysis to what the teacher (and/or the syllabus) appears to recommend.

The influence of the students' social beliefs on their interpretations of the text in the examples that have been used in this section offers some insightful points about how some young students in Uganda read and interpret a literary text. For instance, although some of the students seem to be doubtful about the relevance of the text to their contexts, the very weaknesses they identify in it seem to make them question, interrogate and affirm their own beliefs. The girls who participated in the exchange above, interrogate the relegated roles for girls, while the boys appear to defend the same. It can therefore be argued that some students have the ability to relate literary content to their contextual realities (gender roles, roles as children and religious obligations in society) despite the fact that the curriculum appears to limit their interpretations. While the exchange above seems to be at odds with the compliant roles assigned to girls (as some of the boys point out), it illustrates that students do carry some degree of agency when interpreting the texts they read (Alvermann, 2008; Moje, 2002).

Students' awareness of available reading resources

All the students who participated in the group interviews showed a high awareness of the availability of reading materials in their school. They had knowledge of how to locate books and other resources from the library. During group interviews, students competently described the library procedures and schedules, which resonated with what the school librarians also said during my interviews with them. There was evidence that some of the students transferred the knowledge of the library procedures into practice, whereas some students were selective in how to use the two school libraries as the example below shows:

STUDENT D, S3: You have to have a library card but borrowing of books is mainly done in the afternoon starting at 2pm and returning them is in the morning hours. You get your library card then you are given a small paper where you write your name and registration number then you place them in your library card then you give it to the librarian and they give you the book. We all have library cards.

It is not clear from the statement how or whether the students located actual information in the texts and whether all students accessed the library on a regular basis. The fact that some students were aware of the library resources and the system of accessing the books in the library was a building block for reading within the context of BSS because as Wray and Lewis (2000) argue, it suggested that students had the ability to locate and use information that in the long run could enhance their reading levels by supporting what they learned in the classroom. Jönsson and Olsson (2008) document the poor state of libraries in Uganda and the fact that students rarely appreciate the library cataloguing information; hence it is important to acknowledge that, as my research showed, some young readers in Uganda do have the ability to access and utilise library resources, rather than overgeneralising.

The issue of library awareness needed to be qualified further, however. For example how did students balance their time between the library, other school activities and their busy lesson schedules that started at 8am and ended at 4.30pm? Furthermore, how did they negotiate the limited library space? These two factors seemed to pose challenges of time and space allocated to reading activities at BSS. Analysed data revealed that individual students who attached significance to reading utilised different free periods such as the tea break, the lunch break and the period before they left school, in order to read. As noted by Student A, S2: 'I read newspapers from the school library. From 4.30 to 5.10 we are allowed to borrow and read newspapers.' Other factors such as examinations often influenced the times they read as one student noted: 'For me during school time I only read textbooks from the library but during holidays after exams I just pick Luganda stories' (Student D, S3). Reading textbooks supplemented students' classwork, while reading newspapers could improve their vocabulary and knowledge about topical issues.

More important, however, is that the data shows students consciously allocated time to reading, even outside their school schedule. Although most of the students said that they used the school libraries to read, some students said that they found other spaces in which to do so. For example Student E, S3, said: 'At school there is a small place behind the German [laboratory] where I hide and read'. Student C, S5, stated that: 'For the students who stay in the hostels sometimes we go to the libraries outside the school especially at [the nearby health institution] over the weekends.' Student B, S6, noted:

> Sometimes I even read a novel as a lesson is going on. For example, the teacher is teaching and I have hidden the novel in my notebook or under the desk or I change places and I sit at the back.

Hiding to read or finding spaces outside the school could suggest that the students wanted to control their reading space, perhaps to complement the limited library and classroom spaces. On the other hand, what students such as the one from S6 read privately may not be linked to the syllabus and hence could be perceived as a waste of class time. However, reading privately can help students to consolidate prior knowledge from classroom interactions, as suggested by Wray and Lewis (2000) when they state (albeit in relation to non-fiction reading) that 'remembering is improved by revisiting the information one is trying to remember … This may involve restructuring information into different formats … and using it in different contexts' (23). In addition, the students' responses show how they negotiate the multiple subcultures within the secondary school context to create personal spaces for reading.

The variety in students' reading interests is noteworthy. They suggest that students engage with other literacies in their social environments, such as searching for information online and reading magazines, and that these literacies are not left outside the classroom. In the same way, despite the fact that my findings largely revealed the central role of the teacher and the curriculum in the literacy practices of the students, it can be argued that some of the students at BSS strongly complemented their classroom reading with resources outside the curriculum.

The fact that some students accessed a variety of texts from within and outside the classroom, is a positive indicator for adolescent literacy as recommended by the IRA (2012) and the National Council of Teachers of English (2006). The choice made by some students to read books written in local languages is particularly enlightening about the extent of students' personal interests because although Luganda was taught at BSS, these particular students did not study the subject. Also, it is instructive to note how different activities (being read to in Luganda when young and their preparation for a religious event that is conducted in Luganda) also seem to continue to influence students' reading choices. This echoes some ideas that arose in the reviewed literature in the work of Moje et al. (2008) and Stevens and Bean (2007), that reading is a social action that is influenced by different subcultures and beliefs that students develop over time.

Students' reading choices

However, the data suggests that students' reading choices were still mainly influenced by the prescriptions of the curriculum. In an interview with the S1 class, I noted that the students used phrases such as 'I think' or 'maybe' when asked about who chose the books they read in class. These phrases suggest that they were uncertain about the selection process. They were at the receiving end of the syllabus without any particular input and they trusted their teachers to make the best choices, perhaps because they had never been asked to make any decisions about their subjects themselves. Data from lesson observations showed that most of the students read and completed the literature texts before the lessons and they responded knowledgeably to the teacher's questions about the texts. In two years the S2 class had read five literature texts. The students who participated in the group interview collectively cited *Orphan Boy* (Ocita, 2002) as the most interesting text because as Student D, S2, said: 'It was very short and the characters were Ugandan.' The book has the least complicated plot and simplest language compared to the others they had read. These students' contributions suggested that their reading choices were influenced by the ability to relate to the book in terms of setting and perhaps the accessibility of the language.

The school's influence on students' reading choices was prominent when more than three-quarters of the participants said that they read the Bible on a regular basis. Student A, S3, stated thus: 'We all read the Bible. Reading the Bible is our culture in [BSS].' The use of the word 'culture' is very telling of the attachment that this particular student has to religion and the assumption that everyone in the school reads the Bible. The school mission, core values and vision all rotate around religious ideals. It can be argued that the same ideals appeared to influence students' reading choices, perhaps to keep up with the school image and expectations, which could be translated to mean moral or ethical values. Student A, S5, stated: 'I read inspirational books and stories with moral messages.' However, since Student A also said that 'When I wake up I first read the Bible and even before going to bed', there is arguably a strong influence from the family – perhaps even the community – as well.

Some students were interested in reading books written in local languages, which further emphasised the extent to which their reading choices varied. The major reason for their choice was that they were curious about Luganda in particular since it was the common language they used outside the classrooms. Luganda is not a first language for all the students at BSS, although it was widely spoken by most of them. Other students' interest could simply have been down to curiosity. However, some said they had been read to in local languages by their parents or by teachers when in primary schools and had thus sustained their interest in them. A number of students also said that they had learnt to read a local language as they were being prepared for confirmation by the school pastor. Some of the local literature mentioned included *Njabala* (a popular local story told in Luganda language), *Basajja Mivule* (Mpalanyi, 1984) and *Zinunula Omunaku* (Kawere, 1954). The books cited by the students are some of the most popular in Luganda. It was not clear whether the students could read the local language fluently, because I focused specifically on the English and Literature in English throughout my study. However, books written in English were the first choice for the students, possibly because it was the language of instruction and communication in BSS.

Conclusion

Twaweza (an organisation that works in Uganda, Kenya and Tanzania to assess children's learning achievements, especially in areas of literacy and numeracy) begins a recent document by stating that 'The results of numerous studies assessing learning in children attending basic education in developing countries show that, while millions of children are able to attend school in these countries, schooling does not always lead to learning' (Twaweza, 2017). In addition, some research reports such as Jönsson and Olsson (2008) and Parry (2010) appear to confirm the educational challenges faced by young people especially in Uganda. My own research established that the examination-oriented secondary curriculum had the potential to delimit reading choices and space available to the students. However, as my study suggests, and as Parry (2010) also argues, it is not enough to accept that students often fail to transfer and apply skills between their academic reading and personal domains outside the school. The need to relate classroom content to the students' personal experiences cannot be overemphasised. In my study, the young people's personal responses to texts such as *Lysistrata* appeared to be suppressed in order to meet examination requirements. But, as the evidence suggests, the students here could already read this literary text independently as well, so what is required is for teachers to provide them with the opportunity to bring their ideas to the fore during lessons. Using exploratory questioning techniques and creating an environment conducive for discussions can help to activate students' prior knowledge before the teacher emphasises the interpretation apparently favoured by examinations. The extra interpretations based on students' personal contexts do not in any way work in opposition to the formal approaches; on the contrary, they serve to strengthen them.

English language in Uganda is greatly appreciated but mainly as a means of access to superior employment and a brighter future. Using English appropriately is associated with a good education and it is common practice in many middle-class households in that country to use English as opposed to local languages as a way of communication. Therefore, the suggestion by some of the participants in this study that they prefer reading Luganda texts somewhat contradicts this practice. However, in addition to illustrating that there is some hope for local languages being appreciated by the younger generation, this evidence also affirms the argument made by Moje et al. (2008) that sometimes the need to develop racial identity influences young students' reading choices. It suggests teachers need continuously to draw on students' local cultural contexts when analysing texts. In addition, they need to encourage students to make reading choices outside the prescribed curriculum that they do not have to hide.

Finally, it is often argued that reading should expose young people to a variety of texts, and for students to be competent readers their ability to read should match their cognitive development. In other words, recognising words on paper is not an end in itself; young people should have the ability to move their reading forward to accommodate more complex texts. Therefore, the reading practices of the young people in this chapter are worth documenting because reading in Uganda is still underdeveloped despite efforts in educational reforms to support its improvement. However, as practitioners in teaching and researching reading in the Ugandan context, we need to continue exploring students' reading interests, abilities and common text choices in order to provide appropriate support for them.

Note

1 The classes in secondary schools in Uganda are labelled from Senior One to Senior Six. The word Senior is similar in meaning to Grade or Form. The capital letter 'S' is used to abbreviate the word Senior, thus S1, S2, etc. is used from this point in the chapter onwards.

References

Alvermann, D. E. (2008). Why bother theorizing adolescents' online literacies for classroom practice and research? *Journal of Adolescent & Adult Literacy*, 52 (1), 8–19.

Aristophanes. (2011). *Lysistrata*. Nairobi: East African Educational Publishers Ltd.

Cohen, L., Manion, L. and Morrison, K. (2011). *Research Methods in Education* (7th ed.). New York: Routledge.

Denscombe, M. (2007). *The Good Research Guide* (3rd ed.). McGraw-Hill: Open University Press.

Gee, J.P. (2014). *How To Do Discourse Analysis: A Toolkit* (2nd ed.). New York: Routledge.

IRA, International Reading Association. (2012). *Adolescent Literacy: A Position Statement of the International Reading Association*. Newark: IRA.

Janks, H. (2010). *Literacy and Power*. London: Routledge.

Jönsson, A. and Olsson, J. (2008). Reading culture and literacy in Uganda: The case of the 'Children's Reading Tent'. Retrieved 24 April 2013, from http://bada.hb.se/bitstream/2320/3405/1/08-7.pdf

Kawere, E. K. N. (1954). *Zinunula Omunaku*. Nairobi: Eagle Press.

Kyeyune, R. (2003). Challenges of using English as a medium of instruction in multilingual contexts: A view from Ugandan classrooms. *Language, Culture and Curriculum*, 16 (2), 173–184.

Kyeyune, R. (2011). *Learning to Teach Reading and Mathematics and its Influence on Practice in Uganda: Uganda's Country Report*. Kampala: Makerere University.

Magara, E. and Batambuze, C. (2005). Towards a reading culture for Uganda. *African Journal of Library, Archive and Information Science*, 15 (1), 35–42.

Miles, M. B., Huberman, A. M. and Saldana, J. (2014). *Qualitative Data Analysis: A Methods Sourcebook* (3rd ed.). London: Sage.

Moje, E. B. (2002). Re-framing adolescent literacy research for new times: Studying youth as a resource. *Reading Research and Instruction*, 41 (3), 211–228.

Moje, E., Overby, M., Tysvaer, N. and Morris, K. (2008). The complex world of adolescent literacy: myths, motivations and mysteries. *Harvard Educational Review*, 78 (1), 107–154.

Mpalanyi, S. E. K. (1984). *Basajja Mivule*. Kampala: Mubaka Printers Limited.

National Council of Teachers of English. (2006). NCTE Principles of Adolescent Literacy Reform: A Policy Research Brief. Urbana, IL: NCTE.

Ocita, J. (2002). *Orphan Boy*. Kampala: Fountain Publishers.

Parry, K. (2010). African literacies: Which of them matter, and why? *Reading and Writing*, 1 (1), 9–22.

Simons, H. (2009). *Case Study Research in Practice*. London: Sage.

Stevens, L. P. and Bean, T.W. (2007). *Critical Literacy: Context, Research, and Practice in the K-12 Classroom*. London: Sage.

Twaweza. (2017). *What Makes a Curriculum Effective in Promoting Children's Learning? A Concept Note for Analyzing Basic Curriculum Effectiveness in East Africa*. Dar es Salaam: Tanzania. Retrieved on 28 October 2017 from: www.twaweza.org/uploads/files/ConceptNote Draft08102015mc+rc.pdf

UNEB, Uganda National Examination Board. (2012). *The Achievement of S2 Students in English Language, Mathematics and Biology: NAPE Report*. Kampala: UNEB.

UNESCO, United Nations Educational, Scientific and Cultural Organization. (2014). *Teaching and Learning: Achieving Equality for All*. Paris: UNESCO.

Vavrus, F., Bartlett, L. and Salema V. (2013). Introduction: teaching and researching in tension. In F. Vavrus and L. Bartlett (Eds.), *Teaching in Tension: International Pedagogies, National Policies, and Teachers' Practices in Tanzania*. Rotterdam: Sense Publishers, pp. 1–22.

Verspoor, A. M. (2008). *At the Crossroads: Choices for Secondary Education in Sub-Saharan Africa*. Washington, DC: World Bank.

Wray, D. and Lewis, M. (2000). Extending literacy: Learning and teaching. In M. Lewis and D. Wray (Eds.), *Literacy in the Secondary School*. London: David Fulton Publishers Ltd, pp. 15–28.

9

EXPLORING POST-16 LITERATURE IN ENGLISH IN A MALAYSIAN CLASSROOM

A hermeneutic phenomenological perspective

Jia Wei Lim

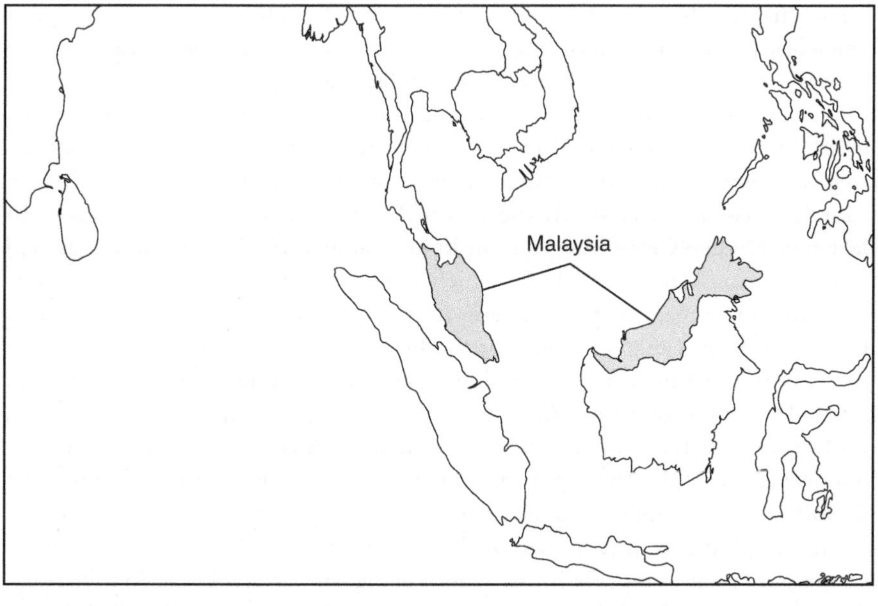

MAP 9

Introduction

This chapter is about research into teacher and student experiences of the literature classroom. As an Advanced-level English literature teacher in Malaysia, I thoroughly enjoyed interacting with students within and beyond the classroom as we discussed the plot, characters and themes of various texts. However, as the years passed, I began to be dissatisfied with my teaching. I was especially struck by how differently I could feel after a particular class: sometimes I left the classroom feeling elated and at other times, utterly disheartened; sometimes I felt that my students could truly grasp what I had to say, but at other times they seemed to struggle tremendously. In trying to find reasons for those differences, I realised that I did not know how to reflect on the effectiveness or impact of my teaching, neither had I given much thought to the nature of teaching and learning the subject itself. Thus, I grew interested in this area of research due to a desire to better understand literary pedagogy.

This chapter first describes the methodological framework I constructed for my research, which was based on hermeneutic phenomenological principles. I approached post-16 literature as a complex phenomenon mainly experienced by teachers and students in the literature classroom. In an attempt to conceptualise literature classroom experiences, I decided to focus on how teachers and students respond to and interact with each other in reading literature texts. Although I included individual readings in my study, here I focus chiefly on social readings of literature such as those that develop out of classroom discussions and activities.

The chapter also provides an example of how I applied this methodological framework to my data. I have used the same framework on two occasions. The first was for my research on two A-level English literature classes that I observed in England and the second for my doctoral study on the development of post-16 English literature in Malaysia. In this chapter, the selected data sample is from the latter. It is one of many interesting observations I made of a Form 6 Literature in English class in Malaysia. At the end of Form 6, students sit for the post-16 Malaysian Higher Certificate of Education examination, locally known as *Sijil Tinggi Pelajaran Malaysia* (STPM), which is equivalent to England's Advanced-level. Students engage with a variety of texts over the course of their STPM studies. The STPM text selection for the literature syllabus currently consists of a collection of 19 poems by a range of poets such as William Wordsworth and Seamus Heaney mostly from Anglophone countries, a group of 12 short stories by Malaysian writers, two plays (one by William Shakespeare and another by a modern American playwright) and, finally, two novels. The observation that I include in this chapter took place in a school that has had a long history of teaching English literature at post-16 level. Indeed, the principal whom I spoke to expressed a sense of pride in the school being one of the few in Malaysia that offers Literature in English as an option for the STPM examination. The literature class for that year had 16 students and Ms Alice was their English literature teacher. This particular observation took place towards the end of their first few months in Form 6 and students were in the midst of revising the poems they had covered that term for the upcoming school examination. In this class, Ms Alice, instructs two students, Yusof and Johari, to be literature teachers. It is an act of role reversal that reveals interesting conceptualisations regarding literature teachers and students. By using discourse analysis to analyse this particular classroom observation, I demonstrate how I used my methodological framework to explore literature teacher and student classroom experiences. Finally, I reflect on the advantages and limitations of the framework with suggestions for future application.

Researching the social sphere of the classroom

Research in reading is a complex undertaking as it can be approached either as a personal activity between one reader and a text or an activity that is done with other individuals as well as a text in a social sphere, such as a classroom (Choo, 2013). This chapter focuses on the latter, specifically post-16 literature as a subject in school. The distinction between a social and individual sphere is echoed in Rosenblatt's (1988) work on a transactional theory of literature. Various other studies have argued that teaching and learning literature occur in a social context that involves a complex negotiation of interpreted meaning between teacher, student and text (Yandell, 2014). Like Yandell, I view the literature classroom as a context where the social identities of a literature teacher and student are acted out in a negotiation of meaning that centres on the act of reading a text. It is an act of meaning-making that also taps into students' aesthetic reading experiences. In his book, *The Social Construction of Meaning: Reading Literature in Urban English Classrooms* (2014), Yandell conducts multiple observations over time in two English classrooms where teachers and students form interpretive communities as they engage with various literature texts. He demonstrates that focusing on teacher and student interaction in the classroom can produce rich insights into teacher and student negotiations of interpreted meaning.

The focus of my research, however, extends a little beyond social negotiations of meaning; I also explore teacher and student conceptualisations and actualisations of literature as a school subject. I suggest that teacher and student interactions, which may include meaning-making as well as other use of discourse within the classroom, do influence how teachers and students conceptualise the subject. For example, even if a teacher tells students that open discussions are encouraged in class, whether or not the discussions happen and what form those discussions take could contribute to teacher and student conceptualisations of literature. Thus, my interest between what is intended and what actually happens in the classroom prompted me to frame teacher and student interaction within the issue of curriculum implementation.

Drawing from hermeneutic phenomenology

Classroom experience and syllabus implementation can be researched in numerous ways. For reasons I hope to make clear in this section, I chose to explore the interactions between the syllabus, teacher and student using a hermeneutic phenomenological approach. I undertook a naturalistic interpretive study that rejected the idea that human behaviour is predictable and governed by law; instead, I wanted to emphasise the importance of understanding the social world of individuals involved in the study and an acknowledgement that the researcher is not entirely objective or separated from the research (Cohen et al., 2011).

Max van Manen has written extensively on the use of phenomenology in educational research. A former school teacher in the Netherlands and currently professor emeritus at the University of Alberta in recognition of his work in research methods, pedagogy and curriculum studies, his work on phenomenology is driven by the desire to bridge the pragmatic North American approach to education and research with an interpretive European approach. In his book *Researching Lived Experience* (1997), he focuses on hermeneutic phenomenology which he argues is:

> a *descriptive* (phenomenological) methodology because it wants to be attentive to how things appear, it wants to let things speak for themselves; it is an *interpretive* (hermeneutic) methodology because it claims that there are no such things as uninterpreted phenomena … the (phenomenological) 'facts' of lived experience are always already meaningfully (hermeneutically) experienced.
>
> (180–181, emphasis in original)

Adopting a hermeneutic phenomenological framework enabled me to focus on literature as a distinct phenomenon while exploring the subjectivity of individual interpretations of teacher and student experiences of literature. Among the eight hermeneutic phenomenology research principles van Manen (1997) says characterises hermeneutic phenomenology, four are particularly relevant to my research.

(i) The study of lived experience

I explore what literature is by focusing on how it is experienced by teachers and students in the classroom. This focus follows the hermeneutic phenomenological interest in an individual's immediate experience of his or her lifeworld (the environment in which the individual lives) to understand the nature of everyday experience. Van Manen provides examples from his lived experience as a teacher and father in order to illustrate how asking phenomenological questions such as 'what is teaching?' can produce a deeper reflective understanding of the said phenomenon. Thus, by phenomenologically asking 'what is literature?', I hoped to delve beyond facts about the subject such as what texts are studied and how the subject is structured to explore what the phenomenon of literature is in the lives of teachers and students.

(ii) The importance of consciousness

An important assumption of phenomenology is that consciousness forms the boundary of one's experience. Although phenomenology emphasises immediate experience as it happens in our consciousness, hermeneutic phenomenology recognises that 'reflection on lived experience is always recollective' (van Manen,

1997: 10). As van Manen illustrates, the individual does not consciously conceptualise anger when he or she is angry. It is when the immediate experience of anger is over that the individual can reflect on it and, in doing so, conceptualise it. This hermeneutic phenomenological principle is alluded to in Harding's (1962) efforts to analyse a reader's experience in reading a literature text. In response to the perspective that readers read texts in order to identify with them or as a form of wish fulfilment, Harding (1962) suggests that readers may also take on the role of a spectator where they reflect on what they have read. This reflection brings with it a sense of distance from the text, which is necessary if one were to consciously think about what was read. In the same way, conscious processing of experience necessitates a move away from that initial point of experience.

Thus, what hermeneutic phenomenology endeavours to do is to get as close as possible to that initial point in lived experience. Accepting that one cannot have full access to immediate experience resonates with my study because I do not claim to be able to encompass what the literature phenomenon is in its entirety. Rather, I recognise that my exploration of the phenomenon relies on teacher and student memories and conceptualisations of their experiences in the literature classroom as well as my own interpretations and analysis. However, I believe that this reliance on memory does not detract from the value of my research. In fact, perhaps the value of literature is found precisely in how it is conceptualised in the memory of one's lived experience. Memory is not a 'distortion of the past' but a mediation of it (Gardner, 2010: 108). Although I only involved a few participants in my exploration of literature, their memories are also drawn from collective experiences of the literature classroom, which provided me with glimpses of what literature classrooms were like in the past and are now.

(iii) The study of essences

What phenomenology aims to uncover is 'the internal meaning structures of lived experience' (van Manen, 1997: 11). The focus is on what, in lived experience, distinguishes the studied phenomenon from other phenomena. Phenomenologists believe that these distinctions form the phenomenon's essence. This idea of essence is important because underlying my research interest is the assumption that experiences of teaching and learning literature are different from those of other subjects. Centring my research on the essence of literature also increases the 'objectivity' of my study, which van Manen defines as being 'oriented' and remaining 'true to the object' (ibid.: 20), while being clear that I present a 'subjective', 'unique and personal' orientation to the phenomenon (ibid.).

(iv) The description of experiential meaning

'Phenomenology attempts to explicate the [experiential] meanings as we live them in our everyday existence, our lifeworld' (van Manen, 1997: 11). Hermeneutic phenomenology as a theoretical perspective emphasises different definitions of meaning at different times. The first category of meaning refers to language. It is through language that our experiences are interpreted, conceptualised and expressed (Gadamer, 1989, 2001; Strauss and Feiz, 2014). The second category focuses on interactions, be they between individuals or between the individual and a text. The third category is meaning as value or purpose that is related to how individuals engage with and conceptualise their experiences. I see this multiplicity of meaning as a strength of hermeneutic phenomenology because it makes me conscious of and allows me to explore various aspects of meaning for participants as well as myself as a researcher.

Applying hermeneutic phenomenological principles to the post-16 literature classroom

Interpretation, conceptualisation and actualisation are three processes through which, I argue, literature teachers and students experience literature in the classroom. I found the three processes drawn from hermeneutic phenomenological principles useful in my research and their application yielded interesting findings about teacher and student literature classroom experiences.

Interpretation

In order to focus on experiences of teaching and learning post-16 literature, the teacher needs to interpret relevant documentation as an 'active participant' in an 'interaction' with the syllabus (Cooper and McIntyre, 1996: 73–74). The teacher assigns meaning to what is read and it is possible that different teachers interpret documents differently. Students also go through the process of interpretation as they interpret teacher action in the classroom in order to form their own conceptualisations of what post-16 literature is. The teacher likewise interprets student action as lessons progress. Even though these interpretations are influenced by a great number of aspects within and beyond the classroom, I have chosen to focus only on how the syllabus and relevant documentation such as examination papers and examiner reports might influence literature teachers and students.

Conceptualisation

A 'concept' in hermeneutic phenomenology is defined as 'an abstraction – a symbol – a representation of an object … or of a behavioural phenomenon' where the 'symbols [are] of phenomena, not the phenomena themselves' (Frankfort-Nachmias and Nachmias, 1996: 26). In my research, the phenomenon is literature, while symbols or concepts within the subject could range from the use of specific literary theories such as postcolonialism and formalism to iconic writers like Shakespeare and V. S. Naipaul. These concepts are elements that teachers and students could consider representative of literature. However, concepts in themselves are not stagnant as they can change with time (Carey, 2011). Therefore, to better reflect the changing nature of concepts, I use the term 'conceptualisation' and its accompanying verb 'conceptualise' to refer to the process involved in the formulation of teachers' and students' literature concepts. Acknowledging that teachers and students go through processes of conceptualisation also allows me to indirectly include elements apart from the syllabus that might influence their literature classroom experiences.

Actualisation

Finally, conceptualisations are made real, or actualised, in the classroom through observable action, be it in spoken, written or visual form. These actions consist of everything teachers and students say and do in the classroom, through which I suggest that their conceptualisations are realised. It is possible that teacher and student action may not fully reflect their conceptualisations of the subject. Bousted (2000) carried out a study in which she interviewed teachers of various subjects as well as observed them in their classrooms. Bousted found that there was a noted difference between what English teachers in her study said and did. Nevertheless, the fact remains that teachers and students respond to each other based on what they observe or, in other words, what the other party actualises. Although classroom interaction forms one of the processes in this study, I also view official documentation such as the syllabus and examination papers as actualisations of the respective examination board's conceptualisations of literature.

Figure 9.1, published in my previous study (Lim, 2015), is an initial representation of how I perceived interpretation, conceptualisation and actualisation to be connected in a continuous cycle. I later refined it after application in my doctoral research (see Figure 9.2). What does not change in Figures 9.1 and 9.2 is that the cycle begins with the teacher's translation of the syllabus and then

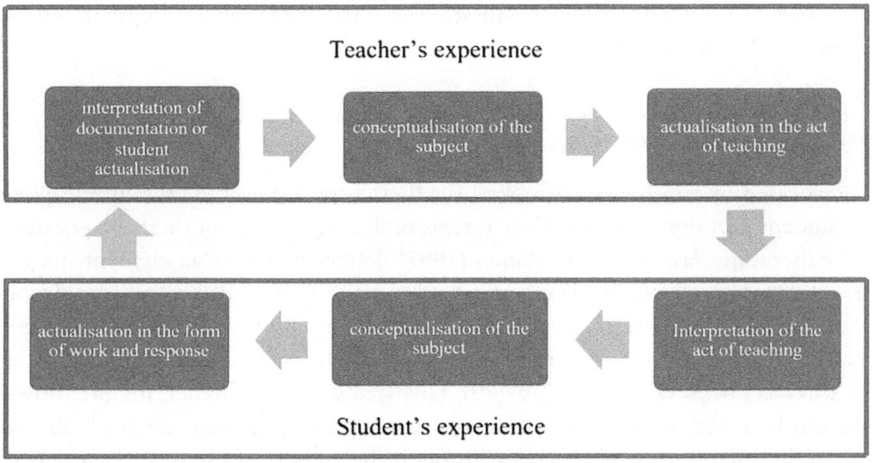

FIGURE 9.1 A cycle of interpretation, conceptualisation and actualisation processes experienced by a teacher and a student in the classroom

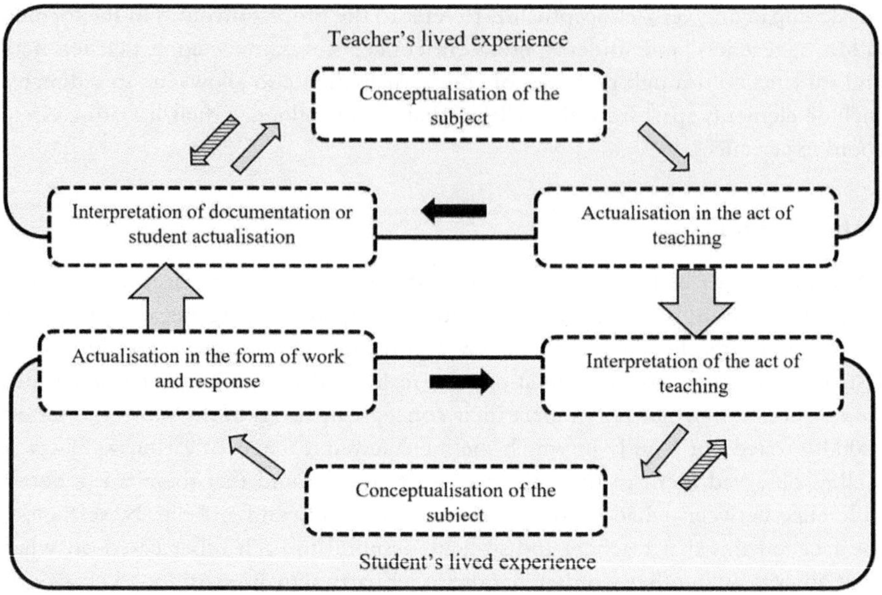

FIGURE 9.2 A revisualisation of the interpretation, conceptualisation and actualisation processes experienced by a teacher and a student in the classroom

follows teacher and student experiences of the subject as it is implemented in the classroom. It is an admittedly simplified representation of what happens in the classroom context because a key limitation in my research is that I could not possibly account for all the influences that shape how teachers and students construct the subject. I chose to take the interpretation of the syllabus as my starting point and end with students' actualisation of their literature conceptualisations in order to bound my analysis.

Interpretive data analysis

As advocated by van Manen, I looked for themes regarding the literature teacher and student identity and what they foreground as significant in their experiences of the literature classroom. Van Manen (1997) defines theme as 'an element (motif, formula or device) which occurs frequently in the text' (78). Themes should be 'uncovered' from experiential meaning, identified and 'isolated' through 'a process of insightful invention, discovery or disclosure … [It] is not a rule-bound process but a free act of "seeing" meaning' (79). This 'free' act of researcher 'insight', however, can be problematic because it seems vague and implies that analysis is almost entirely instinctive, an issue I address through the additional use of two particular discourse analysis tools.

Using two discourse analysis tools to identify interpretations, conceptualisations and actualisations of literature as a school subject

To make the process of 'insightful invention, discovery or disclosure' (van Manen, 1997: 79) more explicit, I used two tools from James Paul Gee's (2014) discourse analysis, namely the identity building tool and significance building tool. A scholar in sociolinguistics and education, Gee defines discourse as an integration of language, action, interaction, values, ideas, beliefs and use of symbols and tools. All those elements play a part in enacting a particular socially situated identity, such as the identity of a literature teacher or student. I applied the identity building tool and significance building tool to identify interpretations, conceptualisations and actualisations about literature as a school subject.

As Eaglestone and English (2013) comment in reference to undergraduates studying English as a degree, what literature students experience in the course of their studies is a '[p]rogression … not simply a matter of assimilating information: it is a matter of acquiring a form of identity' (19). Thus, I use Gee's identity building tool to explore how teachers and students form their own and each other's identities in literature classroom discourse while I use the significance building tool to explore what teachers and students choose to emphasise and value in their literature classroom experiences. The use of both tools involves a close linguistic analysis of participants' use of language in terms of content, grammar and vocabulary as well as an analysis of other forms of discourse such as positionality and gestures (Strauss and Feiz, 2014).

Analysing an extract from an STPM literature classroom observation using discourse analysis tools

For illustrative purposes, I will now show how both the identity building tool and significance building tool were used to analyse an extract from my data. The analysis demonstrates how they can highlight different areas of teacher and student conceptualisations and experiences of literature.

This particular extract in Table 9.1[1] is taken from a classroom observation that took place during the first two periods of the school day with each period lasting 40 minutes. I chose it because it directly addresses literature teacher and student identities and their roles in the classroom. Students had been instructed to come to class prepared with visual organisers containing relevant information and analysis of each poem they had studied that semester. Students were also told by Ms Alice that they would be asked to share those visual organisers with the rest of the class. However, Ms Alice transforms what would have been a set of student presentations to an act of role reversal when she instructs the students to be the teachers. Here, Yusof and Johari take turns to present their notes of William Wordsworth's *The Solitary Reaper* to their classmates.

TABLE 9.1 Extract from a STPM literature classroom observation

Time	*Observation*
7.08am	(*Ms Alice enters the classroom*) **Ms Alice**: I'm going to give you the marker so you're going to be the teacher. **Yusof**: Me! (*raises hand and speaks loudly*) **Ms Alice**: Settle down! Johari, you? No? Later then. Right, Yusof, come to the front. **Yusof**: Yay! I like to be first. **Ms Alice**: We have a new teacher. **Yusof**: Can I bring my book? (*Yusof stands in front of the whiteboard facing the class*) **Stanley**: (*addressing Yusof*) Can we talk *Bahasa Sarawak*?[a] **Yusof**: Of course you can! This is literature class. **Ms Alice**: I'm going to be a student also (*sits down at the teacher's table*).
7.13am	**Yusof**: Before we start, what do you know about *Solitary Reaper*? (*Class laughs*) **Yusof**: What? This is what teacher do. **Debbie**: That's why you're up there! You're supposed to tell us! **Yusof**: No, must ask *mah*! Must understand first. So, first of all, *Solitary Reaper* is written by Wordsword. **Stanley**: Wordsworth! **Yusof**: Wordsworth! Sorry my pronunciation is wrong (*writes 'Wordsworth' on whiteboard*) **Stanley**: Nice handwriting, teacher! **Yusof**: (*continues writing on whiteboard*) Is the rhyming scheme the same? **Stanley**: No. It's… (*Ms Alice looks around to check if others are attentive*) **Yusof**: The persona hears a sad song, or a melancholic (*grins*) song. Why? She sings a sad song even though she is beautiful. This also beautiful thing, so can be fun! That's all I understand from there. And pentameter, yeah, I think it's iambic pentameter. Not sure. **Ms Alice**: Right, thank you teacher (*gets up and walks towards the whiteboard*). (*Yusof returns to his seat*) **Stanley**: Starry, starry night **Ms Alice**: Anyone else want to add something to it? (*writes additional notes on the whiteboard*). Come, Johari. **Yusof**: Yay! New teacher! (*Johari looks at the whiteboard and book. Johari leaves his seat to stand in front*) **Stanley**: (*to Johari*) Talk about themes! **Johari**: So the theme of *Solitary Reaper* is about nature, beauty of nature. And it's also about memory… (*While speaking, Johari often looks at Stanley*) **Johari**: (*mumbles*) mortality (*looks at Ms Alice for response*). **Ms Alice**: Ask the students? **Johari**: Students, do you know what it means?

TABLE 9.1 (*Cont.*)

Time	*Observation*
	Brenda: The song dies. **Ainul**: Past history! **Yusof**: (*answers*) **Ms Alice**: Anyone else want to add in? It's very important that he put it here (*in reference to the words 'themes and structure' Johari wrote on the board*). **Johari**: This is a work of art.
	Stanley: Yo!
7.23am	**Johari**: The place where he writes, the nightingale gives life. So maybe the persona feels alive when she sings. So maybe her song sounds depressing. So he assumes, it's about, maybe, just some random song she knows, or maybe she … So he still think about her singing. **Ms Alice**: Thank you, Johari. (*loud applause from class as Johari returns to his seat*)

[a] *Bahasa Sarawak* translates as 'Sarawak language', which is a mixture of the Malay language and a local dialect.

Using the identity-building tool to explore how teachers and students form their own and each other's identities in literature classroom discourse

Ms Alice sets up the reversal of teacher and student roles from the very beginning of the class by directly telling students 'you're going to be the teacher', symbolised by her passing the marker pen used for writing on the whiteboard to a student. Her choice of where to sit, however, is significant, which is something I comment on later. The first student to present is Yusof who chooses to speak about *The Solitary Reaper* by William Wordsworth. By directly addressing Yusof as 'a new teacher' when he steps forward to stand in front of the whiteboard, Ms Alice implies to the whole class as well as to him that he now has a different role to play. Other students follow suit and address Yusof as teacher throughout his presentation until the end when Ms Alice says 'Thank you, teacher', emphasising once again that Yusof has played the role of the teacher. When it is Johari's turn to present, it is Yusof who first labels Johari as 'a new teacher' and Johari himself, following Ms Alice's suggestion, addresses the class as 'students'. Through such role-switching, a few points come to light in terms of how the identities of a literature teacher and student are understood.

First of all, each perceived role seems to come with access to different types of actions available to them in this classroom. Of note is a short exchange between Yusof and Stanley in which Yusof's new role as a teacher allows both of them to challenge the status quo. In Malaysian schools, it is often advocated that only English be used during English classes as it is seen as a way to encourage students to speak the language. When Yusof takes on the role of a literature teacher, however, the first thing Stanley asks is for permission to speak in their local language. Thus, Stanley's question implies that the teacher has the authority to dictate what language is allowed during a literature class, which can be seen as a challenge to school policy. Yusof's reply, 'Of course you can! This is literature class,' further implies that the literature class and literature teacher are able to challenge existing teaching and learning practices. Moreover, after receiving permission, Stanley does not act upon it, which further indicates that his question was meant as a challenge rather than an actual request. Furthermore, the implication of Stanley's and Yusof's words is that while literature is conceptualised as distinct from their local language, literature does allow for the presence and expression of the local language. This suggests that Yusof's conceptualisation of literature is not limited by an adherence to a particular language.

Another action that is strongly associated with the role of the literature teacher is the use of questions. As literature teachers, Yusof and Johari both present questions to their fellow classmates, although in Johari's case, he was prompted to do so by Ms Alice. Unlike Yusof who questions the class almost immediately after he becomes the literature teacher, Johari looks to Ms Alice for assurance when he is unsure of what he is saying. It is Ms Alice, the real literature teacher, who suggests that Johari address the class as 'students' and ask for their ideas, which Johari subsequently does. Ms Alice's prompting as well as Yusof's and Johari's questions are particularly interesting because in most of my observations, there is rarely any instance of a student addressing a general question to their fellow classmates. Questions either come from the teacher or are communicated via the literature teacher. Thus, it seems that it is the teacher who has the ability to address students as a collective group, which is an act notably absent from a literature student's repertoire.

Aside from access to certain actions, the role reversal also reflects the different expectations literature teachers and students have of each other. Yusof and Debbie, for example, seem to have different ideas of the literature teacher's role and what the teacher should do in the classroom. As a literature teacher, Yusof begins teaching by asking the class questions about what they know even though he was expected by his classmates to carry out Ms Alice's instruction to present his thoughts about the poem. When the class responds to Yusof's question with laugher, Yusof states very plainly that asking questions 'is what teacher do' because teachers 'must understand first'. Therein lies Yusof's expectation that literature teachers ought to first discover what students know and proceed teaching from there. It is certainly possible that such questioning may be read as a situation where students are pressured to demonstrate that they are able to supply the teacher with anticipated answers. However, Yusof's use of the word 'understand' indicates that he perceives the act of questioning as a means to identify where students are in terms of their knowledge in order for teaching to be based and built upon students' current knowledge. Debbie, on the other hand, demonstrates a different expectation of literature teachers where teachers 'tell' students about literature, exclaiming 'you're supposed to tell us!'. Hence, literature is conceptualised as a body of knowledge alien to the student but possessed by the teacher. Although these two ideas are not necessarily contradictory in that teachers know more than students, they do represent different perspectives of what a literature teacher should do in the classroom as well as how the source of knowledge could be conceptualised in literature. Being either a literature teacher or student also seems to necessitate the use of different types of speech and vocabulary. For example, in comparison to Yusof's speech as a student in class throughout my observations, Yusof makes an effort to use a lot of literary terminology such as 'iambic pentameter' when he assumes the role of a literature teacher. Most notably, he grins very widely when he says 'melancholic', which might reflect a sense of self-satisfaction at his success in using a complex word especially in light of the vocabulary he normally uses in the classroom. Thus, literature may be conceptualised as a subject that necessitates the use of such language. Aside from questioning, as explored in the paragraphs above, Yusof also makes it a point to encourage students and comment on the study of literature in general by saying 'so can be fun!'.

Another notable difference between the speech of a literature teacher and student in the classroom as demonstrated in the extract seems to be the length of what they say. Throughout the extract in Table 9.1 and in other observations, literature students tend to respond to questions with short phrases that are not in themselves extended utterances. The short answers may demonstrate that literature teachers are expected to explain and elaborate on points as a way of teaching so literature students volunteer their participation and elaborate only when the teacher prompts them to do so. Such an actualisation of STPM literature teaching and learning may signal a lack of student confidence in their own ideas, a hesitancy to express themselves and, at the same time, demonstrates that the teacher's approval and response remains the key guiding force in the STPM literature classroom. In general, the actualisation of literature in this particular STPM class may be interpreted as a representation of literature that is conceptualised as a subject where the teacher's knowledge and understanding of the text takes precedence over student contributions. Thus, what occurs is not a matter of exploring interpretations of literature texts but rather an acceptance of interpretations shaped and almost entirely determined by the teacher.

This dominance of the teacher is also made prominent by Ms Alice's actions. As previously mentioned, Ms Alice sits down at the teacher's table when she announces that she 'is going to be a student also', even though there are empty seats near the back of the classroom. Perhaps to Ms Alice, being a literature student is less about a physical location in the classroom than it is a demonstration of attitude where students listen to the teacher and are attentive in class. It is more likely, however, that she may have wanted to maintain some form of control over the students as evidenced by how she looked at them from time to time to check if they were listening to their 'new' literature teachers. This monitoring would not have been possible if Ms Alice had sat at the back of the classroom. Thus, the role reversal exercise in this extract was not complete, as Ms Alice's actions demonstrate that she did not entirely relinquish her role as a literature teacher.

Using the significance-building tool to explore what teachers and students choose to emphasise and value in their literature classroom experiences

The significance-building tool focuses specifically on how the language used emphasises and de-emphasises particular elements in a sentence or utterance. Paying close attention to how participants connect different elements and what they highlight may provide some insight into how they engage with their classroom experiences as literature teachers and students. Below are a few examples of what can be gained through an analysis of the same extract with a focus on significance.

One line that begs analysis for significance is Ms Alice's announcement, 'I'm going to give you the marker so you're going to be the teacher', which sets the tone for the class. In her speech, Ms Alice places herself in the position of authority where it is clear that she is the active one who chooses to hand over the lesson to students and places upon students their new roles as literature teachers. Another point of interest in Ms Alice's instruction is her use of the marker pen as a symbol of a literature teacher's identity. She presents the link between holding the marker pen and becoming a teacher as a cause-and-effect relationship where holding the pen makes one the teacher. In other words, it may seem that having access to the whiteboard is exclusive to being a teacher. Therefore, my interpretation of literature actualisation in this class being teacher-centred is able to substantiate my earlier observation of the classroom.

Another example of how using the significance-building tool can illuminate teacher and student classroom experiences is demonstrated through an analysis of Debbie's words. In response to Yusof's question about what the class knows about *The Solitary Reaper*, she says, 'That's why you're up there! You're supposed to tell us!' I discussed the insight her words reveal about teacher and student roles using the previous discourse analysis tool but further analysis of her word choice using the significance tool draws attention to the phrase 'up there'. The phrase shows a distinct physical separation between teacher and students where 'up' could relate to the teacher's perceived superiority over students along with how Debbie perceives the classroom's orientation with 'up' or 'front' being where the whiteboard is. Debbie also emphasises that the teacher is the active force in the classroom when she comments 'You're supposed to tell us!' while the students have a passive role, mostly receiving what is told to them. Debbie's choice of words, especially the word 'supposed', expresses her perception that literature teachers have unquestionable knowledge about literature and are meant to communicate that knowledge to students. Her words imply that teaching and learning in a STPM literature classroom is mostly unidirectional from the teacher to the student. Thus, Debbie seems to conceptualise literature as a subject that is to be acquired passively and does not involve contributions from the students.

Revisiting my research methodology

In this chapter, I have suggested that the literature teachers and students I observed go through three interactive processes of interpretation, conceptualisation and actualisation in the classroom. Focusing on these three processes as a cycle not only allowed me to identify differences and similarities in how various examination boards, teachers and students conceptualise the subject but also illuminated ways to explore how one party influences others. I believe the three processes as represented in Figure 9.1 form an effective lens through which to explore the classroom. However, in the process of writing up my research on my study of STPM literature, I came to understand that the boundaries between these processes are indistinct. Although interpretation may sometimes blur into conceptualisation, the lack of boundary distinctions does not take away from the usefulness of these three processes in identifying crucial gaps that have given rise to misinterpretations between examination board, teacher and student conceptualisations and actualisations of STPM literature in my doctoral research.

Upon reflection, and based on what I have learned through the process of analysing and writing up my research, I have modified Figure 9.1 to better reflect the complexities in which teachers and students engage with their experiences in the literature classroom, which has resulted in Figure 9.2. I have made four significant changes, which I illustrate with brief examples drawn from the general body of my research.

First of all, I have used a dashed outline for the three processes to visually acknowledge that each process is subject to other influences not foregrounded in this framework. For example, a former student of the subject whom I interviewed as part of my research expressed how his actions in the literature classroom were not only based on his conceptualisations of the subject but also by his concern of how his classmates would perceive his actions. It is a limitation I mentioned earlier on in that I am unable to account for every possible influence on these three processes. However, such experiences show that a visual representation of the indefinite boundaries of those processes is appropriate.

Second, I have repositioned the interpretation and actualisation process boxes so that they extend beyond the boundary of lived experience for literature teachers and students. This is done to demonstrate that what the individual interprets originates from external sources. In other words, objects such as the syllabus document do exist beyond the individual's interpretation process. Actualisation, likewise, extends beyond one's lived experience because actions are observed by others. Moving the actualisation box beyond the lived experience boundary mainly allows for the idea that actions may be interpreted differently from the intended meaning. After all, the interpretation of one's actions is not entirely within the actor's control. For example, a former teacher whom I interviewed as part of my research said that he was terrible at teaching literature; however, his former student whom I also interviewed said otherwise. Instead of thinking his teacher was terrible, the student praised him for his ingenious and innovative teaching approach. Therefore, both boxes were moved to better reflect the uncertain nature of interpretation and actualisation.

Third, the interaction between processes of interpretation and conceptualisation also does not merely occur unilaterally. In Figure 9.1, I had indicated that the process of interpretation forms conceptualisations about literature. However, it became clear during my analysis that conceptualisations about the subject also influence one's interpretations just as much as those interpretations inform conceptualisations. Moreover, the process of conceptualisation does not automatically lead to action as those conceptualisations may continue being constructed through interpretations of other objects. At times, it became difficult to distinguish between those processes. For instance, Ms Alice's conceptualisation of STPM literature is certainly shaped by her understanding of the syllabus. However, her interpretation of the syllabus is also influenced by her conceptualisations of what literature teaching and learning is. Thus, striped arrows have been added to Figure 9.2 to demonstrate how they interplay with each other.

Finally, the black arrows are added to portray the self-reflectiveness that individuals in my research demonstrate. For example, the teachers who participated in my study did not only interpret student actualisation while they taught in the classroom; they also reflected upon their own actions as they taught. Ms Alice's responses to my questions about her experience teaching literature, for example, did reveal that she was attentive to her students' actions. However, her attentiveness was not only due to what her students did but also a desire to improve her teaching as she says she often asked herself what else she could do to improve her teaching.

Overall, therefore, I believe Figure 9.2 better acknowledges the complexity by which experiences are interpreted. In comparison to Figure 9.1, Figure 9.2 allows for more consideration of aspects that may inform and guide analysis of literature teacher and student experiences.

Concluding words

My hope in sharing the approach I have used in my research is that it may be valuable to others interested in empirical research particularly on literature teaching and learning. It would also be very interesting to see how this framework may be applied to subjects other than literature as well as to different education contexts. As acknowledged in this chapter, the introduction of the processes of interpretation, conceptualisation and actualisation drawn from hermeneutic phenomenology may not be very distinct but, perhaps, other concerns and approaches may be brought into sharper light through the use of this research perspective. At the very least, perhaps my proposed methodological framework may be used to generate dialogue regarding how drawing on a methodology such as hermeneutic phenomenology can inform empirical research in literature and in other fields.

Note

1 The extract has been edited for ease of reading without compromising the exchange in the classroom as far as possible. Grammatical and syntax errors have not been corrected unless they impede comprehension.

References

Bousted, M. (2000). Rhetoric and practice in English teaching. *English in Education*, 43 (1), 12–23.

Carey, S. (2011). Précis of the origins of concepts. *Behavioral and Brain Sciences*, 34, 113–167.

Choo, S. S. (2013). *Reading the World, the Globe, and the Cosmos: Approaches to Teaching Literature for the Twenty-First Century*. New York: Peter Lang Publishing.

Cohen, L., Manion, L. and Morrison, K. (2011). *Research Methods in Education* (7th ed.). London: Routledge.

Cooper, P. and McIntyre, D. (1996). *Effective Teaching and Learning: Teachers' and Students' Perspectives*. Buckingham: Open University Press.

Eaglestone, R. and English, E. (2013). Journals and student engagement with literary theory. *English in Education*, 47 (1), 18–32.

Frankfort-Nachmias, C. and Nachmias, D. (1996). *Research Methods in the Social Sciences* (5th ed.). London: Edward Arnold.

Gadamer, H. (1989). *Truth and Method* (2nd ed.). London: Sheed and Ward Limited.

Gadamer, H. (2001). *Gadamer in Conversation*. New Haven: Yale University Press.

Gardner, P. (2010). *Hermeneutics, History and Memory*. Oxford: Routledge.

Gee, J. P. (2014). *An Introduction to Discourse Analysis: Theory and method* (5th ed.). Oxford: Routledge.

Harding, D. W. (1962). Psychological processes in the reading of fiction. *British Journal of Aesthetics*, 2 (2), 133–147.

Lim, J. W. (2015). What happens in an English literature classroom? A hermeneutic phenomenological perspective. *Malaysian Journal of ELT Research*, 11 (1), 52–66.

Rosenblatt, L. M. (1988). *Writing and Reading: The Transactional Theory*. Retrieved 24 March 2016 from: www.ideals.illinois.edu/bitstream/handle/2142/18044/ctrstreadtechrepv01988i00416_opt.pdf

Strauss, S. and Feiz, P. (2014). *Discourse Analysis: Putting our Worlds into Words*. New York: Routledge.

van Manen, M. (1997). *Researching Lived Experience: Human Science for an Action Sensitive Pedagogy* (2nd ed.). Ontario: The Althouse Press.

Yandell, J. (2014). *The Social Construction of Meaning: Reading Literature in Urban English Classrooms*. London: Routledge.

10

PRESSURE, PLEASURE AND FUNCTION

Malaysian undergraduates reading across boundaries in a university in England

Su Li Chong

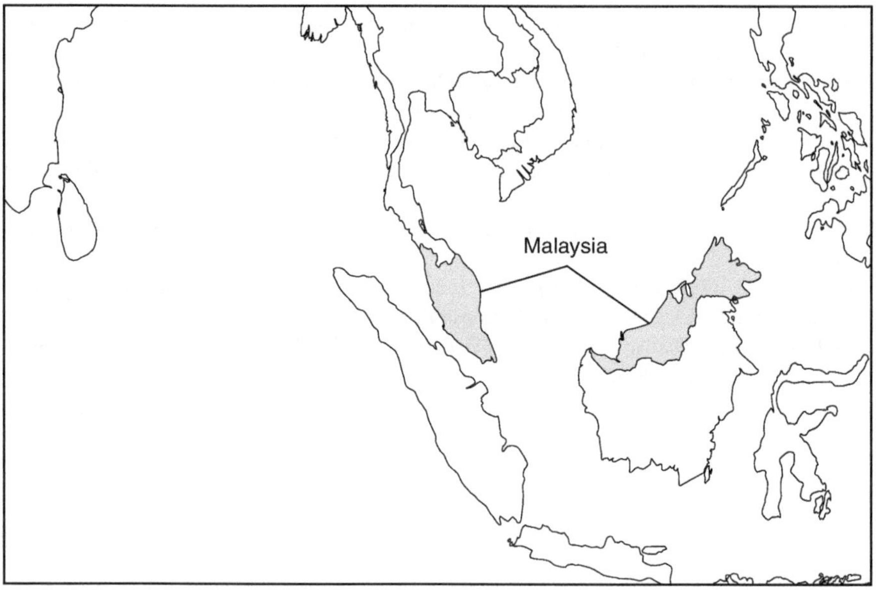

MAP 10.1

In this chapter, I discuss part of an in-depth empirical study that I carried out for my doctoral research, which aimed to understand how Malaysian undergraduates in an English university experienced reading. In my study, I contrasted these undergraduates' perspectives on their past contexts in school with current contexts in the university to show up complex relationships of what it means to read. My

MAP 10.2

exploration of this complexity showed how the reading experience, when seen through the reader's eyes, can contradict and challenge conventional wisdom of what it means to read for pleasure, for functional purposes or under pressure. My study also offers empirical evidence showing how even within boundaries of reading genres and formal spaces, the reader is fundamentally his or her own agent of change. Therefore, if research helps us to see reading experiences as more fluid than hitherto, it also means we need to expand our conception of literacy.

Within the scope of this chapter, notions of space, domains and boundaries underpin my discussion. I have previously written about the concept of space in terms of how it is both ambiguous, yet defined in relation to reading:

> I discuss notions of boundaries ... conceived as offering some sense of tangibility to the reading experience without enforcing a rigid shape to any individual's experience of reading. Instead, this sense of tangibility can be a useful springboard as a means to compare and contrast the reading experiences of individual readers across and between domains and contexts as the experiences take their unique shapes.
>
> (Chong, 2016: 20)

In my study, the term 'domain' refers to academic and non-academic spaces that are associated with formal institutions. For example, schools and universities are obvious domains that shape learning and, by association, reading experience. In this chapter, my discussion of how readers respond to pressure or pleasure, and how they read for functional purposes, is located within and across the boundaries of these domains.

Growing up in Malaysia, I was educated in Malaysian primary and secondary schools. I also spent a number of years in a Malaysian public university to read for my degrees in language education and English literature. I then joined higher education and have served as a lecturer for 20 years. In that time, I have taught English language proficiency, English literature, technical and professional writing, and professional communication skills in Malaysian universities. In most of these courses, a fair amount of reading is expected from the undergraduates. However, my undergraduate students often seem to regard reading as a task that is burdensome and even challenging. This is not to say that the students face any difficulty in reading, but they seem to find it hard to sustain their motivation for reading. Because most Malaysians know and use more than one language, their access to reading materials often cuts across different languages. Malay, English, Chinese and Tamil are the main languages taught in schools, although they are by no means the only ones in use. For young people who can read in multiple languages, my undergraduates' reading experience does not seem as extensive as it could potentially be. This realisation spurred me on to investigate what reading experiences might actually be like for a young adult in a university. I carried out my study with the aim of understanding the reading experience of a small number of multilingual Malaysian undergraduates who were pursuing their degrees in a university in England. The reason for undertaking my study in the United Kingdom was to understand how these undergraduates negotiated their reading choices in a linguistic environment that calls only for the use of English. The undergraduates were between 19 and 23 years old.

In order to understand these undergraduates' backgrounds, it is first necessary to understand notions of literacy and education in the Malaysian system. Malaysia is a developing country whose literacy rates are relatively high. In contrast with other age groups across Malaysia, young adults (15- to 24-year-olds) have the highest literacy rates at approximately 98% (UNESCO Institute of Statistics, 2013). This implies that Malaysia is generally committed to literacy education. Yet, Malaysia does not have education policies that are fully dedicated to it; in Malaysian schools, literacy is taught by way of the language subjects. Therefore, language teaching and learning pedagogies underpin how reading and writing skills are taught (Chong, 2017). One implication of these pedagogies is an assumption that students will use language hierarchically: Malay is assumed to be their national language, while English is their second language and Chinese or Tamil is their ethnic or home language. The teaching of reading also tends to be shaped by these assumptions. Yet, such a reductionist view of language use and reading is unhelpful in providing space to capture what Rosenblatt describes as the fluid transactions and complexities of reading when a reader interacts with texts across different contexts (Rosenblatt, 1978, 1983, 1993). Therefore, my study provided a space to understand the complexities of young people's reading experience.

Theoretical perspective: A transactional theory of reading

Across highly literate societies in the twenty-first century, concerns no longer revolve exclusively around young people's ability or inability to read, but around adolescent readers who choose not to read, in spite of their considerable ability to do so. Aliteracy, a term that is defined as having the ability to read but choosing not to, has become the new literacy problem (Agee, 2005; Goodwin, 1996; Mikulecky, 1978). Alvermann (2004), for example, flags up how a 'transmission model of instruction' (27) in some American classrooms has possibly led to high levels of aliteracy among adolescents. Whether that connection is tenable or not, one of the effects of such discussions about literacy, illiteracy and aliteracy is to assume that they form a linear continuum. However, I argue that such an assumption requires rethinking because the experience of being literate, illiterate or aliterate is intertwined in a very complex way, but also especially when we understand more about reading in different spaces and domains (Chong, 2016). Yet, when we examine current practices in mainstream education, we are continually confronted by a paradox. The scramble to have national education systems internationally recognised (e.g., within the Organisation for Economic Co-operation and Development, 2016) has normalised the practice of regulating, ranking and rating. Such regulatory practices often impose a narrow, domain-driven sense of what education and literacy may mean, which, in turn, may perpetuate the notion that reading experience can only be shaped and dictated by an external, and usually powerful, other.

In the twenty-first century, there has been significant awareness of how 'the conjunction of new technologies of meaning-making' and a 'shift … in "the balance of agency"' has allowed for the exploration of new ways of being literate (Kalantzis et al., 2016: 8). Educators are encouraged to embrace the idea that today's students are less the recipients than the creators of knowledge. Such a tipping shifts traditional notions of what mainstream reading has, for too long, been taken to mean, and offers possible alternative definitions that allow for seeing reading and literacy anew (McKenna et al., 2012).

Research design

My study was underpinned by interpretivist epistemology, which makes the researcher the interpretive tool through which the study is situated and understood. In particular, I assumed that reading is a phenomenon formed by human experience that is transactional, fluid and difficult to predict (Rosenblatt, 1983). Therefore, I adopted a phenomenological perspective to guide my research methodology (Giorgi, 1985). I found the phenomenological perspective to be appropriate because it is designed to examine phenomena that are usually taken for granted. This means that a specific human experience that seems to be common to the general population can be reconsidered through phenomenological lenses so that new meanings about the phenomenon can be generated. In line with this research design, I used a phenomenological interview (Seidman, 2006) and diary-writing as my research methods.

The phenomenological interview that was carried out at least three times with each participant was a good method for capturing the phenomenon of reading in terms of how it occurred in the past and in current time. The first interview was dedicated to the participants' recollections of their language learning experience in primary and secondary school in Malaysia. Intertwined with the recollections of their general language learning experience across the four language modes (i.e., reading, writing, speaking and listening) were the participants' specific recollections of their reading experiences. In the second and third interviews, the talk revolved around their current reading experiences as undergraduates in an English university.

The participants were also asked to keep a weekly diary designed to capture their reading experience across eight to eleven weeks, during term and vacation time. The diary-writing was a useful way to encourage participants to stay closely focused on their reading experiences and sustained the momentum of the research. The diary-writing also captured specific titles of texts they chose to read while in the university. Therefore, diary-writing became a good way to collect data across a period of time.

The data from my study was analysed using both thematic coding and discourse analysis. First, the thematic coding was underpinned by phenomenographic analysis. Phenomenography provided a theoretical structure to analyse how outwardly similar participants might nevertheless fall into contrasting groups and, yet, within those contrasting groups they might share similarities and differences in the way they experienced a particular phenomenon (Marton, 1988). Guided by this theoretical structure, I interrogated the data for how it would cleave along initial themes, which I termed codes. Then, these codes were further analysed and shifted to form broader categories. From categories, they were analysed as abstractions and, from there, conceptions of the reading experience were formed. The code-category-conception analysis is based on the code-to-theory model drawn from the work of Saldaña (2013). Second, I found that discourse analysis was useful in unpacking the finer motifs of the qualitatively different ways in which the participants transacted with selected texts.

This study was carried out entirely in England. In total, eight undergraduates volunteered to take part. During the time of the study, these undergraduates who had previously attended primary and secondary schools in Malaysia, had been living in England for between one and four years. Table 10.1 depicts the participants' profile.

Discussion of findings

The findings drawn from data of the participants' reading experience as school students and later as undergraduates seemed to cleave along two lines. First, their reading experiences appeared to cleave along the initial dichotomous theme of academic and non-academic reading. The participants' recollections about

TABLE 10.1 Participants' profiles

NO.	*PSEUDONYM (GENDER)*	*DEGREE, YEAR OF STUDY*
1	Jen (F)	Engineering, 1st
2	Fong (F)	Mathematics, 2nd
3	Khong (M)	Engineering, 2nd
4	Jon (M)	Engineering, 2nd
5	Jack (M)	Engineering, 3rd
6	Yen (F)	Economics, 1st
7	Zee (F)	Law, 2nd
8	Nick (M)	Law, 2nd

academic-related reading as school students provided a glimpse of the stance and attitude they took when it came to schoolwork. It suggests that overwhelming academic work as well as extra-curricular activities inside and outside school occupied a significant amount of their time. As this was an expected finding, I was curious to learn about what they thought of their non-academic reading and how one domain was associated with the other.

Non-academic reading appeared to have reduced as they progressed in school years. It came as little surprise, therefore, that at least five out of the eight participants attributed their reduction in non-academic reading to lack of time. Table 10.2[1] shows my initial impression of participants' non-academic reading experience as school students. The reading list provided was not exhaustive.

Non-academic reading seemed to be associated with out-of-school activities and the reading material cut across fiction and non-fiction. Non-academic reading also seemed to be relegated to the periphery of mainstream academic reading, especially when participants talked about their secondary school years. In their talk about their past reading choices, hints of aliteracy seemed to be present. I noticed this especially in their talk about lack of time to pursue wider reading. The decision to read was almost exclusively about reading academic texts particularly in terms of school hours, tuition classes, examinations and memorisation drills.

On the whole, the participants seemed to have little autonomy and agency while at school. Going to school and doing well were simply something they had to do. Pressure related to examinations and school appeared to be pervasive. To most of the eight participants, the notion of choosing to read within the domain of school simply translated into a choice of reading academic texts over non-academic texts. They seemed to make a clear separation between the two. If the boundaries were obvious, as they seemed to be here, participants were particularly aware of having to make choices.

While the reading experience across their school years was heavily dominated by academic and non-academic domains, there seemed to be a shift when the undergraduates talked about their reading experience as university students. Here, I saw an overarching and differently dichotomous category that encompassed both

TABLE 10.2 Participants' non-academic reading experiences as school students

Participants	*Non-academic reading experience (by authors/titles/genre)*		*Reading volume across time*
	Primary school	*Secondary school*	
Jack	Picture cards, Sherlock Holmes, Jules Verne, H.G. Wells, G.K. Chesterton, Encyclopaedia	Lord of the Rings (J. R. R. Tolkien), Harry Potter (J. K. Rowling), Andrew Matthews, Dale Carnegie	Reduced
Jen	Picture books, Heidi, Pollyanna, Anne of Green Gables, Little Women, Peter and Jane, Disney stories, Malory Towers, Nancy Drew, Hardy Boys, Harry Potter	Lord of the Rings, Silmarillion, The Hobbit, newspapers	Reduced
Khong	Peter and Jane, Enid Blyton, Roald Dahl, Harry Potter, Narnia, fairy tales, Artemis Fowl	Science fiction, non-fiction, newspapers	Reduced
Jon	Pictures, fairy tales, science-y books (illustrated), general knowledge,	Newspapers, fiction (Angels and Demons), non-fiction (A Brief History of Time, Sun Tzu's Art of War)	Reduced
Fong	Chinese novels, Chinese magazines	Chinese novels, Chinese non-fiction, Chinese newspapers	Not significantly reduced
Yen	Fiction (Enid Blyton, Famous Five) Peter and Jane, Chinese fiction, Malay fiction	Non-fiction (Reader's Digest, The Economist, Times, Chicken Soup series), fiction (James Patterson, Sidney Sheldon, Darren Shan), Chinese fiction	Not significantly reduced
Zee	Picture books, Peter and Jane, Dune, Chinese magazines, Chinese fiction (Huan Chu Ghe Ghe series), Malay novels	English and Chinese manga, English, Chinese and Malay non-fiction and fiction, English and Chinese newspapers	Not significantly reduced
Nick	Enid Blyton, comics, Christian-based fiction	Christian books (John Maxwell, Max Lucado), Bible stories, Self-help (Dale Carnegie), fiction (Goosebumps, Chillers)	Reduced

academic and non-academic reading. I called this dichotomous category 'primary/secondary school' and 'university'. During the time the participants were in primary/secondary school and university, both academic and non-academic reading occurred.

Drawing on the participants' diary entries and the interview data, I was able to put together a profile of their reading choices. This profile represents only a selection of what they read. Table 10.3 shows the selection of titles or topics read and the reasons for reading them.

In Table 10.3, we see that two of the participants, Jack and Khong, appeared to read materials from a similar genre but from different stances. For example, Jack read a textbook on the topic of investments to prepare for an examination while reading another text on practical steps to investing to pursue personal interest. As

TABLE 10.3 Selection of reading titles and the reasons for reading them

Participant	*Academic reading*		*Non-academic reading*	
	Selected titles	*Reason for reading*	*Selected titles*	*Reason for reading*
Jack	Derivatives and Alternative Investments	To prepare for chartered financial analyst exams	One up on Wall Street	To pursue personal interest
Jen	Fluid mechanics handout no. 5	To prepare for supervision	The Hobbit Eyewitness Travel Europe	To pursue personal interest
Khong	Software Engineering and Design handout	To prepare for supervision	Articles on software engineering for international development	To follow-up from a talk
Jon	Linear systems and control	To prepare for exam	Wikipedia	To fulfil a need to know
Fong	Statistical physics	To complement lecture notes	Random articles on Facebook	To read stories shared by others
Yen	Microeconomics	To revise	Norway	To learn about Norway
Zee	The independence and impartiality of the judiciary – the case of Tunisia	To carry out research	A Thousand Splendid Suns	To catch up on fiction reading
Nick	Foskett v. McKeown case	To prepare for revision	Online news (BBC, Huffington Post, freemalaysia.com)	To stay abreast with current issues

TABLE 10.4 Five participants' impressions of boundary-crossing

Participant (Course)	*Perspective on reading domains*
Khong (Engineering)	Both [academic and non-academic reading are] not mutually exclusive in a sense that I could be curious about some academic thing which actually made me read further about it.
Jon (Engineering)	I can't draw Venn diagrams to describe all of this [academic and non-academic reading] cause everything is a blurry blob ... that's sort of entangled together.
Fong (Mathematics)	[Academic reading is] fun. Like you get to understand what is it about then it sort of ... link with what you're studying then if you like the subject, then you feel very contented
Zee (Law)	And some of the non-academic reading that I do I find relates still to the academic reading.
Yen (Economics)	Academic is more technical whereas non-academic is more opinions, stories ... Yes, (I enjoy both).

this notion of boundary-crossing was introduced during my interviews with them, the participants talked increasingly about the blurring of lines. I found that this occurred in at least five of the participants' reading experiences. Using quotations from the interview transcripts, I provide a glimpse of these five participants' impressions of boundary-crossing in Table 10.4.

It seemed that when the domains fused, academic reading did not come across as being unnecessarily burdensome to these participants. In fact, they found academic reading to be pleasurable. In contrast, there were those who found themselves reading academic texts purely for functional purposes but who would avoid reading those texts if there was no external requirement to do so. From here, a dichotomous conception was formed. This conception represented those who, on the one hand, found the academic and non-academic reading domains to be indistinguishable and those who found the academic and non-academic reading to be clearly distinctive. This refers to the way in which the undergraduates identified their reading experiences as being for pleasure or for functional purposes. The conception was termed 'domain-free' and 'domain contingent' reading, respectively. As I have mentioned in the preceding section, the data was analysed using the code-category-conception. Figure 10.1 is an illustration of the development of the data across the code-category-conception theme-based analysis.

Next, I discuss a 'domain-free' conception of reading, which was when the participants experienced reading across boundaries. For these participants, academic and non-academic boundaries blurred at many points. The boundaries that seemed at first to separate domains, ceased to be significant. This had important implications for the way these participants understood reading choices, because when domains did not appear significantly separated, readers did feel they were choosing one over another. Ironically then, the reading choice also ceased to feel

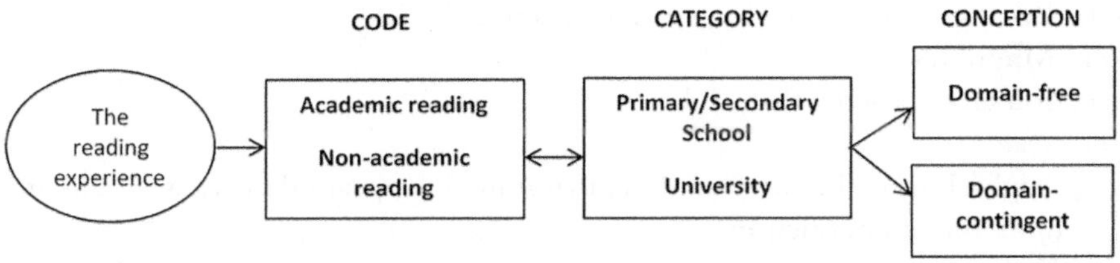

FIGURE 10.1 Analytical development of data

like a choice. This has further implications for the way we understand reading for pleasure and reading for functional purposes. As boundaries blur, the reading transaction could be seen as being less constrained by externally imposed boundaries (e.g., genres or domains) and more as being embodied in a transaction between reader, text and context. In order to better understand the complexities of this reading transaction, I will discuss a particular undergraduate's case, which illustrates how such domain-free reading occurred. Both coding and discourse analysis were used with her interview data.

A case of domain-free reading: Zee

Zee was a conscientious student while in primary and secondary school. Being ethnically Chinese, Zee attended Chinese vernacular primary school. She was, therefore, strongly trilingual and triliterate in Chinese, English and Malay. She seemed aware that she cut a figure of someone who was a keen reader but yet appeared almost shy about it. If she seemed to downplay the intensity of her reading experience when asked about it during the interviews, that intensity came across very clearly in the reading diary that she kept for at least eight weeks.

Zee had known from early on that she wanted to become a lawyer. Unsurprisingly therefore, as a law undergraduate, her reading choices mirrored her academic interests. Predictably, academically determined legal texts consistently showed up across her eight-week reading diary. However, it was her reference to reading one particular text that defied ordinary conventions that drew my attention. It revolved around Zee's experience of reading the Malaysian Federal Constitution (Malaysia: Federal Constitution, 1957).

I first encountered the topic when it came up towards the end of her initial interview. I had asked if there had been any particular text that she was reading in the manner of what is known as 'bedside reading'.

SLC: And do you have, for example, a book that you have that you must read before you sleep (*Zee gives a slight giggle*) or you, anything like that?

ZEE: Er (*hesitates*) no I (*rising tone*) don't (*hesitates*), but very oddly (*laughs*), sometimes (*laughs*), I like to read the Federal Constitution (*laughs*).

SLC: Yeah?

ZEE: Yeah.

SLC: Because then, is that, do you enjoy reading that?
ZEE: Mmmhhh?
SLC: You enjoy reading that, right?
ZEE: Yeah.
SLC: Right. I mean, I know you think that it might appear odd because you might think that it's not fiction …
ZEE: Yeah, it's not fiction, (conventionally thinking) it's not motivational or anything, right, but sometimes when I just want to get away from other things or when I'm feeling very stressed, I just continue reading whichever article I stopped at.
SLC: And why does that give you pleasure? Why is that interesting to you?
ZEE: Er, probably reminds me why I am doing what I am doing now. Yeah, like why, why am I studying law, why am I working so hard now (*laughs*).

The first turn in the interview is my question about Zee's bedside reading. I noted that she gave an involuntary giggle immediately after the word 'sleep'. In the next turn, a few other unexpected elements occurred. Her initial hesitation, followed by a markedly rising intonation before the word 'not', followed by another hesitation, indicated that she had some difficulty saying what she next said. Zee went on to contradict her negation to say, in effect, that she *did* do bedside reading. She read the Malaysian Federal Constitution. She buffered that sentence with the phrase 'very oddly' and there was more laughter.

It was possible that those words were uttered in anticipation of how unusual it may have sounded to me. I seemed to have picked up that notion and responded with the assumption that she might think it 'odd' because it was 'not fiction'. My words indicated that I did have preconceived notions of the division (academic/non-academic versus pleasure/function versus fiction/not fiction), which would have made the Federal Constitution seem like an improbable choice. This observation was important because it revealed that despite the improbability, the Malaysian Federal Constitution still seemed to be a significant text to Zee. The improbability only emerged when it was seen as a non-academic, preferred and pleasurable text. In this light, the text had unexpectedly crossed the academic/non-academic domain boundaries.

Although during this first interview Zee did explain why that text was important to her, I pursued that topic with her across three further interviews so as to understand how such an unlikely text could have had such a central place in her life. In the second interview, I raised the topic once again. The following is an excerpt:

SLC: But again, bottom line is you enjoy doing that?
ZEE: Yah … (*laughs*) I'm such a nerd.
SLC: No, makes me want to read it.
ZEE: Yeah, you should, you really should. You can buy it at any book store in Malaysia (*laughs*).

This excerpt was selected because of what appeared to be the recurrence of Zee's hesitation with regard to her enjoyment in reading the Malaysian Federal Constitution. In response to my question of whether she enjoyed it, Zee's affirmation was followed by laughter and a self-castigating 'I'm such a nerd', with an audible emphasis on the word 'nerd'. On the face of it, it could appear that Zee's response demonstrated embarrassment. However on further inspection, the language in the excerpt revealed something else. If Zee had felt embarrassed about her choice of text, it could be that it was also a co-constructed outcome within our talk. This was because, in the first turn of talk, my own use of the conjunction 'But' immediately indicated that her experience was contrary to common practice. Once again, if she were presumably reading this text by choice, she would probably not be disparaging about it. She would probably not think herself a 'nerd'. Thus it was possible that her phrase 'I'm such a nerd' could have been, albeit silently, preceded by 'You must think ...'. When I carried on to affirm her choice to say that I, too, felt compelled to read it, her quick reply that I 'really should' confirmed her stand.

There was little doubt that Zee considered the Federal Constitution to be an academic text. Her diary across five weeks captured her reading of various other nations' constitutions that also required numerous references to the Malaysian Federal Constitution. In line with Rosenblatt's reading stances, Zee's functional dipping in and out of the Federal Constitution was her taking on a predominantly efferent stance; yet, at the same time, across the three interviews, Zee seemed to describe her stance towards this text as being more than efferent. The specific language she used was very telling. She saw it as having 'sentimental value' (interview 2), where a 'sense of purpose is being hammered home' (interview 2), where she felt 'like [she was] being anchored back somewhere' (interview 2) and how it 'brings [her] back to where [she] think[s] [she's] supposed to be' (interview 3).

The pleasure Zee had felt from reading the text was at one and the same time conventional and unconventional. It was conventional in how 'the reader draws on images and feelings and ideas stirred up by the words of the text', how the transaction became a 'lived experience' (Rosenblatt, 2005: 96). The feelings and 'private meanings' drawn from Zee's accounts of her transactions with the Federal Constitution indicated that a predominantly aesthetic stance was taken. Yet, it was unconventional in the way that there was no plot, characters, climax or denouement within the Malaysian Federal Constitution as it is not a conventional literary text. It must be acknowledged that the absence of narrative characteristics within the text could point to the possibility that the aesthetic stance was, here, aesthetic creation. In fact, there is arguably significant aesthetic creation on the part of the reader when private meanings and emotions can be evoked from transactions with texts that are *not* explicitly designed with obvious aesthetic intent. This provided insight into the problematic and entrenched ways in which labelling texts and genres can govern our responses. It was as if it were legitimate for Zee to say that she enjoyed reading a story book but unacceptable if the text happened to be the Federal Constitution. Her – and evidently my – initial marginalisation of the Federal Constitution belied the significant role it had in her life.

The interview and diary evidence of her experience with this text provided a unique insight into how the academic and non-academic reading domains were criss-crossed when they were embodied in, and by, Zee. The mitigating factor of an individual's interest for what she is apprehending in reading is critical in dissolving boundaries. Ultimately what made Zee's reading of the Federal Constitution stand out was the way in which she transacted with the same text through both the predominantly efferent and predominantly aesthetic stances. This not only supports Rosenblatt's argument that the stances need not be determined by the texts, but also demonstrates that the same reader and the same text can evoke different transactions with the reading when shaped by the context.

Discussion

The undergraduates in my study showed that they consistently experienced what I call situational motivation. This form of motivation encompassed the unpredictable, immeasurable, fluctuating and intertwining notions of pressure, pleasure and function of reading, situated within contexts that were also not constant. Very often, it was the context or situation that ultimately drove the reading choice.

The notion of aliteracy is often taken to refer to individuals who are assumed to 'choose' not to read. This assumption tempts the (empowered) educator to conclude that the (disempowered) student is poorly motivated to read. Yet, such thinking presumes too quickly that reading motivation is predictable, measurable and linearly progressive or, for that matter, regressive. What selected findings from my study demonstrated was that when considering the reading experience, we must account for something as fundamental as the reader's freedom and agency. If young people appear to choose not to read despite being highly literate, their negotiations of reading across domains must be examined. This is because it has a critical impact on the character of their reading experience. These findings compel us to better understand the continuum of academic and non-academic reading because pleasure and pressure in one domain (academic/professional) may critically shape satiation and hunger in another (non-academic/personal) (Wigfield, 1997; Wigfield et al., 2004). Perhaps then, aliteracy is less about motivation than it is about shifting landscapes and changing contexts. And because curricular reading appeals differently to different individuals, 'students need to learn to develop a guiding principle for choice at a point on the (aesthetic-efferent) continuum appropriate to the situation and their purpose' (Rosenblatt, 1993: 383). Thus, an important implication from my study suggests that teachers and students work together to form a unique repertoire that is guided not only by genre and domains but the chemistry of the transaction of reading as it is lived and experienced.

Concluding remark

In keeping up with the changing face of being literate, we will do well to remember that the complexities of reading that involve fluid transactions between the reader, text and context cannot be undermined. For too long, borders have been drawn up for reasons of convenience on the part of policymakers and education managers. The truth of the matter is that meaning-making lies not only in formalised domains seen especially through academic structures and systems, but in the transactions of the reader with making meaningful reading choices.

Note

1 Unless indicated, all reading materials Tables 10.2 and 10.3 were in the English language. All these titles were taken directly from the interviews or diaries, which explains why I have not been able to provide a reference list for any of the texts referred to.

References

Agee, J. (2005). Literacy, aliteracy, and lifelong learning. *New Library World*, 106 (5/6), 244–252.

Alvermann, D. E. (2004). Adolescent aliteracy: Are schools causing it? *Voices in Urban Education: Adolescent Literacy*, 3, 26–35.

Chong, S. L. (2016). Re-thinking aliteracy: When undergraduates surrender their reading choices. *Literacy*, 50 (1), 14–22.

Chong, S. L. (2017). Many languages, whither literacy: Understanding the ontology of reading in multilingually-diverse contexts. *3L: The Southeast Asian Journal of English Language Studies*, 23 (2), 1–13.

Giorgi, A. (1985). Sketch of a psychological phenomenological method. In A. Giorgi (Ed.), *Phenomenology and Psychological Research*. Pittsburgh: Duquesne University Press, pp. 8–21.

Goodwin, L. (1996). *Aliteracy among College Students. Why Don't They Read?* Paper presented at the Annual Meeting of the College Reading Association Charleston South Carolina. Retrieved on 27 October 2017 from: http://files.eric.ed.gov/fulltext/ED410527.pdf

Kalantzis, M., Cope, B., Chan, E. and Dalley-Trim, L. (2016). *Literacies* (2nd ed.). Australia: Cambridge University Press.

Malaysia: Federal Constitution. (31 August 1957). Retrieved on 28 October 2017 from: www.agc.gov.my/agcportal/uploads/files/Publications/FC/Federal_Consti_(BI_text).pdf

Marton, F. (1988). Phenomenography – a research approach investigating different understandings of reality. In R. R. Sherman and R. B. Webb (Eds.), *Qualitative Research in Education: Focus and Methods*. London: Falmer.

McKenna, M. C., Labbo, L. D., Kieffer, R. D. and Reinking, D. (Eds.). (2012). *International Handbook of Literacy and Technology* (Vol. 2). London: Routledge.

Mikulecky, L. (1978). *Aliteracy and a Changing View of Reading Goals*. Paper presented at the annual meeting of the International Reading Association, Houston, Texas. Retrieved on 27 October 2017 from: http://files.eric.ed.gov/fulltext/ED157052.pdf

Organisation for Economic Co-operation and Development. (2016). PISA Participants. Retrieved 9 June 2016, from www.oecd.org/pisa/aboutpisa/pisaparticipants.htm

Rosenblatt, L. M. (1978). *The Reader, the Text, the Poem: The Transactional Theory of the Literary Work*. Carbondale: Southern Illinois University Press.

Rosenblatt, L. M. (1983). The transactional theory of the literary work: implications for research. In C. Cooper (Ed.), *Researching Response to Literature and the Teaching of Literature: Points of Departure*, Norwood, New Jersey: Ablex, pp. 33–53.

Rosenblatt, L. M. (1993). The transactional theory: Against dualism. *College English*, 55 (4), 377–386.

Rosenblatt, L. M. (2005). *Making Meaning with Texts: Selected Essays*. London: Heinemann Educational Books.

Saldaña, J. (2013). *The Coding Manual for Qualitative Researchers* (2nd ed.). London: Sage.

Seidman, I. (2006). *Interviewing as Qualitative Research: A Guide for Researchers in Education and the Social Sciences*. New York: Teachers College Press.

UNESCO Institute of Statistics. (2013). *Adult and Youth Literacy: National, Regional and Global Trends, 1985–2015*. Montreal: UNESCO.

Wigfield, A. (1997). Reading motivation: A domain-specific approach to motivation. *Educational Psychologist*, 32 (2), 59–68.

Wigfield, A., Guthrie, J. T., Tonks, S. and Perencevich, K. C. (2004). Children's motivation for reading: Domain specificity and instructional influences. *The Journal of Educational Research*, 97 (6), 299–310.

CONCLUSION

Evelyn Arizpe and Gabrielle Cliff Hodges

Cumulating intellectual gold

In the Introduction we wrote about the way in which bringing together writing about small-scale qualitative research projects on a common topic – in this case, young adult reading – might be an important way of making such research more visible than it often currently is and, at the same time, potentially doing what Jensen and Rodgers describe as cumulating 'intellectual gold' (2001: 235). Readers who have read all the preceding chapters in this book will now be in a strong position to reflect on the value of the various research projects discussed, which have been conducted in diverse parts of the world. It is hoped they will thereby have gained an idea of some of the rich detail involved in young people's reading. That detail has partly been made visible because the authors themselves were also the researchers and were therefore able to write about what they learnt from their own direct involvement. In addition, however, it stems from the extraordinary variety of research methods that have been used to generate data. These were research methods that helped put the young people at their ease, accorded respect to the participants' own voices and hence seemed to elicit extraordinary insights into what it means to be a young adult reader in today's world.

Research methods and data analysis techniques

It is, perhaps, worth summarising again the research methods that were used. They form an interesting collection. Perhaps the most popular research method was interviewing (both individual and small-group interviews) not least because of the researchers' commitment to getting to know their participants and encouraging them to feel enough rapport to speak about their reading with confidence. Also used were: questionnaires/surveys (Coban; Aramouni; Arizpe and Guerrero Guadarrama);

semi-structured group interviews (Cedeira Serantes; Nambi); small-group discussions (Coban; Spring); think-aloud activities (Cedeira Serantes); drawings or photo-story making (Coban; Arizpe and Guerrero Guadarrama); personal reading history collages; (Cliff Hodges; Arizpe and Guerrero Guadarrama); place-journals with visual and verbal responses to texts (Spring); diary-writing (Chong); classroom observation (Lim); recording numbers of books read and examining the diversity of the texts (Manresa); students' assessments of their reading (Manresa); participant interviews, for example with parents (Arizpe and Guerrero Guadarrama); a field notes journal (Aramouni).

All the research methods arose out of the researchers' theorised methodologies which were either case studies or hermeneutic phenomenology. Within these two approaches, the research methods not only needed skill and subtlety on the part of the researchers to carry them out effectively; they also required some agile use of data analysis to ensure that the nuances of the participants' responses were understood as thoroughly as possible. The most common forms of data analysis were thematic coding and discourse analysis. In one case, it also involved the students as researchers analysing the data they had collected themselves. The researchers were very alert to the fact that they were always researching in vulnerable contexts, albeit some much more so than others. It was therefore imperative to establish, as far as possible, a sense of trust between all those involved in the research process, not only the participants but their parents, teachers and schools as well, especially in places where people were less used to qualitative research and the idea of volunteering for a project.

What all these research methods and data analysis techniques seem to do when brought together is show just how tentative and contingent each reader's personal reading history and preferences may be and how impossible it is, when generating this level of detail, to generalise about young people's reading. Although we hope the research methods are replicable by other researchers in different contexts, the intention within this book has been to use them to explore the rich diversity of young people's reading. That diversity includes not just reading undertaken by committed readers but also the reading of those who, historically, have been neglected (not least because other broad-brush-stroke research methods may have categorised them as reluctant or disaffected rather than, as Chong suggests, aliterate). By contrast, our intention here has been to see what difference it makes to our understanding of adolescent readers and readership to adopt an integrated focus on social, cultural, historical and spatial aspects of young people's reading within a single piece of research in a single context and also across different research in contexts worldwide.

Another strong feature of the research designs outlined in the preceding chapters is the researchers' desire to explore a much wider range of reading material that young adults engage with than has tended to be researched hitherto. A common assumption has previously been that accomplished readers have predominantly read print-based books. Changes in digital technology over the past couple of decades, however, mean that young people now have a much wider range of reading material at their disposal than ever before. They can, for example, still choose to read texts that have traditionally been available for many years such as comics, films, fiction or non-fiction books. However, they can also choose to read traditional texts in online formats as well as accessing websites, fan fiction, newspapers or social media online (e.g., see chapters by Cedeira Serantes; Coban; Chong). Or they can still read their chosen texts in more traditional formats, since print-based books have not simply been replaced by digital forms of reading.

Tentative findings

Reading all the chapters in this book, we are struck by a number of threads that begin to emerge and that we might, perhaps, class cumulatively as golden threads of intellectual wisdom (Jensen and Rodgers, 2001) and hence as very tentative findings. We discuss some of those threads here before going onto suggest what implications they may possibly raise for future research.

In Chapter 1, Cedeira Serantes explicitly notes the need for researchers like her to be reflexive. She recognises that she plays a central part in the research process and hence needs to make sure that her particular role is clearly visible, both to her participants and to anyone reading about her research. All the researchers here, whether adopting a case study approach or drawing on hermeneutic phenomenology, (and also, perhaps, because they have all undertaken doctoral studies), are in some way or other explicit about how they perceive knowledge to be constructed and how their own epistemologies and assumptions must therefore be a visible part of their analysis and interpretation. As researchers with a keen interest in reading themselves, all the authors are aware of their attitudes to their own reading histories and, indeed, appear ultimately to understand them much better as a result of engaging in their research. However, they are also highly conscious of their own and their participants' very different lived experiences, as well as of the ways in which technologies and literacy practices across a wide variety of genres are constantly changing. They realise, therefore, that their studies capture only a brief moment, albeit a very particular one, in time and space, and hence that their accounts are necessarily partial and tentative.

Making adolescent reading choices visible

One of the stated aims of this book has been to ask what we can learn from making adolescent reading choices visible. Visual research methods such as drawing (as a prompt for group discussion), rivers of reading collages or taking photos to create a photo-story montage have all proved to be important sources of data in the research projects described here. They enable not only the researchers but also the young people themselves to see their reading choices clearly and therefore the ways in which they intersect with or diverge from other people's. For example, the notion of how we might learn differently by taking an aerial view of young people's personal reading histories is raised expressly in Chapter 3. However, it is also touched on by Spring, in a fictional context, in Chapter 6 when Junior and his best friend Rowdy, in Sherman Alexie's book (2012), climb a pine tree on their reserve and realise that from their vantage point they can see their entire world, not just part of it. Making reading choices visible is a step in the direction of adopting an ecological way of thinking about reading, one in which all facets can be seen to contribute to the overall organic growth of the process. Hence, the landscape of all readers becomes important, not only of avid or reluctant readers, but also those for whom the boundaries may in the past have been viewed as less straightforward. Moreover, exploring the spaces in between more traditionally conceived boundaries is something that Manresa is particularly concerned to do in her research into the indeterminate space between school reading and personal independent reading outside.

As the earlier list of research methods suggests, the authors have not only made participants' reading choices clear; the participants have also verbalised their ideas about reading, whether in writing or in talk. What much of the research in this book suggests is how valuable the data may be when the visual and the verbal are analysed in conjunction with one another rather than separately. Intersections such as those between visual and verbal ways of generating data are, as we would expect, particularly pertinent when considering sociocultural issues such as class, ethnicity or geopolitics. Differences between young people, even in the same country, can have profound effects on how they may perceive themselves as readers, as Aramouni explains when applying Smith's concept of literacy clubs to her young adult participants in Lebanon. Nambi, too, argues persuasively that participants in school English literature classes may interpret the texts they are studying very differently depending on: their cultural values accrued from families, friends or the media; teachers' commitment to the exigencies of tests and examinations; perceptions of reading for academic purposes versus reading for pleasure; the weight of a school's religious stance. Lim shows through classroom observation how students in a Literature in English class perceive a teacher's role. Chong, meanwhile, through interviews and students' own diary-writing, tests to the limits Rosenblatt's concept of an aesthetic-efferent continuum, showing how an individual reader can read a text normally perceived as highly functional in an aesthetic manner.

In all these contexts, of course, there are always issues of power to contend with as well. Several of the authors explicitly acknowledge power as a factor when they consider their epistemological stances because they know that reading is connected closely with the idea of power. For example, some of the spaces in which people read and learn to read such as schools and libraries are firmly imbued with power such that young readers are seldom free to read where or how they want in these places, never mind choose what they want to read. In many of the countries where authors were researching, the publishing industry proves to be a powerful force, for example when it comes to the availability and perception of writing and publishing in languages other than English. For many of the participants in this research, English is their second or third language. Nevertheless, they are often ambivalent about the importance of English compared with, say, texts published in Luganda or Malay. As the research – perhaps surprisingly – suggests, young people do not necessarily want to read what others may assume they would prefer because it has greater relevance; on the contrary, sometimes they want (like Junior and Rowdy) a lengthier vista, possibly because their own locality is too violent and disturbing, or because they feel it is already familiar to them and they yearn for something different. As ever, the issue is highly complex and it is not possible to generalise about it on behalf of whole cohorts of young readers. On the other hand, seeing the issue repeatedly addressed, as it is in this volume, can help us understand its importance and complexity.

One other way in which some of the researchers here have begun to explore less well-rehearsed aspects of young people's reading is in relation to time. Cedeira Serantes outlines some fascinating features of it in relation to comics reading. Many of her participants do not have a great deal of time for reading so how they employ that time when it is available is of considerable importance. Cedeira Serantes' participants discuss the actual time it takes to read comics, not least because of how they need to navigate both image and text. Chong's university undergraduates are likewise pressed for time, a factor that – as revealed through the reading diaries they keep – they deal with through the choices they make about what to read and why. Far from being reluctant readers, as some of their lecturers appear to presume, they in fact use their time very precisely to read for many different purposes: for academic reasons to further their university studies, but also for other purposes such as keeping abreast of global news or for their own pleasure and satisfaction. Perhaps researchers might explore more fully in the future how both space and time impact on analyses of young people's reading; as yet, we do not know enough.

Adolescent reading in times of crisis

The issue of adolescent reading in times of crisis is one that we feel this book has attempted to address in unusual ways. A great deal of research into young people's reading hitherto has been done in relatively stable contexts such as in research-accessible places within England, Australia, Canada or the United States of America (Manuel and Brindley, 2012). Moreover, young people have tended to be classified within a single national heading; for example, for purposes of surveys such as those conducted by the Programme for International Student Assessment (PISA) (Kirsch et al., 2002), an international survey that aims to evaluate education systems worldwide by testing the skills and knowledge of 15-year-old students. Participants are thus merely Canadian or English or Malaysian. In 2009, one of the foci for the PISA tests was reading, but the results did not offer anything like the individual detail of the research in this book. Here, for example, in Spring's chapter we not only learn about the reading done by Indigenous Aboriginal youth in one small part of Canada; we also read about participants in her earlier doctoral research who were equally diverse in terms of their origins, two of the five being immigrants to Canada from Russia and Korea and a third being a first-generation Canadian with British heritage. Meanwhile, from other chapters in this book we learn that the young readers in Mexico undertaking research with Arizpe and Guerrero Guadarrama responded very differently to the unstable context in which they were living than did the readers in Lebanon facing The Situation. In the former, the participants appear to want to read about their context as a way to help them understand what might have been happening and, indeed, suggest ways they might have tried to cope with it. In the latter, however, the readers seem to want to veer right away from their immediate experiences of difficulty and move into other very different worlds. Even within Mexico, however, we are reminded that the two schools from which the participants are drawn are very different from one another: one is a city school, the other more rural. As we write the closing pages of this book, however, we are mindful of the ways in which the research contexts being referred to are continuing to shift due to political unrest and upheaval. One tentative finding therefore appears to be that different young readers may well respond unexpectedly to the contexts in which they find themselves reading. The responsibility of researchers, as our authors have done here, is to find out what those differences may be, not simply to make assumptions.

Young adult readers' experiences within and beyond school and university

Because of the age range of the participants involved in the research outlined in this book, another of the golden threads that begins to emerge is the evidence these young people provide about their experiences as readers as they move through the upper levels of school and on into university. Rather than being perceived as lacklustre in the face of all the reading they must do, the young adults are revealed by the research to be skilful and adept. Moreover, the customary view of readers as isolated or solitary proves not to be valid either. Instead, there is a strong emphasis here on the social nature of reading, through sharing and belonging to a community of readers, as well as relating to characters and the writers of texts. It is perhaps here, too, that Rosenblatt's ideas about reading as a transaction and as an event in time and place (1978/1994, 1985) come fully into their own. Reading is an engagement by a reader with a text out of which arises a reading. No two readings of the same text can therefore possibly ever be identical; no rereading of the same text by the same reader can ever be what it was the previous time because the reader has changed. There are, of course, definite consequences of this understanding of reading as a transaction and as a social process for future research, both in terms of methodologies and research methods. We cannot continue to conduct research that ignores the ecology of reading.

As several of the authors in this book remind us, gender issues are seldom very far away when reading is in focus. Cedeira Serantes' participants discuss with her the gendered expectations that many people have about comics readers and seek to dispel some of the myths that have accumulated around the topic. One of the potential advantages of small-scale qualitative research such as we have discussed in this volume is the way it also often shows readers as individuals who are not, first and foremost, being defined by their gender. Instead, their reading is being determined by other matters altogether such as the course of study they are following, the friendships they value, their teachers.

Another important factor that emerges from the research and which has begun to be written about (e.g., Martens, 2016) but will also require further investigation in the future is the materiality of texts and the difference that makes to readers. The researchers here listen to what young adult readers say about the various physical sensations they experience, whether wanting to own a text for its qualities as a material object, or the different ways of reading engendered by the physicality of the text, for example: a Chinese newspaper online; fanfiction on dedicated websites; comics in a comics store. Nor should the more longstanding issue of reading, enjoying and collecting series fiction be forgotten. Many young readers are well-known to be avid collectors of series fiction, most recently, for example, the Harry Potter series, which participants in this research have experienced in a wide range of places across the world. It reinforces the point made by Watson (2000) that choosing to read and collect series fiction is not done by chance; it is a deliberate process, one – of course – in which many adults likewise engage.

Implications for teaching and further research into young adult reading

Finding out about what young readers think is a challenge that every single researcher here has been keen to address. Work by González, Moll and Amanti (2005) argues the fundamental importance of teachers learning about what children and young people already know and think so that their prior knowledge can be seen as vital funds contributing to the understanding they are accruing. There are serious implications here for any adults involved in young people's reading – whether teachers, librarians, authors, bookstore workers or parents. If, as these projects suggest, young adults read very variously, even while their reading also displays commonalities, then what adults need to do is find out more. They need to find out more about readers with whom they come into immediate contact, but also about young adults who read further afield.

In the quotation from Teresa Cremin at al.'s work (2015) in Chapter 3 of this book, we see the candid astonishment that some of the teachers involved in the project expressed. They simply had not realised how much the children in their classes already knew. Once they did, the whole basis of their teaching would shift accordingly. That is not the case in lessons, however, where ideas about what constitutes knowledge are informed by academics such as Hirsch (1988). For him, the students' own knowledge – precisely because they have already acquired it – is not as powerful as new knowledge, which it is assumed they will learn from their teachers. This kind of approach appears to be the polar opposite to how researchers in this book approach their participants: whatever their stated ideas about reading, those participants have often been selected because the researchers think they do already know a great deal about reading and will therefore have plenty to share;

where they are more reticent, these chapters show the researchers still taking great care to accord them all the highest levels of respect.

There is a longstanding tradition of classroom talk in English, literature and literacy lessons that considers finding out what learners know to be an essential pedagogical approach. However, the same cannot necessarily be said for the teaching of English everywhere, as the findings of Nambi and Lim, for example, attest. In the context of some schools and classrooms, teachers (especially in the examination years) are very concerned to do what they perceive to be the right thing by their students to help them gain good results (a situation that currently pertains in many classrooms across the world, including in England, as a result of high-stakes testing, performance management and external pressures on schools to attain highly in league tables). The research methods we have already written about earlier in this chapter are expressly designed to establish and build up the necessary rapport that the researchers know they need if they are to elicit intricate responses about what young readers know and can do, in all kinds of contexts, including such classrooms as the above. What the research shows is that despite their teachers' desires to help their students, the students were (necessarily, as Rosenblatt would argue) engaging directly in their own transactions with the literature and thinking through the ideas being generated for themselves. However variously students respond, their perspectives help us to understand more about all young readers, not just those involved here.

Some of the many research methods described in these chapters are replicable by others and adaptable for readers of different ages and in varied contexts. Others – for example one-to-one interviews or classroom observation – might be harder to scale up easily. Whatever route researchers of the future decide to follow, what we hope is that their work can build on the insights this book affords. The research described here has done precisely what so many larger-scale reading research projects in the past have called for as they reach their conclusions: undertaken in-depth, student-centred, qualitative research to learn more about what young adult readers themselves say they do.

We suggest that the findings may also make a difference to those young adult readers themselves, not just to the researchers. What participants often gain by the inclusive methodologies and methods the researchers adopt is greater metaliterary understanding. Activities such as collage-making of personal histories can enable students themselves to realise – sometimes for the first time – the various routes and trajectories that comprise their personal reading histories. (Indeed, the adults with whom they construct their collages are often acquiring metaliterary awareness of a similar kind at the same time.) Other ways in which participants may be strengthened by involvement in these research projects is their growing understanding of the role reading may play in their sociocultural contexts. As we have seen from some of the most volatile places in which young adults read, the texts they encounter can help them understand the situations in which they find themselves living; they may, equally, turn them away from what they face on a day-to-day basis and lead them to want to look in an altogether different direction.

Either way, while it is true that 'textual lives' are, as Margaret Mackey describes them, 'fleeting and fragmentary' (2016: 507), she also argues that 'the qualities of individual location feed into the activity of reading' both at a level that is intensely personal *and* 'social and collective' (495) so that reading research must attend to both the generic and the particular.

As we wrote in the Introduction, one of the chief aims of this publication is to enable readers to understand the diversity of young adult reading as it has been researched by different people in many different parts of the world. A reader reflecting on all the projects described here is offered a relatively unusual opportunity to compare and contrast the various ways in which young adult readers describe their reading and are subsequently written about. It is, therefore, possible to gain insight into how young readers perceive themselves and others and to realise that all readers appear to be different from one another. The studies are, however, only small-scale, conducted as they mostly were for doctoral degrees. Moreover, the researchers have had to be highly selective and have only written here about a small part of their larger projects. We are in the presence of minutiae, but finely textured minutiae nonetheless. Future enquiries, conducted by these same researchers or others who may feel enthused by what they have read to take the research further for themselves, could afford to do so on a larger scale to see how any findings might be different. In the meantime, coming back to Mackey, we feel that her concept of 'mapping' the reading process encapsulates much of what this book has done and also points the way forward:

> Our developing literacy is idiosyncratic and unique as well as embodied and universal. It is, in this sense, impossible to tell a general story; at the same time, every unique story is thus general in the truth of its uniqueness. To map what happens as we respond to textual constructions is at best a partial enterprise; yet I believe there is merit in creating even an incomplete map. The process of mapping itself illuminates the territory.
>
> (2016: 508)

References

Alexie, S. (2012). *The Absolutely True Diary of a Part-Time Indian*. New York: Hachette Book Group.

Cremin, T., Mottram, M., Collins, F. M., Powell, S. and Drury, R. (2015). *Researching Literacy Lives: Building Communities between Home and School*. London: Routledge.

González, N., Moll, L. and Amanti, C. (Eds.), (2005). *Funds of Knowledge: Theorizing Practices in Households, Communities and Classrooms*. Mahwah, New Jersey: Lawrence Erlbaum Associates.

Hirsch, E. D. (1988). *Cultural Literacy: What Every American Needs to Know*. London: Vintage Books.

Jensen, J. and Rodgers, R. (2001). Cumulating the intellectual gold of case study research. *Public Administration Review*, 61 (2), 235–246.

Kirsch, I., de Jong, J., LaFontaine, D., McQueen, J., Mendelovits, J. and Monseur, C. (2002). *Reading for Change: Performance and Engagement across Countries*. Paris: Organisation for Economic Co-operation and Development.

Mackey, M. (2016). *One Child Reading: My Auto-Bibliography*. Edmonton: University of Alberta Press.

Manuel, J. and Brindley, S. (Eds.), (2012). *Teenagers and Reading*. Kent Town, Australia: Australian Association for the Teaching of English.

Martens, M. (2016). *Publishers, Readers, and Digital Engagement*. London: Palgrave Macmillan.

Rosenblatt, L. M. (1978/1994). *The Reader, the Text, the Poem: The Transactional Theory of the Literary Work*. Carbondale and Edwardsville: Southern Illinois University Press.

Rosenblatt, L. (1985). Viewpoints: Transaction versus interaction – a terminological rescue operation. *Research in the Teaching of English*, 19 (1), 96–107.

Watson, V. (2000). *Reading Series Fiction: From Arthur Ransome to Gene Kemp*. London: RoutledgeFalmer.

INDEX